Concepts and Applications of Fuzzy Inference System

Concepts and Applications of Fuzzy Inference System

Edited by **Frank West**

New York

Published by NY Research Press,
23 West, 55th Street, Suite 816,
New York, NY 10019, USA
www.nyresearchpress.com

Concepts and Applications of Fuzzy Inference System
Edited by Frank West

© 2015 NY Research Press

International Standard Book Number: 978-1-63238-092-0 (Hardback)

Printed in the United States of America.

Contents

Preface

This book aims to compile all important researches on the versatile and wide subject of engineering and management using Fuzzy Inference System (FIS). The book talks about the theoretical approaches of FIS, deals with the functions of FIS in management related issues and discusses FIS usage in mechanical and factory engineering issues. It also describes FIS relevance to image forming and related issues.

The researches compiled throughout the book are authentic and of high quality, combining several disciplines and from very diverse regions from around the world. Drawing on the contributions of many researchers from diverse countries, the book's objective is to provide the readers with the latest achievements in the area of research. This book will surely be a source of knowledge to all interested and researching the field.

In the end, I would like to express my deep sense of gratitude to all the authors for meeting the set deadlines in completing and submitting their research chapters. I would also like to thank the publisher for the support offered to us throughout the course of the book. Finally, I extend my sincere thanks to my family for being a constant source of inspiration and encouragement.

Editor

Section 1

Application to Power System Engineering Problems

A Multi Adaptive Neuro Fuzzy Inference System for Short Term Load Forecasting by Using Previous Day Features

Zohreh Souzanchi Kashani
Young Researchers Club, Mashhad Branch,
Islamic Azad University, Mashhad
Iran

1. Introduction

Load forecasting had an important role in power system design, planning and development and it is the base of economical studies of energy distribution and power market. The period of load forecasting can be for one year or month (long-term or medium-term) and for one day or hour (short-term) [1, 2, 3, and 4].

For short-term load forecasting several factors should be considered, such as time factors, weather data, and possible customers' classes. The medium- and long-term forecasts take into account the historical load and weather data, the number of customers in different categories, the appliances in the area and their characteristics including age, the economic and demographic data and their forecasts, the appliance sales data, and other factors [17].

The time factors include the time of the year, the day of the week, and the hour of the day. There are important differences in load between weekdays and weekends. The load on different weekdays also can behave differently. For example, in Iran, Fridays is weekends, may have structurally different loads than Saturdays through Thursday. This is particularly true during the summer time. Holidays are more difficult to forecast than non-holidays because of their relative infrequent occurrence.

Several techniques have been used for load forecasting that among its common methods we can refer to linear-regression model, ARMA, BOX-Jenkis[5] and filter model of Kalman, expert systems [6] and ANN [1-4,7]. According to load-forecasting complex nature, however its studying by linear techniques cannot meet the need of having high accuracy and being resistant. Adaptive neural-fuzzy systems can learn and build any non-linear and complex record through educational input-output data.

Then neural-fuzzy systems have many applications in studying load forecasting and power systems according to the non-linear and complex nature of power nets. Among them we can refer to load-peak forecasting and daily network load-curve forecasting.

The east of Iran power plant consumed load information was used for simulation of consumed load forecasting system. The effect of weather forecasting information in consumed load was considered by entering Mashhad climate information gathered from weather forecasting department of the province.

2. A review of previous works

Certain days load model (formal and informal vacations) is completely different from load model of working days of week (Saturday to Wednesday), but is very similar to its near Fridays. Short-term load forecasting by using fuzzy system cannot have a good function for load forecasting of days by itself since load model of special off-days has a big difference to a usual days. As usual days load model is different regarding the surface and the shape of curve, therefore we need an expert system for adjusting the primary forecasting which apply necessary information for results correction by using an expert person's experience.

On the other hand the power price is a signal with high frequency at competitive market; multi season changes, calendar effect weekends and formal vacation) and the high percentage of unusual prices are mostly during periods of demand increase [8]. The behavior of load curve for different week days is different and in sequential weeks is similar to each other. In this paper, authors use ARMA[1] and ANFIS[2] models for power signal forecasting. A compound method is also suggested in [9] based on neural network that forecast power price and load simultaneously. In [10, 11], PSO[3] has been used for forecasting that in these papers it is in the form of long-term. In [12], the method of neural network learning and SVR[4] is presented in order to a faster forecasting. A local learning method is introduced here and KNN[5] is used for model optimizing. In [13], power load model is also mentioned as a non-linear model and a method is suggested that has the capability of non-linear map.

This paper purpose is introducing SVR with a new algorithm for power load forecasting. SVR and ANN are used for error reduction.

2.1 Short-term load forecasting methods

As we use short term load forecasting in our method, review some important methods here.

A large variety of statistical and artificial intelligence techniques have been developed for short-term load forecasting [17].

Similar-day approach. This approach is based on searching historical data for days within one, two, or three years with similar characteristics to the forecast day. Similar characteristics include weather, day of the week, and the date. The load of a similar day is considered as a forecast. Instead of a single similar day load, the forecast can be a linear combination or regression procedure that can include several similar days. The trend coefficients can be used for similar days in the previous years.

Regression methods. Regression is the one of most widely used statistical techniques. For electric load forecasting regression methods are usually used to model the relationship of

---

[1] Autoregressive moving average
[2] Adaptive Neural- Fuzzy Inference System
[3] Particle swarm optimization
[4] Support vector regression
[5] K-nearest neighbor

load consumption and other factors such as weather, day type, and customer class. Engle et al. [18] presented several regression models for the next day peak forecasting. Their models incorporate deterministic influences such as holidays, stochastic influences such as average loads, and exogenous influences such as weather. References [19], [20], [21], [22] describe other applications of regression models to loads forecasting.

Time series. Time series methods are based on the assumption that the data have an internal structure, such as autocorrelation, trend, or seasonal variation. Time series forecasting methods detect and explore such a structure. Time series have been used for decades in such fields as economics, digital signal processing, as well as electric load forecasting. In particular, ARMA (autoregressive moving average), ARIMA (autoregressive integrated moving average), ARMAX (autoregressive moving average with exogenous variables), and ARIMAX (autoregressive integrated moving average with exogenous variables) are the most often used classical time series methods. ARMA models are usually used for stationary processes while ARIMA is an extension of ARMA to non-stationary processes. ARMA and ARIMA use the time and load as the only input parameters. Since load generally depends on the weather and time of the day, ARIMAX is the most natural tool for load forecasting among the classical time series models. Fan and McDonald [23] and Cho et al. [24] describe implementations of ARIMAX models for load forecasting. Yang et al. [25] used evolutionary programming (EP) approach to identify the ARMAX model parameters for one day to one week ahead hourly load demand forecast. Evolutionary programming [26] is a method for simulating evolution and constitutes a stochastic optimization algorithm. Yang and Huang [27] proposed a fuzzy autoregressive moving average with exogenous input variables (FARMAX) for one day ahead hourly load forecasts.

Neural networks. The use of artificial neural networks (ANN or simply NN) has been a widely studied electric load forecasting technique since 1990 [28]. Neural networks are essentially non-linear circuits that have the demonstrated capability to do non-linear curve fitting. The outputs of an artificial neural network are some linear or nonlinear mathematical function of its inputs. The inputs may be the outputs of other network elements as well as actual network inputs. In practice network elements are arranged in a relatively small number of connected layers of elements between network inputs and outputs. Feedback paths are sometimes used. In applying a neural network to electric load forecasting, one must select one of a number of architectures (e.g. Hopfield, back propagation, Boltzmann machine), the number and connectivity of layers and elements, use of bi-directional or uni-directional links, and the number format (e.g. binary or continuous) to be used by inputs and outputs, and internally.

The most popular artificial neural network architecture for electric load forecasting is back propagation. Back propagation neural networks use continuously valued functions and supervised learning. That is, under supervised learning, the actual numerical weights assigned to element inputs are determined by matching historical data (such as time and weather) to desired outputs (such as historical electric loads) in a pre-operational "training session". Artificial neural networks with unsupervised learning do not require pre-operational training. Bakirtzis et al. [29] developed an ANN based short-term load forecasting model for the Energy Control Center of the Greek Public Power Corporation. In the development they used a fully connected three-layer feed forward ANN and back propagation algorithm was used for training.

Input variables include historical hourly load data, temperature, and the day of the week. The model can forecast load profiles from one to seven days. Also Papalexopoulos et al. [30] developed and implemented a multi-layered feed forward ANN for short-term system load forecasting. In the model three types of variables are used as inputs to the neural network: season related inputs, weather related inputs, and historical loads. Khotanzad et al. [31] described a load forecasting system known as ANNSTLF. ANNSTLF is based on multiple ANN strategies that capture various trends in the data. In the development they used a multilayer perceptron trained with the error back propagation algorithm. ANNSTLF can consider the effect of temperature and relative humidity on the load. It also contains forecasters that can generate the hourly temperature and relative humidity forecasts needed by the system. An improvement of the above system was described in [32]. In the new generation, ANNSTLF includes two ANN forecasters, one predicts the base load and the other forecasts the change in load. The final forecast is computed by an adaptive combination of these forecasts. The effects of humidity and wind speed are considered through a linear transformation of temperature. As reported in [32], ANNSTLF was being used by 35 utilities across the USA and Canada. Chen et al. [4] developed a three layer fully connected feed forward neural network and the back propagation algorithm was used as the training method. Their ANN though considers the electricity price as one of the main characteristics of the system load. Many published studies use artificial neural networks in conjunction with other forecasting techniques (such as with regression trees [26], time series [33] or fuzzy logic [34]).

Expert systems. Rule based forecasting makes use of rules, which are often heuristic in nature, to do accurate forecasting. Expert systems, incorporates rules and procedures used by human experts in the field of interest into software that is then able to automatically make forecasts without human assistance.

Expert system use began in the 1960's for such applications as geological prospecting and computer design. Expert systems work best when a human expert is available to work with software developers for a considerable amount of time in imparting the expert's knowledge to the expert system software. Also, an expert's knowledge must be appropriate for codification into software rules (i.e. the expert must be able to explain his/her decision process to programmers). An expert system may codify up to hundreds or thousands of production rules. Ho et al. [35] proposed a knowledge-based expert system for the short-term load forecasting of the Taiwan power system. Operator's knowledge and the hourly observations of system load over the past five years were employed to establish eleven day types. Weather parameters were also considered. The developed algorithm performed better compared to the conventional Box-Jenkins method. Rahman and Hazim [36] developed a site-independent technique for short-term load forecasting. Knowledge about the load and the factors affecting it are extracted and represented in a parameterized rule base. This rule base is complemented by a parameter database that varies from site to site. The technique was tested in several sites in the United States with low forecasting errors.

The load model, the rules, and the parameters presented in the paper have been designed using no specific knowledge about any particular site. The results can be improved if operators at a particular site are consulted.

Fuzzy logic. Fuzzy logic is a generalization of the usual Boolean logic used for digital circuit design. An input under Boolean logic takes on a truth value of "0" or "1". Under fuzzy logic an input has associated with it a certain qualitative ranges. For instance a transformer load may be "low", "medium" and "high". Fuzzy logic allows one to (logically) deduce outputs from fuzzy inputs. In this sense fuzzy logic is one of a number of techniques for mapping inputs to outputs (i.e. curve fitting).

Among the advantages of fuzzy logic are the absence of a need for a mathematical model mapping inputs to outputs and the absence of a need for precise (or even noise free) inputs. With such generic conditioning rules, properly designed fuzzy logic systems can be very robust when used for forecasting. Of course in many situations an exact output (e.g. the precise 12PM load) is needed. After the logical processing of fuzzy inputs, a "defuzzification" process can be used to produce such precise outputs. References [37], [38], [39] describe applications of fuzzy logic to electric load forecasting.

Support vector machines. Support Vector Machines (SVMs) are a more recent powerful technique for solving classification and regression problems. This approach was originated from Vapnik's [40] statistical learning theory. Unlike neural networks, which try to define complex functions of the input feature space, support vector machines perform a nonlinear mapping (by using so-called kernel functions) of the data into a high dimensional (feature) space. Then support vector machines use simple linear functions to create linear decision boundaries in the new space. The problem of choosing an architecture for a neural network is replaced here by the problem of choosing a suitable kernel for the support vector machine [41]. Mohandes [42] applied the method of support vector machines for short-term electrical load forecasting. The author compares its performance with the autoregressive method. The results indicate that SVMs compare favorably against the autoregressive method. Chen et al. [43] proposed a SVM model to predict daily load demand of a month. Their program was the winning entry of the competition organized by the EU Load NITE network. Li and Fang [44] also used a SVM model for short-term load forecasting.

3. Consumed load model

The load forecasting art is in selecting the most appropriate way and model for and the closest ones to the existing reality of the network among different methods and models of load forecasting, by studying and analyzing the last procedure of load and recognizing the effective factors sufficiently and maximizing each of them, and then in this way it forecasts different time periods required for the network with an acceptable approximation. It should be accepted that there is always some error in load forecasting due to the accidental load behavior but never this error should go further than the acceptable and tolerable limit. Relative accuracy has a particular importance in load forecasting in power industry. Especially when load forecasting is the basis of network development planning and power plant capacity. Since, any forecasting with open hand causes extra investment and the installation capacity to be useless and vice versa any forecasting less than real needs, faces the network with shortage in production and damages the instruments due to extra load.

Consumed load model is influenced by different parameters such as weather, vacations or holidays, working days of week and etc. in order to build a short-term load forecasting system, we should consider the influence of different parameters in load forecasting, which it can be full field by a correct selection of system entries. Selection of these parameters depends on experimental observations and is influenced by the environment conditions and is determined by trial and error.

4. Reviewing the predictability of time series by the help of lyapunov exponent[6]

Chaos is a phenomenon that occurs in many non-linear definable systems which show a high sensitivity to the primary conditions and semi random behavior. These systems will remain stable in the chaotic mode if they provide the Lyapunov exponent equations.

4.1 Background

Detecting the presence of chaos in a dynamical system is an important problem that is solved by measuring the largest Lyapunov exponent. Lyapunov exponents quantify the exponential divergence of initially close state-space trajectories and estimate the amount of chaos in a system.[50]

Over the past decade, distinguishing deterministic chaos from noise has become an important problem in many diverse fields, e.g., physiology [51], economics [52]. This is due, in part, to the availability of numerical algorithms for quantifying chaos using experimental time series. In particular, methods exist for calculating correlation dimension (D2) [53], Kolmogorov entropy [54], and Lyapunov characteristic exponents. Dimension gives an estimate of the system complexity; entropy and characteristic exponents give an estimate of the level of chaos in the dynamical system.

The Grassberger-Procaccia algorithm (GPA) [53] appears to be the most popular method used to quantify chaos. This is probably due to the simplicity of the algorithm [55] and the fact that the same intermediate calculations are used to estimate both dimension and entropy.

However, the GPA is sensitive to variations in its parameters, e.g., number of data points [56], embedding dimension [56], reconstruction delay [57], and it is usually unreliable except for long, noise-free time series. Hence, the practical significance of the GPA is questionable, and the Lyapunov exponents may provide a more useful characterization of chaotic systems.

For time series produced by dynamical systems, the presence of a positive characteristic exponent indicates chaos. Furthermore, in many applications it is sufficient to calculate only the largest Lyapunov exponent ($\lambda 1$). However, the existing methods for estimating $\lambda 1$ suffer from at least one of the following drawbacks: (1) unreliable for small data sets, (2) computationally intensive, (3) relatively difficult to implement. For this reason, we have developed a new method for calculating the largest Lyapunov exponent. The method is reliable for small data sets, fast, and easy to implement. "Easy to implement" is largely a subjective quality, although we believe it has had a notable positive effect on the popularity of dimension estimates.

For a dynamical system, sensitivity to initial conditions is quantified by the Lyapunov exponents. For example, consider two trajectories with nearby initial conditions on an attracting manifold. When the attractor is chaotic, the trajectories diverge, on average, at an exponential rate characterized by the largest Lyapunov exponent [58]. This concept is also generalized for the spectrum of Lyapunov exponents, λi (i=1, 2, ..., n), by considering a small

---

[6] Lyapunov exponent

n-dimensional sphere of initial conditions, where n is the number of equations (or, equivalently, the number of state variables) used to describe the system. As time (t) progresses, the sphere evolves into an ellipsoid whose principal axes expand (or contract) at rates given by the Lyapunov exponents.

The presence of a positive exponent is sufficient for diagnosing chaos and represents local instability in a particular direction. Note that for the existence of an attractor, the overall dynamics must be dissipative, i.e., globally stable, and the total rate of contraction must outweigh the total rate of expansion. Thus, even when there are several positive Lyapunov exponents, the sum across the entire spectrum is negative.

Wolf et al. [59] explain the Lyapunov spectrum by providing the following geometrical interpretation. First, arrange the n principal axes of the ellipsoid in the order of most rapidly expanding to most rapidly contracting. It follows that the associated Lyapunov exponents will be arranged such that

$$\lambda_1 > \lambda_2 > \ldots > \lambda_n$$

where λ_1 and λ_n correspond to the most rapidly expanding and contracting principal axes, respectively. Next, recognize that the length of the first principal axis is proportional to $e^{\lambda_1 t}$; the area determined by the first two principal axes is proportional to $e^{(\lambda_1 + \lambda_2)t}$; and the volume determined by the first k principal axes is proportional to $e^{(\lambda_1 + \lambda_2 + \cdots + \lambda_k)t}$. Thus, the Lyapunov spectrum can be defined such that the exponential growth of a k-volume element is given by the sum of the k largest Lyapunov exponents. Note that information created by the system is represented as a change in the volume defined by the expanding principal axes. The sum of the corresponding exponents, i.e., the positive exponents, equals the Kolmogorov entropy (K) or mean rate of information gain [58]:

$$K = \sum_{\lambda i > 0} \lambda i$$

When the equations describing the dynamical system are available, one can calculate the entire Lyapunov spectrum. The approach involves numerically solving the system's n equations for n+1 nearby initial conditions. The growth of a corresponding set of vectors is measured, and as the system evolves, the vectors are repeatedly reorthonormalized using the Gram-Schmidt procedure. This guarantees that only one vector has a component in the direction of most rapid expansion, i.e., the vectors maintain a proper phase space orientation. In experimental settings, however, the equations of motion are usually unknown and this approach is not applicable. Furthermore, experimental data often consist of time series from a single observable, and one must employ a technique for attractor reconstruction, e.g., method of delays [60], singular value decomposition.

As suggested above, one cannot calculate the entire Lyapunov spectrum by choosing arbitrary directions for measuring the separation of nearby initial conditions. One must measure the separation along the Lyapunov directions which correspond to the principal axes of the ellipsoid previously considered. These Lyapunov directions are dependent upon the system flow and are defined using the Jacobian matrix, i.e., the tangent map, at each point of interest along the flow [58]. Hence, one must preserve the proper phase space orientation by using a suitable approximation of the tangent map. This requirement, however, becomes unnecessary when calculating only the largest Lyapunov exponent.

If we assume that there exists an ergodic measure of the system, then the multiplicative ergodic theorem of Oseledec [61] justifies the use of arbitrary phase space directions when calculating the largest Lyapunov exponent with smooth dynamical systems. We can expect that two randomly chosen initial conditions will diverge exponentially at a rate given by the largest Lyapunov exponent [62]. In other words, we can expect that a random vector of initial conditions will converge to the most unstable manifold, since exponential growth in this direction quickly dominates growth (or contraction) along the other Lyapunov directions. Thus, the largest Lyapunov exponent can be defined using the following equation where d(t) is the average divergence at time t and C is a constant that normalizes the initial separation:

$$d(t) = Ce^{\lambda_1 t}$$

For experimental applications, a number of researchers have proposed algorithms that estimate the largest Lyapunov exponent [55,59], the positive Lyapunov spectrum, i.e., only positive exponents [59], or the complete Lyapunov spectrum [58]. Each method can be considered as a variation of one of several earlier approaches [59] and as suffering from at least one of the following drawbacks: (1) unreliable for small data sets, (2) computationally intensive, (3) relatively difficult to implement. These drawbacks motivated our search for an improved method of estimating the largest Lyapunov exponent.

4.2 Calculation of lyapunov exponent for time series

In order to calculate Lyapunov exponent for those systems which their equation is not determined and their time series is not available, different algorithm is suggested [45-49].

The algorithm proposed by Wolf [48], seeks the time series of close points in the phase space. These points went round the phase space or got divergent rapidly. Close points in the same direction are selected.

The differential coefficient is in the direction of the maximum development and their average logarithm on the route of phase space yields the biggest Lyapunov exponent. Suppose that series of $x_0, x_1, x_2,...$ x_k is available and the interval between them is obtained as $t_n - t_0 = n_\tau$ that τ is the interval between two successive measurement. If the system has chaotic behavior, we can explain divergence of the adjacent routes based on the difference range between them, as following.

$$d_0 = |x_j - x_i| \tag{1}$$

$$d_1 = |x_{j+1} - x_{i+1}| \tag{2}$$

$$\vdots$$

$$d_n = |x_{j+n} - x_{i+n}| \tag{3}$$

It is supposed that d_n will increase exponential by n increase:

$$d_n = d_0 e^{\lambda n} \tag{4}$$

So by calculating its logarithm we have:

$$\lambda = \frac{1}{n} \mathrm{Ln} \frac{d_n}{d_0} \tag{5}$$

There should be at least one Lyapunov exponent bigger than zero to have chaos, the existence of positive value of λ means the chaotic behavior of system. Therefore, in order to Table 1 we can expect system to forecast.

Winter	Fall	Summer	Spring
0.07563	0.05428	0.0444	0.0523

Table 1. Lyapunov exponent for seasons of one year

5. Preparing the input data

First step in the process of electricity load forecasting is to provide last information of the system load being studied. After preparing the input data matrix, it is turn of classification. The reason of this classification is the existence of completely determined models in different days that were referred to in many references. Among different days of weeks, Saturday to Thursday which are working days in Iran, have the same load model. Fridays have also their own particular model and have a low level of load. Special days have a completely different model, too. So it seems necessary at the first look that each of these classes should be analyzed separately. We consider 2 groups of features that refer to previous days; 2, 7, and 14 day ago, and 2, 3, 4 day ago.

6. Adaptive neural- Fuzzy inference system

ANFIS, proposed by Jang [14, 15], is an architecture which functionally integrates the interpretability of a fuzzy inference system with adaptability of a neural network. Loosely speaking ANFIS is a method for tuning an existing rule base of fuzzy system with a learning algorithm based on a collection of training data found in artificial neural network. Due to the less tunable use of parameters of fuzzy system compared with conventional artificial neural network, ANFIS is trained faster and more accurately than the conventional artificial neural network. An ANFIS which corresponds to a Sugeno type fuzzy model of two inputs and single output is shown in Fig. 1. A rule set of first order Sugeno fuzzy system is the following form:

Rule i: If x is Ai and y is Bi then $f_i = p_i x + q_i y + r_i$.

ANFIS structure as shown in Figure 1 is a weightless multi-layer array of five different elements [15]:

- Layer 1: Input data are fuzzified and neuron values are represented by parameterized membership functions;
  - $O_{1,i}$ is the output of the ith node of the layer 1.
  - Every node i in this layer is an adaptive node with a node function

$$O_{1,i} = \mu A_i(x) \text{ for } i = 1, 2, \text{ or}$$

$$O_{1,i} = \mu B_{i-2}(x) \text{ for } i = 3, 4$$

- x (or y) is the input node i and A_i (or B_{i-2}) is a linguistic label associated with this node
- Therefore $O_{1,i}$ is the membership grade of a fuzzy set (A1,A2,B1,B2).
- Typical membership function:

$$\mu A(x) = \frac{1}{1+|\frac{x-ci}{ai}|2bi}$$

- a_i, b_i, c_i is the parameter set.
- Parameters are referred to as premise parameters.

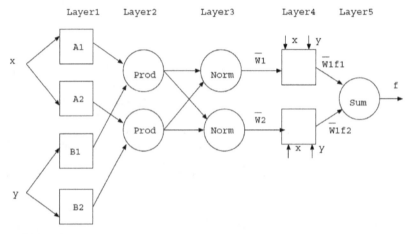

Fig. 1. ANFIS architecture

- Layer 2: The activation of fuzzy rules is calculated via differentiable T-norms (usually, the soft-min or product);
  - Every node in this layer is a fixed node labeled Prod.
  - The output is the product of all the incoming signals.
  - $O_{2,i} = w_i = \mu A_i(x) \cdot \mu B_i(y)$, $i = 1, 2$
  - Each node represents the fire strength of the rule
  - Any other T-norm operator that perform the AND operator can be used
- Layer 3: A normalization (arithmetic division) operation is realized over the rules matching values;
  - Every node in this layer is a fixed node labeled Norm.
  - The ith node calculates the ratio of the ith rulet's firing strenght to the sum of all rulet's firing strengths.
  - $O_{3,i} = \bar{w}_i = \frac{w_i}{w_1+w_2}$, $i = 1, 2$
  - Outputs are called normalized firing strengths.
- Layer 4: The consequent part is obtained via linear regression or multiplication between the normalized activation level and the output of the respective rule;
  - Every node i in this layer is an adaptive node with a node function:

$$O_{4,1} = \bar{w}_i f_i = \bar{w}_i(p_x + q_i y + r_i)$$

- $\bar{w}_i$ is the normalized firing strenght from layer 3.
- $\{p_i, q_i, r_i\}$ is the parameter set of this node.
- These are referred to as consequent parameters.
- Layer 5: The NFN output is produced by an algebraic sum over all rules outputs.
  - The single node in this layer is a fixed node labeled *sum*, which computes the overall output as the summation of all incoming signals:
  - overall output = $O_{5,1} = \sum \bar{w}_i f_i = \frac{\sum_i w_i f_i}{\sum_i w_i}$

The main objective of the ANFIS design is to optimize the ANFIS parameters. There are two steps in the ANFIS design. First is design of the premise parameters and the other is consequent parameter training. There are several methods proposed for designing the premise parameter such as grid partition, fuzzy C-means clustering and subtractive clustering. Once the premise parameters are fixed, the consequent parameters are obtained based on the input-output training data. A hybrid learning algorithm is a popular learning algorithm used to train the ANFIS for this purpose.

- ANFIS uses a hybrid learning algorithm to identify the membership function parameters of single-output, Sugeno type fuzzy inference systems (FIS).
- There are many ways of using this function.
- Some examples:

$$[FIS,ERROR] = ANFIS(TRNDATA)$$

$$[FIS,ERROR] = ANFIS(TRNDATA,INITFIS)$$

7. The proposed method for power consumed load forecasting

Since fuzzy methods and systems were presented for using in different applications, researchers noticed that making a fuzzy powerful system is not a simple work. The reason is that finding suitable fuzzy rules and membership functions is not a systematic work and mainly requires many trails and errors to reach to the best possible efficiency. Therefore the idea of using learning algorithms was proposed for fuzzy systems. Meanwhile learning of fuzzy network proposed them as the first goals for being unified in fuzzy methods in order to make the development and usage process of fuzzy systems automatic for different applications. Function estimation by using the learning methods is proposed in neural networks and neural-fuzzy networks.

In the suggested methods we forecast load consume and its improvement by the help of the offered method. One of the famous neural-fuzzy systems for function estimation is ANFIS model. We used this system for power consumed load forecasting in this paper too, but with this difference that we used one separate adaptive neural-fuzzy system for each season of the year. Although at the time of training these systems data overlapping is considered, because data of each season of the year is not completely independent and there is some similarities between the first days of a season with its previous season regarding the amount of load consumption. Figure 2 shows the diagram of multi adaptive neural-fuzzy system (multi ANFIS).

As it is shown too, in the Figure 2, we us a switch for any subsystem of a season be thought in lieu of that season. Therefore the time of system training and testing will decrease and the entrance of extra data is prevented.

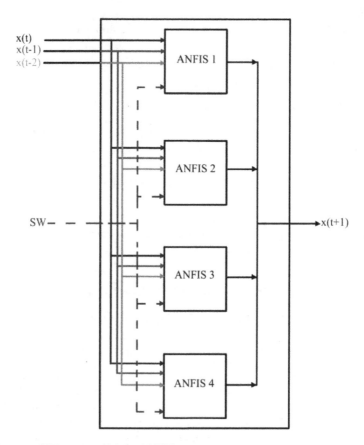

Fig. 2. Implemented Diagram of Multi ANFIS

8. Result

In the proposed method we classified day into two categories. We divide the season days into two groups of working days (Saturday to Thursday) and holidays that their load consumption is different from other days.

Here we also calculated the output of Multi ANFIS based on the features of previous day, one time with 2, 7, and 14 day ago and another time with 2, 3, and 4 day ago. You can see the results in Table 2 and 3.

The amount of the accuracy of the performance of any of calculation methods in load forecasting is determined by measuring the obtained values of system model and comparing it with real data.

Mean Absolute Percentage Error (MAPE) is used for studying the performance of every mentioned method with the data of related test. MAPE is determined by following relation:

$$MAPE= 1/N \ (\sum_{i=1}^{N} APE_i) \qquad (6)$$

$$APE= | \ (V(forecast)-V(actual))/ \ V(actual) \ | *100\% \qquad (7)$$

MAPE for working days	load consumption forecasting
1.5409	Spring
2.1869	Summer
2.4575	Fall
1.5116	Winter

Table 2. Power load consumption forecasting for the working days (saturday to thursday) with 2, 3, and 4 day ago

MAPE for working days	Load consumption forecasting
0.9602	Spring
0.8568	Summer
1.1392	Fall
1.3015	Winter

Table 3. Power load consumption forecasting for the working days (saturday to thursday) with 2, 7, and 14 day ago

As it is obvious of the above Tables, making working days separate from holidays with using previous days features (2, 7,and 14 day ago) yields a better result, in load consumption forecasting.

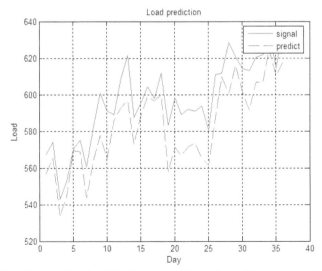

Fig. 3. Power load forecasting for Working days (Saturday to Thursday) of fall with features of 2, 3, and 4 day ago

Also in order to compare, the diagram of daily load forecasting curves for fall through both groups is shown in Figures 3 and 4. It should be mentioned that MATLAB software is used for load forecasting and simulation.

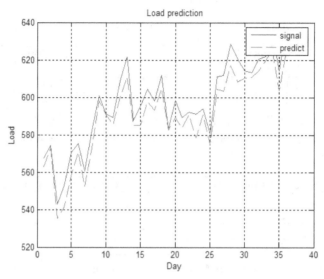

Fig. 4. Power load forecasting for Working days (Saturday to Thursday) of fall with features of 2, 7, and 14 day ago

9. Conclusion and suggestion

Comparing mentioned methods above shows that separation of working days from holidays has a better result in load consumption forecasting. As shown in Figure 5 we can

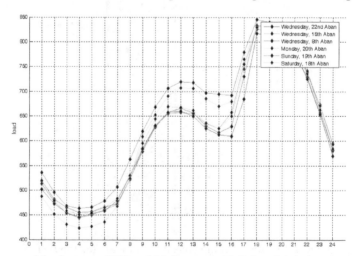

Fig. 5. Compare of the feature of 2, 7 and 14 day ago with 2, 3 and 4 day ago

see that using the features of 2, 7 and 14 day ago are better than 2, 3 and 4 day ago. A cyan and yellow line are refer to 3 and 4 day ago. We can see that these features cannot have good effect on load forecasting.

According to this that in most proposed methods load consumption time series data is used; it seems that we can obtain better results by using time series data of one or more parameters effective in load consumption [16] also with load consumption time series. Accurate load forecasting is very important for electric utilities in a competitive environment created by the electric industry deregulation.

10. References

[1] Huang, S.J. and K.R. Shih, 2003. Short term load forecasting via ARMA model identification including non- Gaussian process consideration. IEEE Trans. Power Syst., 18: 673-679.

[2] Kandil Nahi, Rene Wamkeue, Maarouf saad and Semaan Georges, 2006. An efficient approach for short term load forecasting using artificial neural networks. Int. J. Electric Power Energy syst., 28: 525-530.

[3] Mandal Paras, Tomonobu Senjyu, Naomitsu Urasaki, Toshihisa Funabashi, 2006. A neural network based several hours ahead electric load forecasting using similar days approach. Int. J. Elect. Power Energy Syst., 28: 367-373.

[4] Topalli Ayca Kumluca, Ismet Erkmen and Ihsan Topalli, 2006. Intelligent short term load forecasting in Turkey. Int. J. Electric. Power Energy Syst., 28: 437-447.

[5] Moghram, I. and S. Rahman, 1989. Analysis and evaluation of five short term load forecasting techniques. IEEE Trans. Power Syst., 4: 1484-1491.

[6] Rahman, S. and R. Bhatnager, 1988. An expert system based algorithm for short term load forecast. IEEE Trans. Power Sys., pp: 392-399.

[7] Senjyu, T., H. Takara, K. Uezato and T. Funbasi, 2002. One hour ahead load forecasting using neural network. IEEE Trans. Power sys., 17: 113-118.

[8] F. J. Nogales, J. Contreras, A. J. Conejo and R. Espinola, "Forecasting Next-Day Electricity Prices by Times Series Models", IEEE Transaction On Power Systems, Vol. 17, no.2, May 2002.

[9] Amjadi N, Daraeepour A, "Mixed price and load forecasting of electricity markets by a new iterative prediction method", Electric power systems research, 2009.

[10] Niu D, Li J, Liu D, "Middle-long power load forecasting based on particle swarm optimization", computers and mathematics with applications, 2009.

[11] Alrashidi M, Elnaggar K, "Long term electric load forecasting based on particle swarm optimization", applied enery, 2009.

[12] He W, "Forecasting electricity load with optimized local learning models", Electrical power and energy systems, 2008.

[13] Hong W-C, "Electric load forecasting by support vector model", Applied Mathematical Modelling, 2009.

[14] Jang, J.S.R., C. T. Sun and E. Mizutani. Neuro-Fuzzy and Soft Computing, Prentice Hall, Upper Saddle River, NJ, USA. 1997.

[15] Jang, J.S. ANFIS: Adaptive-network-based fuzzy inference system, IEEE Trans. on System, Man, and Cybernetics, vol. 23, pp.665-685, May/June, 1993.

[16] Souzanchi-K Z, Yaghobi M, Akbarzadeh-T M, "Modeling and Forecasting Short_term Electricity Load based on Multi Adaptive Neural-Fuzzy Inference System by Using Temterature", 2nd International conference on Signal Processing Systems(ICSPS), 2010.

[17] E A. Feinberg, D Genethliou. LOAD FORECASTING, APPLIED MATHEMATICS FOR POWER SYSTEMS Load Forecasting

[18] R.F. Engle, C. Mustafa, and J. Rice. Modeling Peak Electricity Demand. Journal of Forecasting, 11:241–251, 1992.

[19] O. Hyde and P.F. Hodnett. An Adaptable Automated Procedure for Short-Term Electricity Load Forecasting. IEEE Transactions on Power Systems, 12:84–93, 1997.

[20] S. Ruzic, A. Vuckovic, and N. Nikolic. Weather Sensitive Method for Short-Term Load Forecasting in Electric Power Utility of Serbia. IEEE Transactions on Power Systems, 18:1581–1586, 2003.

[21] T. Haida and S. Muto. Regression Based Peak Load Forecasting using a Transformation Technique. IEEE Transactions on Power Systems, 9:1788–1794, 1994.

[22] W. Charytoniuk, M.S. Chen, and P. Van Olinda. Nonparametric Regression Based Short-Term Load Forecasting. IEEE Transactions on Power Systems, 13:725–730, 1998.

[23] J.Y. Fan and J.D. McDonald. A Real-Time Implementation of Short-Term Load Forecasting for Distribution Power Systems. IEEE Transactions on Power Systems, 9:988–994, 1994.

[24] M.Y. Cho, J.C. Hwang, and C.S. Chen. Customer Short-Term Load Forecasting by using ARIMA Transfer Function Model. Proceedings of the International Conference on Energy Management and Power   Delivery, 1:317–322, 1995.

[25] H.T. Yang, C.M. Huang, and C.L. Huang. Identification of ARMAX Model for Short-Term Load Forecasting: An Evolutionary Programming Approach. IEEE Transactions on Power Systems, 11:403–408, 1996.

[26] D.B. Fogel. An Introduction to Simulated Evolutionary Optimization. IEEE Transactions on Neural Networks, 5:3–14, 1994.

[27] H.T. Yang and C.M. Huang. A New Short-Term Load Forecasting Approach using Self-Organizing Fuzzy ARMAX Models. IEEE Transactions on Power Systems, 13:217–225, 1998.

[28] M. Peng, N.F. Hubele, and G.G. Karady. Advancement in the Application of Neural Networks for Short-Term Load Forecasting. IEEE Transactions on Power Systems, 7:250–257, 1992.

[29] A.G. Bakirtzis, V. Petridis, S.J. Kiartzis, M.C. Alexiadis, and A.H. Maissis. A Neural Network Short-Term Load Forecasting Model for the Greek Power System. IEEE Transactions on Power Systems, 11:858–863, 1996.

[30] A.D. Papalexopoulos, S. Hao, and T.M. Peng. An Implementation of a Neural Network Based Load Forecasting Model for the EMS. IEEE Transactions on Power Systems, 9:1956–1962, 1994.

[31] A. Khotanzad, R.A. Rohani, T.L. Lu, A. Abaye, M. Davis, and D.J. Maratukulam. ANNSTLF–A Neural-Network-Based Electric Load Forecasting System. IEEE Transactions on Neural Networks, 8:835–846, 1997.

[32] A. Khotanzad, R.A. Rohani, and D. Maratukulam. ANNSTLF– Artificial Neural Network Short-Term Load Forecaster–Generation Three. IEEE Transactions on Neural Networks, 13:1413–1422, 1998.

[33] T.W.S. Chow and C.T. Leung. Nonlinear Autoregressive Integrated Neural Network Model for Short-Term Load Forecasting. IEE Proceedings on Generation, Transmission and Distribution, 143:500–506, 1996.

[34] S.E. Skarman and M. Georgiopoulous. Short-Term Electrical Load Forecasting using a Fuzzy ARTMAP Neural Network. Proceedings of SPIE, 181–191, 1998.

[35] K.L. Ho, Y.Y. Hsu, F.F. Chen, T.E. Lee, C.C. Liang, T.S. Lai, and K.K. Chen. Short-Term Load Forecasting of Taiwan Power System using a Knowledge Based Expert System. IEEE Transactions on Power Systems, 5:1214–1221, 1990.

[36] S. Rahman and O. Hazim. Load Forecasting for Multiple Sites: Development of an Expert System-Based Technique. Electric Power Systems Research, 39:161–169, 1996.

[37] S.J. Kiartzis and A.G. Bakirtzis. A Fuzzy Expert System for Peak Load Forecasting: Application to the Greek Power System. Proceedings of the 10th Mediterranean Electrotechnical Conference, 3:1097– 1100, 2000.

[38] V. Miranda and C. Monteiro. Fuzzy Inference in Spatial Load Forecasting. Proceedings of IEEE Power Engineering Winter Meeting, 2:1063–1068, 2000.

[39] S.E. Skarman and M. Georgiopoulous. Short-Term Electrical Load Forecasting using a Fuzzy ARTMAP Neural Network. Proceedings of SPIE, 181–191, 1998.

[40] V.N. Vapnik. The Nature of Statistical Learning Theory. NewYork, Springer Verlag, 1995.

[41] N. Christiani and J.S. Taylor. An Itroduction to Support Vector Machines and Other Kernel-Based Learning Methods. Cambridge University Press, Cambridge, 2000.

[42] M. Mohandes. Support Vector Machines for Short-Term Electrical Load Forecasting. International Journal of Energy Research, 26:335–345, 2002.

[43] B.J. Chen, M.W. Chang, and C.J. Lin. Load Forecasting using Support Vector Machines: A Study on EUNITE Competition 2001. Technical report, Department of Computer Science and Information Engineering, National Taiwan University, 2002.

[44] Y. Li and T. Fang. Wavelet and Support Vector Machines for Short-Term Electrical Load Forecasting. Proceedings of International Conference on Wavelet Analysis and its Applications, 1:399– 404, 2003.

[45] Gencay R, Dechert W.D., (1992), "An Algorithm for the n-Lyapunov exponents of an n-dimensional unknown dynamical system" Physica D 59:142 57.

[46] Nychka D.W., Ellner S., (1992), "Finding chaos in a noisy system", J R Stat Soc B., 54:399–426.

[47] J. C. Sprott, "Chaos and Time-Series Analysis", Oxford University Press, USA.

[48] Wolf, A., Swift, J.B., Swinney, H., L., and Vastono, J.A., (1985), "Determining Lyapunov exponent from a time series", Physical D 16, PP. 285-317.

[49] Michael T. Rosenstein, James J. Collins, and Carlo J. De Luca," A practical method for calculating largest Lyapunov exponents from small data sets"

[50] M Rosenstein, J Collins, C Luca, A practical method for calculating largest Lyapunov exponents from small data sets, 1992

[51] G. W. Frank, T. Lookman, M. A. H. Nerenberg, C. Essex, J. Lemieux, and W. Blume, Chaotic time series analysis of epileptic seizures, Physica D 46 (1990) 427.

[52] P. Chen, Empirical and theoretical evidence of economic chaos, Sys. Dyn. Rev. 4 (1988) 81.

[53] P. Grassberger, and I. Procaccia, Characterization of strange attractors, Phys. Rev. Lett. 50 (1983) 346.

[54] P. Grassberger, and I. Procaccia, Estimation of the Kolmogorov entropy from a chaotic signal, Phys. Rev. A 28 (1983) 2591.

[55] S. Ellner, A. R. Gallant, D. McCaffrey, and D. Nychka, Convergence rates and data requirements for Jacobian-based estimates of Lyapunov exponents from data, Phys. Lett. A 153 (1991) 357.

[56] J. B. Ramsey, and H.-J. Yuan, The statistical properties of dimension calculations using small data sets, Nonlinearity 3 (1990) 155.

[57] A. M. Albano, J. Muench, C. Schwartz, A. I. Mees, and P. E. Rapp, Singular-value decomposition and the Grassberger-Procaccia algorithm, Phys. Rev. A 38 (1988) 3017.

[58] J.-P. Eckmann, and D. Ruelle, Ergodic theory of chaos and strange attractors, Rev. Mod. Phys. 57 (1985) 617.

[59] A. Wolf, J. B. Swift, H. L. Swinney, and J. A. Vastano, Determining Lyapunov exponents from a time series, Physica D 16 (1985) 285.

[60] N. H. Packard, J. P. Crutchfield, J. D. Farmer, and R. S. Shaw, Geometry from a time series, Phys. Rev. Lett. 45 (1980) 712.

[61] V. I. Oseledec, A multiplicative ergodic theorem. Lyapunov characteristic numbers for dynamical systems, Trans. Moscow Math. Soc. 19 (1968) 197.

[62] G. Benettin, L. Galgani, and J.-M. Strelcyn, Kolmogorov entropy and numerical experiments, Phys. Rev. A 14 (1976) 2338.

Fault Diagnosis in Power Distribution Network Using Adaptive Neuro-Fuzzy Inference System (ANFIS)

Rasli[1], Hussain[2] and Fauzi[1]
[1]Universiti Teknologi Malaysia
[2]Universiti Kebangsaan Malaysia
Malaysia

1. Introduction

Fault diagnosis in power distribution system is an initial action in preventing power breakdown that will affect electrical consumers. Power utilities need to take proactive plan to ensure customer satisfaction and continuous power supply. Power breakdown is a problem to utilities as well as energy users and there are a lot of factors that can cause interruption to the power system. Power distribution system is exposed to approximately 80% of overall faults that come from a wide range of phenomena including equipment failure, animals, trees, severe weather and human factors (Marusic & Gruhonjic-Ferhatbegovic, 2006). Whenever any of these factors befall the power system, costumers will experience power failure which will disturb their daily transactions. Since customers need smooth and reliable power supply, utilities have to develop an electrical power that has quality, reliability and continuous availability; they are responsible for the planning of power restoration properly in order to maintain high market place. Most engineers in power distribution system have decided that power breakdown is related to system reliability issues (Richard, 2009).

One problem when breakdown occurs is the long time taken to provide reenergized power after fault. To quote some examples are the power breakdown that occurred in Keningau, Sabah, East Malaysia on July 5, 2009 in which about 2 to 3 hours were taken for repairing. A power failure also happened in Lembah Klang, West Malaysia on January 13, 2005 for 5 hours that affected many industries (Fauziah, 2005). In Cameron, Middle of Africa, the engineers had taken 2 hours to detect the fault location in AES-SONEL Ngousso substation on April 2006 (Thomas & Joseph, 2009). This phenomenon has to be considered seriously by power utilities so as to overcome frequent breakdowns and provide power restoration plan effectively. If they are unable to solve the problem effectively, they will lose consumers' confidence and power system maintenance will highly increase. In addition, power system that has low reliability encourages repeated significant faults. The faults require time for restoration. There is an index to control the duration within power interruption, which is called the customer average interruption duration index (CAIDI). Therefore, power utilities are urged to aim for low index value so that the system reliability can be maintained (Richard, 2009).

The first step for implementing power restoration plan is by developing a precise and an accurate fault diagnosis in power distribution system. Usually, fault diagnosis involves several tasks such as fault types classification, fault location determination and power restoration plan. Firstly, the types of fault must be classified. Then, the fault location can be determined accordingly. The fault location in power distribution system is very important in order to plan power restoration through power system reconfiguration by using operational states of circuit breakers (CB) and line isolators (LI). With such plan, it can fully help power operators to make a decision immediately for further action in power restoration.

The remaining parts of the chapter are organized as follows. Section 1 explains the introduction of the chapter followed by the literature review in Section 2. In Section 3, the concept of adaptive neuro-fuzzy inference system is addressed clearly. Next the ANFIS design for fault types classification and fault location determination is described in Section 4. The results of fault diagnosis are presented in Section 5. Finally conclusions are given in Section 6.

2. Literature review

Many research works on fault diagnosis incorporate artificial intelligent approaches which process the information from alarms and protection relays in power distribution and transmission systems (Zhiwei et al., 2008; Souza et al., 2004; Mohamed & Mazumder, 1999; Binh & Tuyen, 2006). An expert system has been implemented in cooperation with SCADA and EMS to develop a more efficient and precise centralized fault diagnosis system in transmission networks (Sekine et al., 1992). The approach registers information such as fault location, causes of fault and identifies unwanted operation of protection devices. Voltage and current sensors are installed on transmission lines for real time implementation and this involves a high cost. Artificial neural network (ANN) based fault diagnosis method in the distribution system is then developed to locate the fault, identify the faulty protection devices and isolate the faulty sections. Fault location and fault states of lines and bus sections are obtained using the information from alarm relays (Mohamed & Mazumder, 1999). This technique provides effective information to the operator for decision making but most distribution systems are not completely equipped with alarm relays.

A combination of ANN and fuzzy logic has been used to process the information from alarms and protection relays (Souza et al., 2004) for the purpose of identifying the faulty components and line sections. A wavelet based ANN approach is developed for fault detection and classification (Silva et al., 2006). The approach uses oscillographic data from fault recorders and therefore requires communication networks between remote power system and digital fault recorders. A substation fault diagnosis system has been developed using the Petri net theory (Jingbo & Longhua, 2006). In this method, the information from circuit breakers and faulty protection devices are configured based on mathematical formulations to calculate the precise fault section. Two Petri net concepts, namely, neural Petri net and fuzzy neural Petri net are used for locating faults at the lines or sections (Binh & Tuyen, 2006). However, these methods are not suitable for fault diagnosis in distribution systems due to lack of information of alarm and protective relays.

A new and accurate fault location algorithm using adaptive neuro-fuzzy inference system (ANFIS) has been developed for a network with both transmission lines and under-ground cables (Sadeh & Afradi, 2009). It uses fundamental frequency of three-phase current and neutral current as inputs while fault location is calculated in terms of distance in kilometer. Although it gives a good performance, there are some imperfections in the fault location due to the wide range in distance. An ANN based fault diagnosis method has been implemented in an unbalanced underground distribution system (Oliveira, 2007). The method uses fundamental voltage and current phasors as inputs to the ANN for locating faults in the line sections. Another ANN based approach which combines the ant colony optimization algorithm has been developed for fault section diagnosis in the distribution systems (Zhisheng & Yarning, 2007). The method locates faults in terms of the line sections but the exact fault points are still not known.

3. The concept of adaptive neuro-fuzzy inference system

Adaptive neural fuzzy inference system (ANFIS) is based on fuzzy logic modeling and uses artificial neural network as the learning algorithm. The system can teach, change the data environment or respond to the remote stimulus for adapting to the change of data environment (Michael, 2005). ANFIS produces constant and linear target by using respective zero and first-order polynomial equations and is also known as a Sugeno-type of fuzzy inference system (FIS).

ANFIS approach targets only one output from several given inputs. The target is manipulated through the performance of the membership function curve according to a particular data input. The curve parameters are identified based on the respective weighted values via the product in between the created learning rules. A ratio between the individual and overall weighted values is calculated. The ratio is gained by using the parameters of output membership function then, finally ANFIS predicts the target by producing an overall gained value as an output. Membership function parameters in input and output sides are adjusted through a learning process to get the targeted values. ANFIS uses hybrid algorithm that consists of a combination between back-propagation and least-square estimation techniques (Jang, 1993). The techniques are implemented in artificial neural network as a learning algorithm that gives very fast convergence and more accurate in ANFIS target.

3.1 ANFIS's learning processes

The ANFIS model exhibits a predicted target whenever it is trained by using at least two columns of data. The last column is the target data and also as an output of the trained ANFIS, while the rest of the columns are the input data. Thus, an ANFIS structure has a single output with at least one column of input data. For the best prediction and high reliability of its performance, the model needs more elements in the column of the input data. However, this situation will also cause the processing time for learning to be slow. For that reason, the ANFIS has to be configured in a high speed processor. Every element in each row of the input data is called data variable in which the linguistic values of the relationship between them is by the rule of 'IF-THEN'. A total of the rule is proportional to the membership function value and the number of column data is linked by the following equation:

$$F^D = P \tag{1}$$

where,
D : Total number of column for the input data
F : Number of membership functions
P : Number of rules

The data is classified as training data and testing data in ANFIS's learning process. Testing data should be in the range of training data for the purpose of testing procedures. The number of training epoch also gives a good result in predicting the target. Accurate targets consider a minimum prediction error from the result of ANFIS training. The error can be reduced by adjusting the variable membership function (MF) and epoch parameters. With increasing in number of MF and epoch, the error will reduce accordingly. Sometimes, no reducing in error can be noticed even though the epoch was increased up to 5000 and above. This is due to the way the data is assembled. Therefore effective input data assembly will result good prediction. For this work, effective configuration of the data has been reached by preparing a wide data range between their elements and arranging the data from small to large values.

During the training process, MF parameters are varied so as to yield the ANFIS's output as target values. The minimum error percentage is a small difference between target and prediction values and it is used to measure the success level of a training process. ANFIS performs a hybrid learning algorithm in the training process which is a combination of two algorithms namely back-propagation and least square estimate (Jang, 1993). The hybrid method improves the bad features of individual algorithm and both are popular in ANN implementation.

In hybrid learning algorithm, MF parameters are adjusted to identify the best prediction value. The parameters determine the size of MF curve as shown in Fig.1. The curve of 'gbell' shape has been selected in the learning process due to its high performance in giving a precise prediction (Jang, 1993). There are MF curve in input and output parts of ANFIS model. Back-propagation algorithm takes responsibility to vary MF parameter in input side of the model, whereas least square estimate (LSE) takes into consideration on the output side as a linear line. In MF parameters, the input side varies, whereas for output, they are static and vice versa.

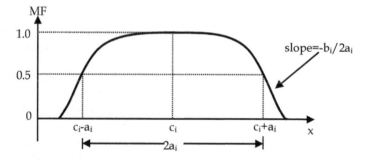

Fig. 1. Gbell shape for MF curve in input side

The prediction values are performed after the MF parameters in both sides of the ANFIS model converge the values according to the given training epoch (Mitra et al., 2008). Fig.2

and 3 show the effect of different epoch and change of MF curve's shape with respect to the prediction error in initial and final learning process.

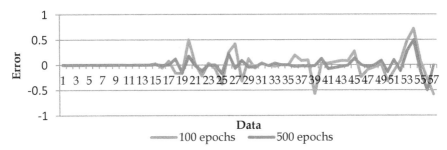

Fig. 2. Prediction errors according to different training epoch

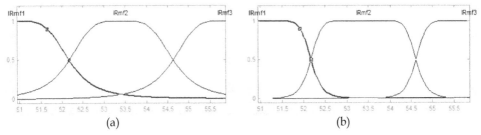

Fig. 3. (a) Initial stage and (b) MF curve of input side on final stage

ANFIS's learning process can be implemented easily by using the provided source code in Matlab such as 'newfis', 'evalfis' and editfis'. A trained ANFIS model is formatted with a file extension of '.fis' to represent an ANFIS module. On the other hand, the file is represented as a module for a particular task where all modules are configured accordingly based on a hierarchy layout to form a fault diagnosis system in power distribution network. The '.fis' file is also a flexible module that can reform when the data changes or new data is added without restructuring the model physically. ANFIS has a capability of producing very fast result in prediction even when handles a large size of input data. Therefore, the system is compliable to most application especially in adaptive control as well as ANFIS in implementing fault diagnosis. Each ANFIS module for a particular task is programmed by using source codes in Matlab. The programming is developed for every task in fault diagnosis and then the tasks are integrated in another programming to perform a simulation tool for fault diagnosis in power distribution network.

3.2 Development of ANFIS model

A basic ANFIS model is shown in Fig.4 in which the model is illustrated in five blocks of learning stages. This model is an example of ANFIS development model for power restoration plan that consists of two inputs and two membership functions. So, there are four fuzzy 'IF-THEN' rules to show the relationship between fault locations in 'x, y' coordinates and it also shows the operational status of CB and LI in the power distribution network. So, the target is '1' for operating while '0' for non-operating state of the devices.

In this chapter, an ANFIS model has been developed with 27 fuzzy 'IF-THEN' rules for the task of power restoration plan as shown in Fig.5 and 8 rules in determining the fault location. Since, the number of block functions represent the rules for every input data, it is difficult to describe the operational process of the model due to lack of space. However, a basic ANFIS model is shown in Fig.4 for that purpose. There are five stages of ANFIS operational process that includes fuzzification, 'IF-THEN' rules, normalization, defuzzification and neuron addition.

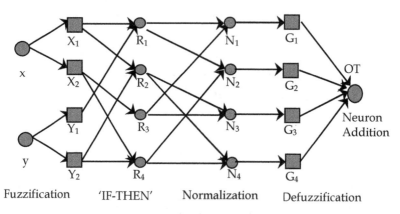

Fig. 4. A basic ANFIS model with two inputs data and two MFs.

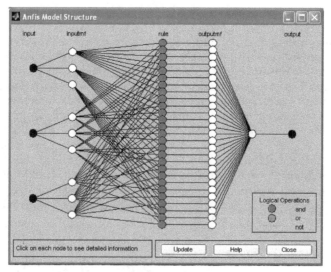

Fig. 5. An ANFIS model structure for the task of power restoration plan

3.2.1 Fuzzification

Referring to Fig.4, the fuzzification stage is located at the first stage of receiving of the input signal. Its function is to convert the input signal to fuzzy signal in which the signal is yielded via the input side of the MF curve. The curve is performed by using the following equations:

$$X_i(x) = \frac{1}{1 + \left(\frac{x - c_i}{a_i}\right)^{2b_i}} \tag{2}$$

$$Y_i(y) = \frac{1}{1 + \left(\frac{y - c_i}{a_i}\right)^{2b_i}} \tag{3}$$

where, $X_i(x)$ and $Y_i(y)$ are fuzzied values for each input data, whereas a_i, b_i and c_i are MF parameters for respective representative of middle, width and slope of the curve as shown in Fig.1. These parameters are varied accordingly to get a suitable curve in order to get fuzzy signal.

3.2.2 Stage of 'IF-THEN' rule

An output signal from the fuzzification stage becomes an input to the stage of the 'IF-THEN' rule. In this stage, the fuzzy signal is gained by using equation (4) up to (7).

$$R_1 = X_1(x) \times Y_1(y) \tag{4}$$

$$R_2 = X_1(x) \times Y_2(y) \tag{5}$$

$$R_3 = X_2(x) \times Y_1(y) \tag{6}$$

$$R_4 = X_2(x) \times Y_2(y) \tag{7}$$

R_1, R_2, R_3 and R_4 are real values for every 'IF-Then' rule.

3.2.3 Normalization

Next, the output signal from the stage of 'IF-THEN' rule will be an input signal to the normalization stage. In this stage, every gained signal are divided to the total of gained signal by the following equation,

$$N_i = {R_i}/{R_T} \qquad i = 1, 2, 3, 4 \tag{8}$$

where, $R_T = R_1 + R_2 + R_3 + R_4$

3.2.4 Defuzzification

The next process is signal defuzzification in which the output signal from the normalization stage becomes an input signal to this defuzzification stage. In this stage, a normalized signal is gained again through a linear equation that is formed from the MF of the output signal as shown in the following equation,

$$G_i = N_i(p_i x + q_i y + r_i) \qquad i = 1, 2, 3, 4 \tag{9}$$

with p_i, q_i and r_i being the MF parameters for the linear signal.

3.2.5 Neuron addition

The last process in the ANFIS operation is called neuron addition in which all defuzzification signals, G_i are added together as shown below:

$$OT = \sum G_i \qquad\qquad i = 1, 2, 3, 4 \qquad\qquad (10)$$

OT is a predicted value.

3.3 Good features of the ANFIS

The advantages of ANFIS are compared to other artificial intelligent techniques such as an artificial neural network (ANN) and an expert system (ES). The advantages are as follows; i) ANFIS gives a high precision in classification and prediction models. This precision when compared to the index error that is presented between ANFIS and ANN show the error of 0.036 and 0.32 respectively (Jang, 1993). ii) ANFIS has adaptive features to solve wrong data problem that involves new power network configuration. The scenario is rather difficult to solve using expert system due to fixed rules. iii) ANFIS has an effective learning process on the training data while considering optimization in its implementation (Jang, 1993; De Souza et al., 2003).

4. The ANFIS design for fault types classification and fault location determination

The development of fault diagnosis in power distribution network implements the ANFIS approach because of its compact structure, very fast training process and precise prediction. A developed fault diagnosis requires a compact ANFIS model development with significant tasks. The tasks involve fault types classification, fault location determination and identification of an operational state of CB and LI for power restoration plan. Every task is represented by an ANFIS model that is structured based on a hierarchy of power distribution network. Post-fault three-phase root mean square (RMS) current is applied to the model to produce the respective task at the output. For the purpose of developing fault diagnosis in power distribution network, such fault current is only used as the model input. If a measured current is more than the current without fault in a network, surely there is some fault in the power network. Fig.6 shows a block diagram of the fault diagnosis development that consists of four ANFIS modules. The modules are stated as ANFIS1 to ANFIS4 when representing the diagnosis tasks. From the figure, post-fault 3-phase current from the faulty power network is injected to ANFIS1 that is responsible for predicting the target in integer 1 to 10 when representing the types of fault.

Meanwhile, fault location is identified according to geometry coordinates. The same fault current as an input to the ANFIS1, is also applied to ANFIS2 and ANFIS3 modules in which they are developed to produce the output in X and Y coordinates respectively. In other words, the modules represent precise fault point in the power network. The technique of geometry coordinate gives better accuracy in producing the fault location compared to the cut-off faulty line approach (Butle-Pury & Moratti 2006). Furthermore, Fig.6 shows a position of ANFIS4 module for restoration power plan in the network. The input signal to this module is from fault location identification whereas the operational states of CB and LI are the module output. The states are considered for the purpose of determination of a new power network configuration. Faulty lines must be isolated before proceeding to the power restoration plan. Binary codes are used to show the states in which digit '1' represents CB and LI in 'close' whereas digit '0' is in 'open' switch.

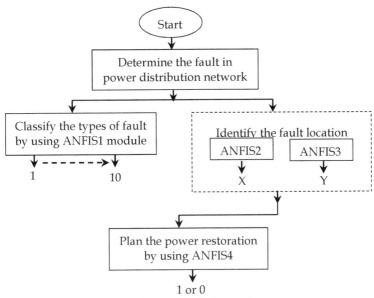

Fig. 6. A block diagram of the procedures in fault diagnosis system

4.1 Fault types classification

Usually, the types of power fault are classified accordingly such as a phase to ground, a phase to phase, two phases to ground and three-phase faults. Fig.7 shows ANFIS1 module

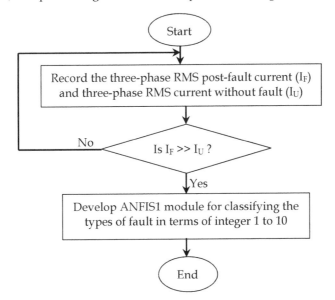

Fig. 7. A procedure in fault types classification

development that is responsible for the task of predicting various types of fault in terms of integer 1 to 10 as follows, 1- red phase to ground fault (AG), 2 – yellow phase to ground fault (BG), 3 – blue phase to ground fault (CG), 4 – Three-phase fault (3P), 5 – red phase to yellow phase fault (AB), 6 – yellow phase to blue phase fault (BC), 7 – blue phase to red phase fault (CA), 8 – red and yellow phases to ground fault (ABG), 9 – yellow and blue phases to ground fault (BCG), 10 – blue and red phases to ground (CAG).

4.1.1 ANFIS1 design for fault types classification

Fig.8 shows the design of an ANFIS1 model that is structured according to the type of fault and represented by the integers 1 to 10. The model consists of ten ANFIS modules which are labeled as ANFIS1-1 to ANFIS1-10. The first module conducts A phase to ground fault (AG) prediction in integer 1 and follows by ANFIS1-2 in integer 2 for 'BG', ANFIS1-3 in integer 3 for 'CG' and so on. ANFIS1-4 to ANFIS1-10 modules represent respective 3P, AB, BC, CA, ABG, BCG and CAG faults. Table 1 shows some relationship parameters between the input and output of ANFIS1's signals.

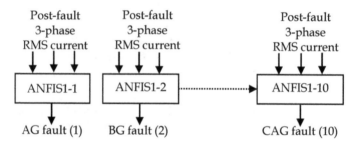

Fig. 8. ANFIS1 design for fault types classification

ANFIS modules	Input	Output
ANFIS1-1	Post-fault 3-phase RMS current	1 – AG fault
ANFIS1-2	"	2 – BG fault
ANFIS1-3	"	3 – CG fault
ANFIS1-4	"	4 – 3P fault
ANFIS1-5	"	5 – AB fault
ANFIS1-6	"	6 – BC fault
ANFIS1-7	"	7 – CA fault
ANFIS1-8	"	8 – ABG fault
ANFIS1-9	"	9 – BCG fault
ANFIS1-10	"	10 – CAG fault

Table 1. Input and output parameters from every ANFIS1 module.

4.1.2 A Procedure for classifying the types of fault

Fig.9 shows a procedure for classifying various types of fault in power distribution network through developing an ANFIS1 model. The first step is the preparation of power network in

XY coordinate layout. The selected power distribution network is a 47 buses practical system. Then, by using the commercial software of PSS-ADEPT, the network is analyzed to record a post-fault 3-phase RMS current for each identified fault point. These points are fault location in XY coordinates for every feeder and radial lines including loads. The post-fault current data is used to train ANFIS1-1 to ANFIS1-10 modules according to respective target output that are integers 1 up to 10. The integers are representative of 10 types of fault. There are 163 selected coordinates for fault points with two fault resistors in the 47 buses practical power network. Therefore, it has about 2462 simulations in generating the data set. Table 2 shows a distribution data for training, testing and classifying the types of fault in the practical system.

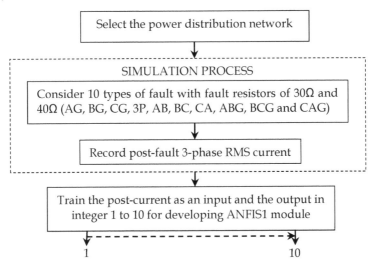

Fig. 9. A procedure for developing ANFIS1 in fault types classification

ANFIS1 module	Generated data set	Trained data set	Number of ANFIS input	Number of ANFIS output
ANFIS1-1 to ANFIS1-3	465	445	3	1
ANFIS1-4	177	157	3	1
ANFIS1-5 to ANFIS1-10	182	162	3	1

Table 2. The training and testing data for classifying the types of fault in a 47 buses practical system

4.2 Fault location identification

Referring to Fig.10, ANFIS2 and ANFIS3 are developed to identify fault location in respective X and Y coordinates. According to previous literature, most of the methods in identifying the fault location for power distribution network are in fault distance from a substation or zone. This approach considers geometrical coordinates in determining fault location in which it produces more accurate and precise fault location identification. From

Fig.10, three-phase RMS post-fault current with (I_F) and without (I_U) fault are compared to investigate the fault in the power system. If current is I_F higher than current I_U, the current I_F is recorded with the merging fault type.

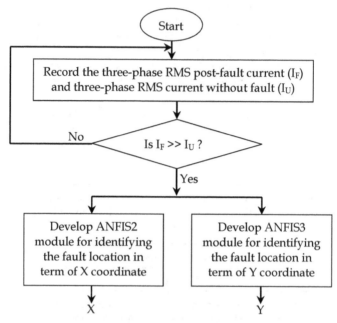

Fig. 10. A procedure for identifying fault location

4.2.1 ANFIS2 and ANFIS3 designs for identifying fault location

The structure of ANFIS2 and ANFIS3 are configured according to selected fault points as shown in Fig.11. For a 47 buses practical system, there are 163 fixed fault points with 64 'X' coordinates and 45 'Y' coordinates. Thus, the total coordinate point is 109. Those points are

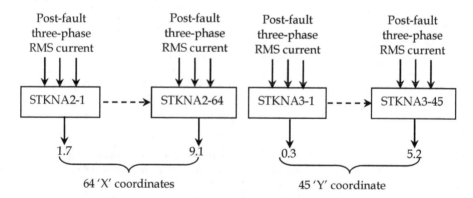

Fig. 11. ANFIS2 and ANFIS3 design for identifying fault location in a 47 buses practical system

represented by each ANFIS module. ANFIS2 consists of 64 modules that are labeled as ANFIS2-1 up to ANFIS2-64 whereas for ANFIS3, its total module is 45 from ANFIS3-1 to ANFIS3-45. The signal input to the ANFIS2 and ANFIS3 is a three-phase RMS post-fault current while the signal output is in terms of X and Y coordinates respectively as shown in Fig.11. Table 3 shows the input and output parameters of the 47 buses practical system.

ANFIS module	Input	Output
ANFIS2-1	Post-fault 3-phase RMS current	1.7
↓		↓
ANFIS2-64	"	9.1
ANFIS3-1	"	0.3
↓		↓
ANFIS3-45	"	5.2

Table 3. Input and output parameters of ANFIS2 and ANFIS3 for identifying fault location in a 47 buses practical system

4.2.2 A procedure for identifying fault location

The procedure for locating fault in a power distribution network by the implementation of ANFIS2 and ANFIS3 modules is clearly shown in Fig.12. The first stage is a selection of power network for testing. Then the network layout is drawn in XY plane for locating the selected fault points along the feeder and radial lines. Fig.13 presents an example of the layout. The detail specification of the network is in the next sub-section. This network layout is embedded in fault analysis simulation software such as PSS-ADEPT to collect the fault current data at each fault point.

Next, the three-phase RMS post-fault current is collected at the main substation through a simulation of fault analysis to the selected power distribution network. The fault analysis is applied to every point of the fixed coordinates while considering 10 types of fault and several fault resistors (R_f). For example, by using three fault resistors and 163 fault points, there are 1335 simulations for single fault to ground and about 486 simulations for double fault to ground. Meanwhile, about 643 simulations are required for phase to phase and three-phase faults. Therefore, the total simulation is about 2464 for power distribution network in the 47 buses practical system. The data collected is arranged in such a way that it has three columns of input parameters and one column of target values. The target is either X or Y coordinates in which they are used to train ANFIS2 and ANFIS3 respectively.

By identifying the fault location in terms of 'XY' coordinates, more precise and accurate location not only in terms of distance from the feeding substation can be yielded. The structure of ANFIS2 and ANFIS3 are quite simple so they undergo a very fast process in the training stage. However, the simulation process should be done repeatedly due to too much fixed fault points in selected power distribution network. If any network has more feeder and radial lines with long line distance, the fault point should also be more. Thus, the number of ANFIS models will also increase.

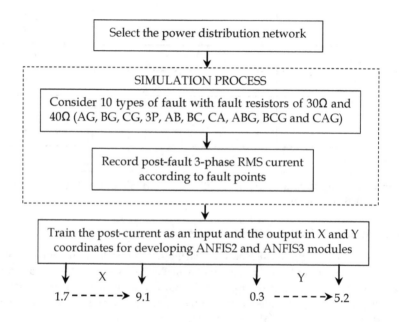

Fig. 12. A procedure for developing ANFIS2 and ANFIS3 in fault location identification

4.2.3 The 47 buses practical system

A single line diagram of the 47 buses practical system is illustrated in Fig.13. The system has seven 11 kV feeders and four 33 kV feeders including 87 CBs and 9 LIs in 11 kV feeder. In this chapter, only 11 kV feeders are used for simulating and testing in order to observe the performance of the developed fault diagnosis system. There are about 2464 line data of three-phase RMS post-fault current that is recorded during the simulation stages. Bus B1 is a power source bus in which it is located on coordinate (1, 2.2) while a monitoring bus B2 is coordinated on (1.8, 2.7). B2 is used for recording the three-phase RMS post-fault current during fault.

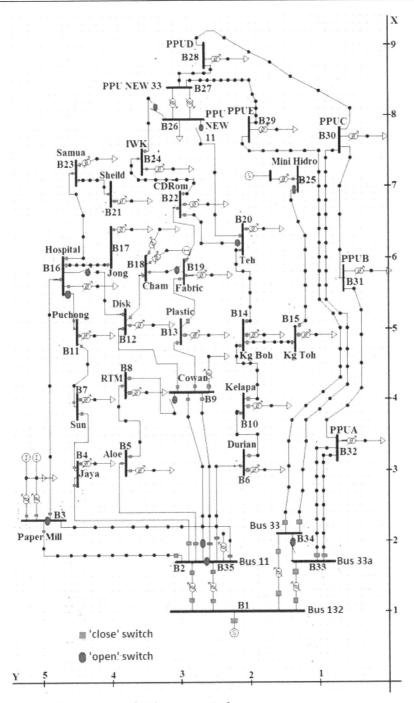

Fig. 13. A single line diagram of 47 buses practical system

4.3 Power restoration plan

Power restoration is a very important consideration in the development of fault diagnosis system especially in a distribution network. Hence, easy and fast action must be taken seriously to plan a power restoration procedure so that the power can be reenergized immediately in a safe and proper manner. This problem can be solved using the ANFIS approach by applying the operational states of CB and LI as shown in Fig.14. This simple technique uses only fault points in XY coordinates and the target is in operational states of CB and LI. These parameters are trained to develop the ANFIS4 model. The power restoration plan considers some requisite processes before developing the ANFIS4 module which are as follows: make sure the power network has a support feeder or a radial that is the nearest to fault feeders. No service loads due to line isolation (NSL) must be calculated in volt-ampere (VA). In addition, the total of loads in the supported feeder (TSL) and actual capacity of the feeder (CSF) should be defined clearly. If NSL is smaller than the differentiation between CSF and TSL, the power restoration plan will be carried to the next action.

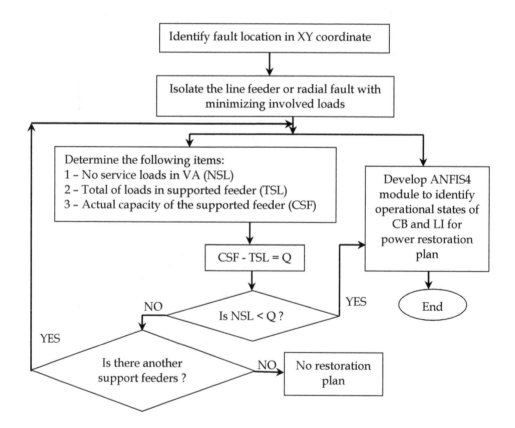

Fig. 14. A procedure for planning power restoration

4.3.1 ANFIS4 design for planning power restoration

Fig.15 shows an ANFIS4 design in a power restoration plan in a 47 buses practical system. The design has 93 modules namely ANFIS4-1 to ANFIS4-93 according to the total of CB and LI in the power network. The input and output data to the ANFIS4 are XY coordinates and binary number respectively. The binary represents the operational states of CB and LI as listed in Table 4. Digit '1' indicates 'close' position while '0' is for 'open' position.

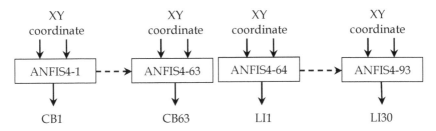

Fig. 15. ANFIS4 design for power restoration plan

ANFIS module	Input	Output
ANFIS4-1	Post-fault 3-phase RMS current	1 or 0
↓	"	↓
ANFIS4-93	"	1 or 0

Table 4. Input and output parameters for ANFIS4 module in power restoration plan

4.3.2 A procedure to train ANFIS4 for power restoration plan

There are several steps in developing ANFIS4 as well as collecting and training the data for the purpose of power restoration plan. The steps are as follows:

i.   Isolate the fault feeder or radial with the minimized load.
ii.   Identify the non-service loads (NSL) in volt-ampere (VA).
iii. Identify support feeder or radial that is available to the fault feeder and determine its load total (TSL).
iv.   Identify the support feeder capacity (CSF) in the power distribution network.
v.   Calculate the difference between CSF and TSL.
vi.   If NSL is greater than the difference, identify another support feeder or radial. If the feeder is available, repeat steps (iii) to (vi). But if the feeder is not available, the power restoration plan cannot proceed.
vii. If the NSL is smaller than the difference, the plan shall be implemented with a procedure as shown in Fig.16.

In this case, a 47 buses practical system has been selected for developing and testing the ANFIS4 module. There are 59 fixed fault points in the selected network, so the collected data has about 5487 lines which includes 63 CBs and 30 LIs in the practical system. Each line consists of three rows including X, Y coordinates and the integer '1' or '0' represents an operational state of CB and LI. The point coordinates are the input signal to the ANFIS4 whereas the integer is the output. Due to the 93 devices for all CBs and LIs, the ANFIS4 modules should be developed regarding to the numbers of the device. Thus, the modules are labeled as ANFIS4-1 to ANFIS4-63 for all CBs and followed by ANFIS4-64 to ANFIS4-93 for all LIs. Table 5 shows a distribution of the data set for each module to train them.

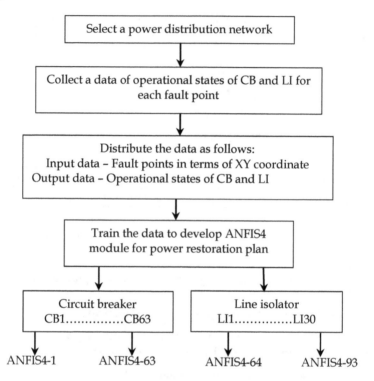

Fig. 16. A procedure for developing ANFSI4 module in power restoration plan

ANFIS1 module	Generated data set	Trained data set	Number of ANFIS input	Number of ANFIS output
ANFIS4-1	80	59	2	1
⋮	"	"	2	1
↓	"	"	2	1
ANFIS4-93	"	"	2	1

Table 5. A distribution of the data set for power restoration plan

5. The result of fault diagnosis

Fault diagnosis performance is measured through a precision and accuracy of ANFIS prediction. The measurement is in percentage error for ANFIS1, ANFIS2 and ANFIS3 while in absolute error for ANFIS4. The 47 buses practical system is used to test the ANFISs. The prediction results from ANFIS1, ANFIS2 and ANFIS3 are presented for practical systems that consist of 1232 test data sets. Meanwhile, ANFIS4 predicts about 2743 test data sets for the same system. The number of test data set is taken from 50% of overall data training.

5.1 The result on ANFIS1 prediction for classifying types of fault

Fig.17 shows the curve of a percentage error and a real target value for ANFIS1 prediction in classifying fault types in 47 buses practical system. The average percentage error for such power systems is 2E-5. Meanwhile, the maximum percentage error for the same power system is 0.52%. From the result on ANFIS1 in classifying the types of fault in terms of integer 1 to 10, it can be said that the ANFIS module is able to show precise prediction.

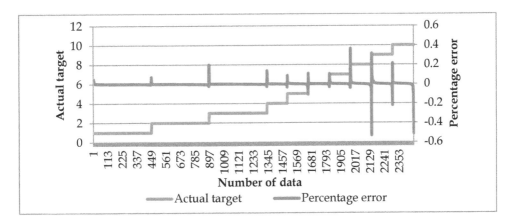

Fig. 17. The result on ANFIS1 prediction for classifying types of fault in the 47 buses practical system.

5.2 The result of ANFIS2 for identifying fault location in terms of X coordinate

The average percentage error of 1.2E-5% is the result of ANFIS2 prediction for identifying the fault location in terms of X coordinate as shown in Fig.18. From the figure, the maximum percentage error is 1.8% in the 47 buses practical system. As a conclusion based on the result, it can be seen that the developed ANFIS2 module is more precise in predicting the fault location than the developed ANN (artificial neural network) module with the same data.

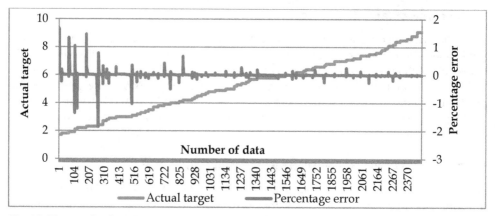

Fig. 18. The result of ANFIS2 prediction for identifying fault location in terms of X coordinate in the 47 buses practical system.

5.3 The result of ANFIS3 for identifying fault location in terms of Y coordinate

Fig.19 shows the result of ANFIS3 for identifying the fault location in terms of Y coordinate in the 47 buses practical system. It is found that about 2.1E-2% is the average percentage error and 10.7% is the maximum percentage error of the ANFIS3 prediction. As a conclusion, ANFIS3 has a high precision for identifying the fault location in terms of Y coordinate based on the average percentage error for 2464 numbers of data training in the system.

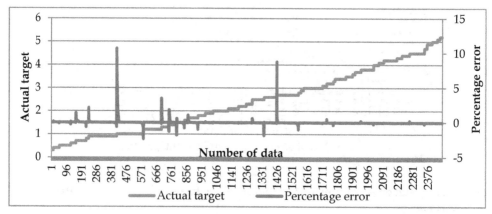

Fig. 19. The result on ANFIS2 prediction for identifying fault location in terms of Y coordinate in the 47 buses practical system.

5.4 The result on ANFIS4 for planning power restoration

Fig.20 shows the result on ANFIS4 prediction in determining the operational states of CB and LI for power restoration plan. Both devices are provided in the 47 buses practical system as a test network for the task. The result shows that the average absolute and maximum absolute errors are 1.14E-7 and 0.028 respectively. Referring to the Fig.20, B1 up to B26 represent 26 buses in the 11 KV of practical system. According to the result, ANFIS4 module gives a high accuracy in the prediction of the operational states of CB and LI for power restoration plan.

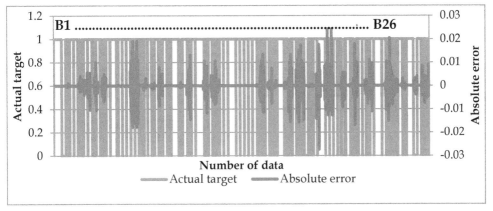

Fig. 20. The result on ANFIS4 prediction for determining operational states of CB and LI for power restoration plan in 47 buses practical system.

6. Conclusion

In general, this chapter describes an accurate method for identifying various fault types as well as the location for the purpose of power restoration plan using the operational states of CB and LI in the power distribution system. For this purpose, the ANFIS approach has been developed by using the representative integers 1 to 10 in classifying ten types of fault. This adaptive approach is also implemented to identify the fault location in power distribution system in terms of geometrical coordinates. Since the developed ANFIS modules are a useful fault diagnosis tool in completing the task, this approach is continuously developed for power restoration plan through network reconfiguration by controlling the operational states of CB and LI. The performance of ANFIS is tested on a 47 buses practical system in which it shows more precision when predicting the target for the developed fault diagnosis system.

7. Acknowledgment

This work of research has been financially supported by the Univerti Kebangsaan Malaysia (UKM) and the Universiti Teknologi Malaysia (UTM).

8. References

Binh, P.T.T., & Tuyen, N.D. (2006). Fault Diagnosis of Power System Using Neural Petri Net and Fuzzy Neural Petri Nets, *Power India Conference, IEEE*, pp. 5, ISBN 0-7803-9525-5, New Delhi, India, n.d.

Butler-Purry, K.L. & Marotti, M. (2006). Impact of Distributed Generators on Protective Devices in Radial Distribution Systems, *Proceedings of the IEEE Power Engineering Society in Transmission and Distribution Conference*, pp. 87-88, ISBN 0-7803-9194-2, Dallas, Texas, USA, May 21-24, 2006

Fauziah, A. (January 2005). PM Mahu Laporan Segera – TNB Diarah Siasat Terperinci Punca Gangguan Bekalan Elektrik, In: *Utusan Malaysia*, 14.01.2005, Available from http://www.utusan.com.my/utusan/info.asp?pub=Utusan_Malaysia&sec=Berita _Utama

Jang, J.-S.R. (1993). ANFIS: Adaptive Network Based Fuzzy Inference System. *IEEE Transaction on Systems, Man and Cybernetic*, Vol.23, No.3, pp. 665-685, ISSN 0018-9472

Marusic, A. & Gruhonjic-Ferhatbegovic, S. (2006). A Computerized Fault Location Process for Overhead Radial Distribution Feeders, *IEEE Mediterranean Conference on Electrotechnical*, pp. 1114-1117, ISBN 1-4244-0087-2, Benalmadena, Malaga, Costa del Sol, May 16-19, 2006

Michael Negnevitsky. (2005). *Artificil Intelligent: A Guide to Intelligent System*, Addison-Wesley, ISBN 0-321-20466-2, Harlow, England

Mitra, P., Maulik, S., Chowdhury, S.P. & Chowdhury, S. (2008). ANFIS Based Automatic Voltage Regulator with Hybrid Learning Algorithm. *International Journal of Innovations in Energy Systems and Power*, Vol. 3, No.2, pp. 1-5, ISSN 1913-135X

Mohamed, A. & Mazumder. (1999). A Neural Network Approach to Fault Diagnosis in a Distribution System. *International Journal of Power and Energy systems*. Vol.19, No.2, pp. 129-134, ISSN 1078-3466

Oliveira, K.R.C. (2007). *Advanced Intelligent Computing Theories and Applications with Aspects of Artificial Intelligent*, Springer Berlin, ISBN 978-3-540-74201-2

Richard, E.B.(2009). *Electric Power Distribution Reliability*. CRS Press, ISBN 978-0-8493-7567-5, USA

Sadeh, J. & Afradi, H. (2009). A New and Accurate Fault Location Algorithm for Combined Transmission Lines Using Adaptive Network-Based Fuzzy Inference System. *Journal of Electric Power System Research*, Vol.79, No.11, pp. 1538-1545, ISSN 0378-7796

Sekine, Y., Akimonto, Y., Kunugi, M. & Fukui, C. (1992). Fault Diagnosis of Power System. *Proceedings of the IEEE*. Vol.80, No.5, pp. 673-683, ISSN 0018-9219

Silva, K.M., Souza, B.A. & Brito, N.S.D. (2006). Fault Detection and Classification in Transmission Lines Based On Wavelet Transform and ANN. *IEEE Transaction on Power Delivery*, Vol.21, No.4, pp. 2058-2063, ISSN 0885-8977

Souza, J.C.S., Meza, E.M., Sebilling, M.T. & Do Corato, M.B. (2004). Alarm Processing in Electrical Power Systems through a Neuro-Fuzzy Approach. *IEEE Transaction on Power Delivery*, Vol.19, No.2, pp. 537-544, ISSN 0885-8977

Thomas Tamo Tatiesa & Joseph Voufo. (2009). Fault Diagnosis on Medium Voltage (MV) Electric Power Distribution Networks: The Case of The Downstream Network of The AES-SONEL Ngousso Sub-Station. *Journal of Energies*, Vol.2, No.2, pp. 243-257, ISSN 1996-1073

Zhisheng Zhang & Yarning Sun, 2007. Assessment on Fault-Tolerance Performance Using Neural Network Model Based on Ant Colony Optimization Algorithm for Fault Diagnosis in Distribution Systems of Electric Power Systems, *The 8th International Conference on Software Engineering, Artificial Intelligent, Networking and Parallel Distributed Computing*, pp. 712-716, ISBN 0-7695-2909-7, Qingdao, China, July 30 – August 1, 2007

Zhiwei Liao, Fushuan Wen, Wenxin Guo, Xiangzhen He, Wei Jiang, Taifu Dong, Junhui & Binghua Xu. (2008). An Analytic Model and Optimization Technique Based Methods for Fault Diagnosis in Power System. *The 3rd International Conference on Electric Utility Deregulation and Restructuring and Power Technologies*, pp. 1388-1393, ISBN 978-7-900714-13-8, Nanjuing, China, April 6-9, 2008

3

Fuzzy Inference System in Energy Demand Prediction

Thair Mahmoud, Daryoush Habibi,
Octavian Bass and Stefan Lachowics
School of Engineering, Edith Cowan University,
Australia

1. Introduction

Fuzzy Inference Systems (FIS) have been widely used in many applications including image processing, optimization, control and system identification. Among these applications, we would like to investigate energy demand modelling. Generally, developing an energy demand model is the challenge of interpreting the historical use of energy in an electric power network into equations which approximate the future use of energy. The developed model's equations are coded and embedded into a processor based system, which predicts the output when a certain type of input occurs. However, the range and quality of prediction is still limited within the knowledge supplied to the model. The major concern about the energy demand modelling is to categorize the type of prediction in short or long-term prediction. In addition, it is crucial to categorize the type of the power network to be modelled. Since identifying the useful historical operation data for setting the model parameters is crucial in modelling, the operation history of the modelled systems must to be analysed. In simple terms, modelling energy demand is the art of identifying the right modelling technique and system's operation parameters. The operation parameters differ based on the type and size of the modelled system. So, taking into consideration why the system is modelled will justify the selection of modelling techniques. Among the reasons for modelling energy demand is managing the use of energy through an Energy Management System (EMS).

For EMS, most of the Artificial Intelligence (AI) methods will lack robustness in terms of their programming and their required computation resources, especially when the EMS is designed to perform on-line quick response tasks. Artificial Neural Network (ANN) might be good candidate among modelling techniques, as there has to be a compromise between robustness of the method and its required computation resources for a specific type of modelling. However, there are a few reasons why ANNs are not suitable for our proposed discussion: their limited adaptability within limited computation resources, their training time and their models' complexity, especially when we deal with highly non-linear systems. Looking at our case study and the reasons this scenario is modelled, we have found that Fuzzy Inference Systems (FIS) are the most appropriate for modelling the energy demand in this specific system, since model development, model parameters, model adaptation capability and computation resources requirements are met. The reason behind choosing FIS to model the energy demand is the flexibility to control the prediction performance and the complexity of the model. Fuzzy modelling and reasoning systems have been widely utilised in literature because of their applicability and modelling performance. The use of Adaptive Neuro Fuzzy Inference Systems (ANFIS) gives the fuzzy modelling two extra valuable advantages: the training time and prediction accuracy compared to other modelling techniques. Fuzzy modelling has been successfully applied in different types of applications including electricity and gas demands, economics and finance, weather and meteorology studies, health and population growth, geographic information systems, traffic and transport systems, etc.

In the recent years, energy demand prediction modelling has been widely investigated, especially when its smartgrid applications have been rapidly grown, and energy price change has been rapidly correlated to the energy demand prediction. Different smart prediction mechanisms have been introduced in literature. (McSharry 2007) has developed a day-ahead demand prediction models, and (Alireza Khotanzad 2002) has introduced a new short-term energy demand prediction modelling technique which integrates the real-time energy price change in the prediction models. (Amir-Hamed Mohsenian-Rad 2010) have also introduced the real-time price environment modelling to perform an optimised residential load control, where a fundamental bid-based stochastic model is presented to predict electricity hourly prices and average price in a given period by (Mazumdar 2008). Among the prediction mechanisms we aim at addressing the use of Fuzzy Inference systems in developing short-term demand prediction models, which can be applied in SmartGrid and electronic market applications.

The objective of this chapter is to review the use of fuzzy logic in modelling the energy demand in a specific electric network after analysing its demand characteristics. This chapter will also discuss the use of FIS to improve the prediction performance and adapt the prediction to the real time effects. We consider a real electric power system by modelling its energy demand and verifying the prediction output results. The next section will consider the system's operation data while selecting the most effective modelling parameters, highlighting the use of FIS in modelling, choosing the suitable data clustering method and detailing learning, training and verification for different type of demand patterns.

2. Fuzzy modelling

Fuzzy modelling is a widely utilised and targeted modelling method. It attracts attention from academic and industrial research sectors because of its applicability and flexibility in interpreting the human decision in many complex computer controlled applications. Despite that its complexity has been mainly considered in modelling, as the number of developed fuzzy rules affects the modelling performance, fuzzy modelling is still one of the most efficient modelling techniques. Its main modelling concept is the same as that used in other modelling techniques, which is building mathematical expressions based on historical operation data for the modelled system. It is considered an effective technique to establish an FIS from a given nonlinear input-output set of data, when in fuzzy modelling, the data is partitioned in the input space and an optimal fuzzy rule table and membership functions are developed.

The data partition is performed using data clustering methods. A data clustering method is applied to partition the input-output set of data into a set of clusters. Depending on the type of clustering method, different type and number of clusters can be identified.

A range of data clustering methods have been illustrated in literature such as the nearest neighbourhood clustering method (Wang 1994), Gustafson-Kessel clustering method(Donald and William 1978), Gath-Geva clustering method (Gath and Geva 1989), fuzzy c-means (FCM) clustering method (Frank Höppner 1999), the mountain clustering method (Yager and Filev 1994) (Yager and Filev 1994), and Fuzzy Subtractive Clustering Method (FSCM) (Chiu 1994). However, the main problem of fuzzy modelling comes from the difficulties of choosing the right range of parameters which leads to the number of rules. In other words, the inaccurate parameter settings would deteriorate the prediction accuracy. Good fuzzy modelling parameter settings come from a good understanding of the modelled system and its modelling problems. The main justification for this problem is that when the number of clusters is increased, the prediction output will have strong alignment with the modelled data. As when the number of clusters equals to the number of data, the developed clusters will specifically resemble the training data characteristics, and lose the generality of resembling the system operation characteristics. Consequently, the clusters will mostly resemble a part of the operation data. Therefore, the prediction will miss other kind of operation data that differ from data modelled despite their availability within the modelled data range, which will result in a high prediction error. In contrast, when the number of clusters is reasonable, the prediction will cover the training data regions, as well as any other types of operation data, as far as they are located within the range of the training data. The prediction however will result in an acceptable range of error, which is fairly accepted by all research communities.

In other terms, a suitable parameters choice is the key solution for a successful fuzzy modelling, which will be based on an optimized number of rules and prediction accuracy level. This problem can be solved by analysing the modelled system operation history and identifying suitable modelling parameters. In addition, having experience about fuzzy modelling will help the modelling process. However, trial and error may be applied for output tuning in most of the modelling cases.

In comparing fuzzy modelling with ANN, it has been concluded that to select the right modelling method, it is crucial to consider the type and the size of the system, the amount of system's historical operation data and the required computation resources. Regarding the type and the size of our case study, it has been found that fuzzy modelling will suit the modelling process. More details about the case study and data analysis are explained in the case study section in this chapter. Full details about the fuzzy modelling process are also explained in modelling methodology section in this chapter. In this chapter we aim at discussing the use FIS as a tuner fuzzy system. The next section describes the main operation principles of Self-Tuning Fuzzy Systems STFS and the use of FIS to improve the prediction accuracy or to adapt the prediction to the external effects.

3. Self tuning fuzzy systems

In modern automation, adaptability has become crucial in implementing smart applications. In the way, that they resemble the human sense of adaptive thinking. Usually, ANN is highly utilised in implementing adaptive systems. However, self tuning and adaptive algorithms are not restricted to ANN, they can also be implemented through fuzzy logic and other optimization techniques. The specific tuning mechanism implementation is subject to the type of the problem or the system to be processed. The tuner and main systems may share the same input parameters, or they may receive two different types of inputs from external sources depending on nature of operation. Self-tuning systems have practically unlimited applications, and they have been widely utilised in academic and industrial applications.

Basically, a STFS is an on-line adaptive output fuzzy system, where its output is changed depending on the type of input and the pre-defined knowledge in the fuzzy tuning system. Generally speaking, a fuzzy system is called tuneable when any of its parameters (input/output scaling factors, membership functions shape and type or fuzzy rules) are changed instantly. It is a combination of general and tuner fuzzy, where the tuner FIS tunes the general system' parameters. Although sometimes both systems have the same input parameters, but they still perform different independent jobs. The main reason using STFS in modelling is to perform a short term prediction and to add the safe prediction estimations to the predicted output. This can be achieved by adapting the prediction to the external effects through a pre-defined knowledge based system.

By looking at our modelled case study, it has been noticed that the model has highly non-linear characteristics. So, developing a model for a high precision prediction is a major challenge. Hence it is required to focus on the model prediction accuracy to consider its weak-points. By considering the energy demand in the targeted case study, modelling knowledge could be added regardless of its availability in the supplied operation data. Using the self-tuning fuzzy system will help in adding the missing knowledge to the operation history data. For such kind of systems, a possible design with external input parameters from external data sources to tune the main fuzzy model output based on a knowledge base could be implemented. In this chapter we aim at utilising the real-time demand change measure to investigate the FIS ability to adapt the prediction output to the actual demand change. Alternatively, in our modelling discussion we also use the main fuzzy system's input parameters to tune the prediction based on a knowledge base system. Similarly, the tuning part may use different mechanisms, e.g. rules, membership functions or output scale tuning. The Weights Adjusting Method (WAM), which is the method that adjusts the output of the main system, is derived from the process needs for adaptation. WAM is set to adjust the weights of the output of the main system and its tuner based on the needed amount of adaptation. Depending on the tuner's fuzzy rule base, a suitable WAM can be derived. Although even when different types of models are discussed in our modelled electric network, only one WAM is applied. For simplicity, we aim at utilising an output scale adaptation design. The full design details are explained in the Modelling Methodology section, whereas the results will be discussed from the prediction improvement point of view and the adaptation performance in the Summary section. In the next two sections, the details about modelling twelve-month load patterns in a real electric network are presented. Additionally, the twelve models are equipped with twelve different tuner fuzzy systems to improve their prediction accuracy or to adapt their prediction to the external effects, depending on the purpose of the modelling.

4. Case study

The electrical energy use of the power network of the Joondalup campus of Edith Cowan University (ECU) in Western Australia has been selected in this study to evaluate the robustness of the proposed modelling technique. Just like most commercial buildings that the energy demand may depend on several independent variables, each having different weightings. Accept when it comes to a university type load profile, a few extra variables may affect the load change patterns. So, it is highly advantageous to analyse the historical operation data of the modelled system to indentify the effective variables. The ECU's electric network has nine substations serving 32 buildings. The minimum daily demand in this university does not drop below 500 kWh at any time, while the maximum daily demand may go up to 3500 kWh in summer daytime. Identifying the critical issues in the network is very important before proceeding in modelling. Fig. 1 shows Load changes in the ECU's Joondalup campus in January 2009.

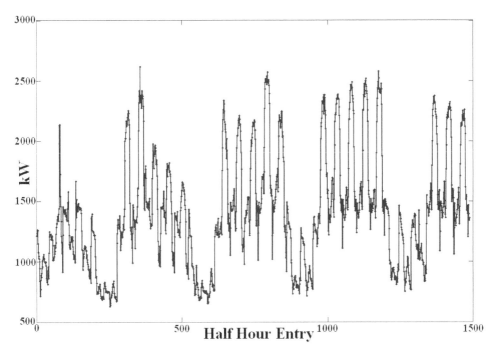

Fig. 1. Load changes in the ECU's Joondalup campus in January 2009.

By monitoring the load change in Fig.1, several load change patterns have been indentified including the weekdays, weekends and hours correlation. In addition, we can identify other important modelling factors e.g. weather, date, hours, order of the day (Monday, Tuesday,...,etc.) and type of the day (working day or weekends/holidays). It has also been noticed that big load changes are infrequent. In this modelling strategy, these big load change events are ignored. It is assumed that such big load changes need to be predefined or have warning settings assigned in order to avoid system overloads. From analysing these effective factors, we could draw a correlation picture about the load change in the ECU's Joondalup Campus and other effective parameters. For more details about load change analysis, Fig. 2 shows the correlation between a 30 minutes interval load change and other identified factors in the ECU's Joondalup campus in January 2009. Fig.2 includes 1500 entry of the correlated information data.

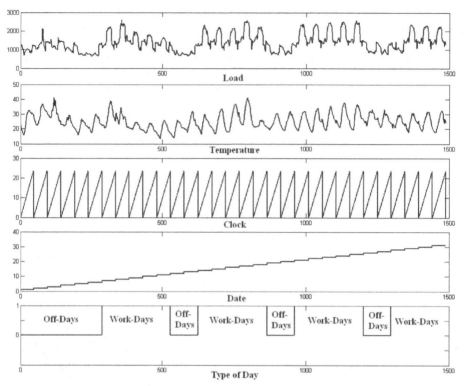

Fig. 2. Load change correlation with the effective factors for ECU's Joondalup campus in January 2009.

By spotting at the critical load change correlation among the identified parameters in Fig.2, several ideas about the energy use scenarios can be obtained. It is also noticeable that there is a big correlation between the daylight time, temperature, type of the day and the monthly order of the day. In Fig.2, only the effective load change parameters mentioned previously are illustrated. Theoretically, other load change parameters could be identified by analysing the university work hours, the nature of activities and the weekly time table in the university. From analysing the university weekly time-table, we could introduce another variable, which is the weekly order of the day. Although this parameter would have an effective load change contribution to the university's energy usage for a certain time of the year, namely the teaching period, but it rarely affects the load change in the remaining times of the year. On an average, it would require higher computation resources and would not indicate the load change effectively throughout the whole year. Therefore, it has been concluded not to consider this parameter among the modelling parameters. The next section details the modelling process and illustrates some hints about the fuzzy modelling.

5. Modelling methodology

This section covers the methodology to model the energy demand measured at 30 minute intervals in the ECU's Joondalup Campus. Basically, the model is developed by combining two modelling systems: the main FIS which is developed from modelling the input-output data using FSCM and ANFIS, and the second FIS system which is either developed by using the correlation between the energy demand and the temperature throughout the day, or by using the knowledge about the real-time demand change with its ability to achieve safe adaptation to the main model's output.

To improve the prediction accuracy and reduce the model complexity, the annual energy demand of the ECU's Joondalup Campus has been proposed to be split into twelve monthly models, represented by twelve different demand pattern models. Each model represents a one month demand model. Fig. 3 illustrates the proposed annual energy demand prediction structure for ECU's Joondalup campus, it also illustrates the possible extra added input to improve the prediction accuracy when possible.

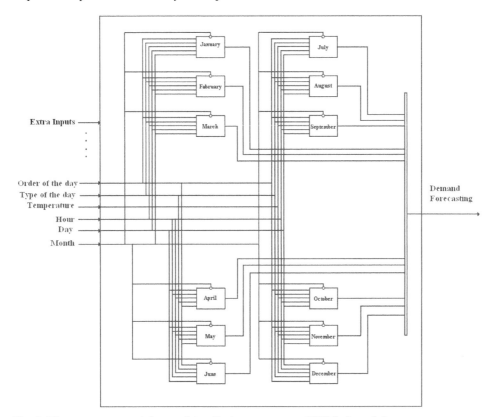

Fig. 3. The energy annual demand prediction structure of ECU's Joondalup campus

Splitting the annual demand model into twelve spilt sub-models gives the prediction the ability to cope with the twelve different load change patterns. In addition, it reduces the computation resources, when only one month model is active at a time. Thus the modelling uses twelve separate modelling methodologies depending on the load change analyses for the individual months. Regarding building the two FIS, their methodology is explained in the following subsections:

5.1 Main fuzzy system

In this subsection, we discuss the use of FIS in modelling. In this investigation, we aim at utilising data clustering methods to perform the fuzzy modelling. Data clustering methods divide the supplied data into different groups based on identified common characteristics in each group. However, these characteristics are identified based on the type of data clustering method. In literature, several types of data clustering methods have been discussed including the on-line and off-line methods. In our investigation, we aim at utilising off-line data clustering methods in modelling.

We aim at clustering the historical operation data of the targeted electric network to develop the demand prediction models. At the end of clustering, a fuzzy reasoning system will be developed. We aim at using ANFIS for developing our targeted fuzzy models. The complete modelling process is illustrated in Fig. 4.

In our modelling example, we use Fuzzy Subtractive Clustering Method (FSCM) (Chiu 1994). It is a method where each of the supplied data is tested under the condition that it has the highest density among the tested individuals. Every individual data is considered to be a candidate for the cluster centring. The individual density is evaluated as follow:

$$P_i = \sum_{j=1}^{n} e^{-\alpha \|x_i - x_j\|^2} \tag{1}$$

where

$$\alpha = \frac{4}{r_a^2} \tag{2}$$

The data density for a specific cluster centre candidate is evaluated from the number of nearer individuals that contribute to the cluster centre. The highest density is identified to become a first cluster centre. The cluster size is decided when FSCM parameters are set to cover a range of data individuals in the cluster's neighbourhood. The radius r_a , which is also referred by Range of Influence (ROI), defines the range of neighbourhood for the clusters extraction. Each of the developed clusters is a basis of a fuzzy rule that describes the system attitude, when the number of these clusters is the number of the fuzzy rules in the modelled network. When the first cluster centre is found, the next highest density is evaluated. Let the new investigated cluster centre to be x_i, and P_i be its density measure. When every data individuals is x_c, the next cluster centre is identified as follow:

$$P_i = P_i - P_{c1} e^{-\beta \|x_i - x_{c1}\|^2} \tag{3}$$

$$\beta = \frac{4}{r_b^2} \tag{4}$$

$$r_b = 1.5 r_a \tag{5}$$

Where P_{c1} is the next density point to be examined, and x_{c1} is the next data point to be examined. where r_b is a constant, which has the influence of reducing the density measure. r_b is defined based on the experience of data clustering. Usually, it is larger than r_a to avoid closely placed clusters. Sometimes, trial and error is used to select the best value of r_b. However, the value of r_b is set to $1.5 r_a$ as illustrated in literature (Chiu 1994), and r_a is set based on the experience about the data clustering. In our investigated cases different values were applied depending on the type of the problem. It is clearly noticed that ROI value decides the number of membership functions, thus influencing the complexity of the developed network. Table 1 illustrates the full details about r_a settings for the investigated cases.

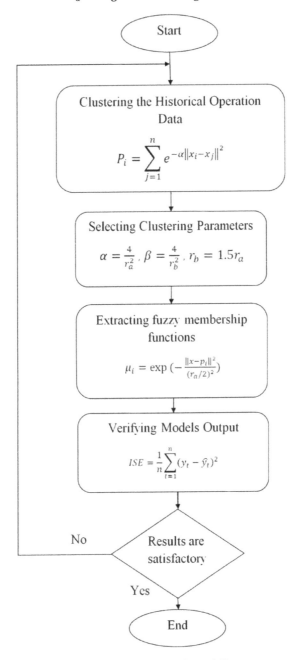

Fig. 4. Selecting suitable FSCM parameters in ANFIS modelling

The next stage is to repeat the above estimation process to identify other cluster centres. The process of indentifying clusters is repeated until the amount of new identified density is equal of less to 0.15 of the highest identified density. More information about FSCM parameters details is found in (Chiu 1994).

The identified data clusters can be easily utilised as fuzzy rules' centres in the zero-order Sugeno fuzzy models. When a data individual is located within the cluster range, a membership function between that particular data individual and its cluster centre is derived. Data affiliation to the cluster centres is derived as follow:

$$\mu_i = \exp(-\frac{\|x-p_i\|^2}{(r_a/2)^2})$$

(6)

where x is the cluster centre and p_i is the input set of data.

By clustering temperature, hour, day and load change data, random FSCM parameters values e.g. Influence Range, Squash, Accept Ratio and Reject Ratio are applied.

These values selection may have strong effects on the complexity of the developed models. Table 1 shows the number of membership functions and the selected ROI values for each of the twelve month models.

Months\Membership Functions ranges	ROI	Rules	Membership Fctn.
January	0.35	28	112
February	0.4	23	92
March	0.5	14	56
April	0.33	40	160
May	0.44	17	68
June	0.4	25	100
July	0.45	20	80
August	0.48	19	76
September	0.43	18	72
October	0.5	11	44
November	0.5	16	64
December	0.41	20	80

Table 1. ROI Values and Complexity of the 12 Month Models

After clustering is made, the developed membership functions are trained. Then, when the developed network is being trained, a simple test will be carried to verify the prediction accuracy of the developed models. To increase the range of prediction in the developed models, the historical operation of three years set of data (2007, 2008 and 2009) is used. The three years data has been divided into three different groups. The first set of data is used to extract the clusters, which is taken as a 90% of the 2007 and 2008 historical data. The second set of data, which is used to train the developed fuzzy systems, has been taken as a whole set of 2007 and 2008 data. Finally, the third set of data, which is used to verify the success of the developed model, has been taken as the 2009 operation data. Fig. 5 shows the data utilization in developing the demand models in this work.

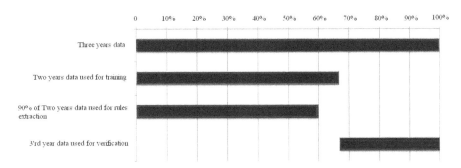

Fig. 5. Modelling data utilization for the ECU's Joondalup Campus energy consumption

After the rules which relate the input-output data have been developed, the developed clusters have been utilised in neuro-fuzzy networks to develop a zero-order Sugeno FIS, which will perform a 30 minutes ahead short-term prediction. In conventional fuzzy systems, trial and error is applied to tune the developed membership functions of the input-output universe of discourse of the fuzzy system. When ANN is used to tune the membership functions, an automated selection process based on the performance index is performed. The membership functions are trained to resemble the training data characteristics. In neuro-fuzzy networks, their networks structure is changed accordingly with the operation scenarios. Neuro-fuzzy networks however utilise the ability of learning of the neural networks to get the best tuning process with better performance and less time (Kandel 1993). Since the fuzzy systems have the property of universal approximation, it is expected that the equivalent neuro-fuzzy networks representation have the same property as well.

Adaptive Neuro Fuzzy Inference System (ANFIS) is another candidate to perform the fuzzy membership functions tuning. ANFIS structure was firstly proposed by (Jang 1993), where other models of ANFIS were proposed by (Chin-Teng Lin 1996) and (Wang and Mendel 1992). Fig. 6 illustrates the ANFIS structure with its learning mechanism.

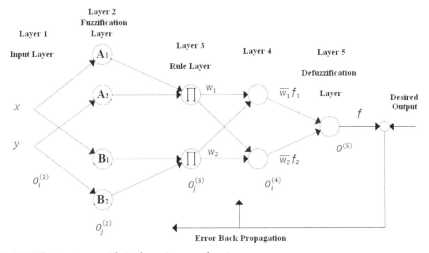

Fig. 6. ANFIS structure with its learning mechanism

where f is the output of the net, x and y are the inputs to this net. The weights of layer 3 are represented by $(\overline{w}_1, \overline{w}_2)$, and the weights of layer 4 are represented by $(\overline{w}_1 f_1, \overline{w}_1 f_2)$, where the used rules of Sugeno ANFIS in this model are expressed in the following form:

$$If\ x\ is\ A_1\ and\ y\ is\ B_1 \quad THEN\ f_1 = p_1 x + q_1 y + r_1$$

$$If\ x\ is\ A_2\ and\ y\ is\ B_2 \quad THEN\ f_2 = p_2 x + q_2 y + r_2$$

Where (p_i, q_i, r_i) are the parameters that are determined and referred to as the consequent parameters. More details about ANFIS parameters can be found in (Jang 1993).

In conventional neuro-fuzzy networks, back-propagation algorithm is used to adjust the network parameters, while in ANFIS the adjusting mechanism is performed by the Hybrid Learning Algorithm (HLA). HLA is basically combined of two identification methods, the least-squares method to identify consequent parameters for the forward pass in layer 4 and the back-propagation method for the backward pass to identify the premise parameters by the gradient descent in layer 2. This combination achieves faster convergence than that of the original back-propagation method. Table 2 illustrates the hybrid learning passes with their identified parameters:

Parameters\Direction	Forward pass	Backward Pass
Premise parameters	Fixed	Gradient descent
Consequent parameters	Least-square estimator	Fixed
Signals	Node outputs	Error signals

Table 2. Two passes in the hybrid learning procedure for ANFIS (J. S. R. Jang 1997).

Finally, when verification result is within an acceptable error bound, the modelling procedure is concluded. Fig. 7 illustrates the developed input membership functions for the four inputs zero-order Sugeno fuzzy system of January's operation of the ECU's Joondalup Campus power network.

From Fig 7, and from the developed Sugeno-fuzzy system for January demand prediction, the developed rules are explained as following:

If *(Temperature is Temperature in Cluster n) and (Hour is Hour in Cluster n) and (Day is Day in Cluster n) and (Day-type is Day-type in Cluster n)* **Then** *(Demand is Demand in Cluster n)*

Where $0 < n \leq$ number of developed rules.

Finally, for the other 11 months of the year, their developed models have different input-output ranges based on the pattern of operation and weather change throughout the four seasons of the year in city of Joondalup. Although other effective modelling parameters have been nominated for the proposed models, experimental investigations have been applied to use three-, four- and five-input modelling parameters for the demand prediction performance improvement, we stick to choosing the four-input modelling parameters, which has been successfully approved to be an optimal selection, from the prediction complexity and prediction improvement point of view, for the developing demand prediction models for the targeted power network.

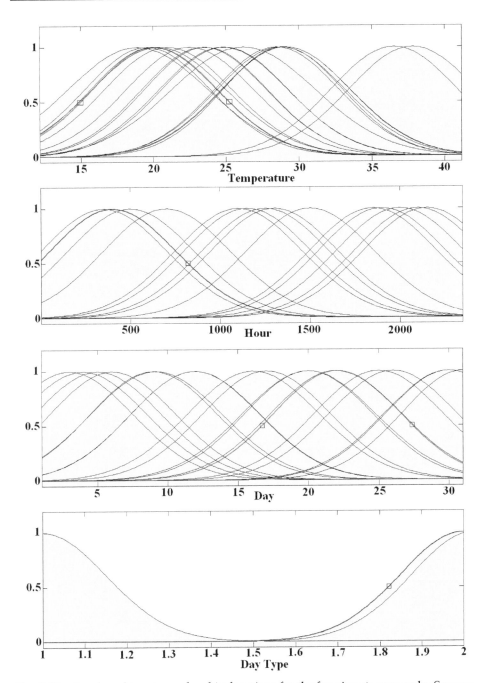

Fig. 7. The developed input membership functions for the four inputs zero-order Sugeno fuzzy system of January's operation of the ECU's Joondalup Campus power network.

5.2 The self-tuning fuzzy system

In this subsection, we aim at discussing two tuning mechanisms which have the ability to improve the prediction accuracy and adapt the prediction to the external effects such as the real-time demand change:

5.2.1 Parallel self tuning fuzzy system

First, we will look at improving our prediction results, based on our knowledge of the energy demand conditions, which could have been partially missed in the given historical operation data. We aim at using the self tuner fuzzy system to improve the prediction accuracy. Fig. 8 illustrates a main fuzzy system with its tuner fuzzy system combination.

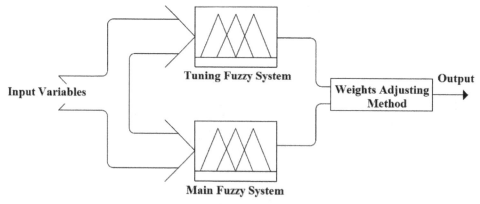

Fig. 8. Self-Tuning fuzzy system (self tuning fuzzy system)

For this system, it is required to enhance the performance of the prediction model by using the knowledge of the system performance, safe operation estimations and actual important needed decisions. In this work, two of the model inputs are selected to develop the fuzzy rule-based system. The rule-based system is developed to have a smooth transition between the specified operation cases in the decision making. In this work generally, we investigate the use of a one rule based system the twelve-month models. Table 3 illustrates the propose rule based system in this investigation.

Hour\Temperature	V. Cold	Cold	L. Warm	Room temp.	Warm	Hot	V. hot
Midnight	S. low	Normal	Normal	S. High	High	V. High	V. High
Dawn	Normal	S. High	High	V. High	V. High	Vv High	Vv High
Morning	Low	S. Low	Normal	Normal	S. High	High	V. High
Afternoon	V. Low	V. Low	Low	Low	S. Low	Normal	Normal
Sunset	V. Low	Low	S. Low	Normal	S. High	High	V. High
Evening	Low	S. Low	S. Low	Normal	S. High	High	V. High
Night	S. Low	Normal	S. High	High	V. High	V. High	Vv. High

Table 3. Self tuning fuzzy rule-based system

To cope with the operation pattern changes through the twelve months of the year, different membership functions are proposed for every month models: all twelve-month models have the same membership functions shape, but with different input/output ranges. Fig. 9 shows the proposed membership function design for the tuning fuzzy system of the January prediction.

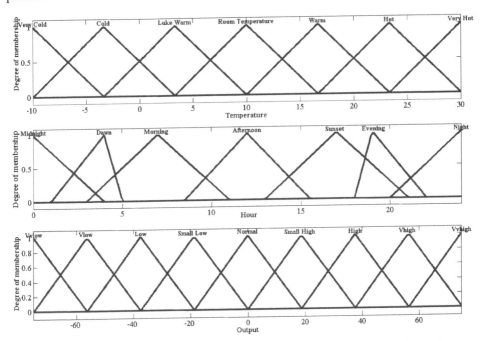

Fig. 9. Membership functions design for the tuning fuzzy system of January demand prediction model

Table 4 illustrates the membership function design for the twelve monthly prediction fuzzy systems.

Months\Membership Functions ranges	Temperature	Hour	Output
January	[-10 30]	[0 24]	[-75 75]
February	[-10 35]	[0 24]	[-75 75]
March	[-10 20]	[0 24]	[-50 50]
April	[15 35]	[0 24]	[-30 30]
May	[0 20]	[0 24]	[-40 40]
June	[0 25]	[0 24]	[-50 50]
July	[-20 20]	[0 24]	[-50 50]
August	[5 20]	[0 24]	[-30 30]
September	[-20 20]	[-4 24]	[-30 30]
October	[30 70]	[0 18]	[-200 200]
November	[10 50]	[-4 18]	[-100 100]
December	[-10 20]	[-4 18]	[-100 100]

Table 4. Membership function design ranges for the 12 monthly demand prediction tuning fuzzy systems

The twelve-month models have different self-tuning fuzzy designs. From the twelve designs, different prediction improvements are carried out. Conservatively, we would like to spot on the weakest prediction region throughout January in Fig. 10, which shows the demand prediction for the 17th to the 21st of January 2009 using ANFIS and Self-Tuning Fuzzy System. The amount of prediction improvement is calculated by evaluating the Integral Square of Error (ISE). ISE is evaluated as follow:

$$ISE = \frac{1}{n}\sum_{t=1}^{n}(y_t - \hat{y}_t)^2$$

where n is the number of entries, t is the time at each entry, y_t is the actual demand and $\hat{y}_t$ is the predicted value. From the equation above, the results show that the self-tuning fuzzy system has an enhanced prediction accuracy error. Table 5 shows the amount of ISE in each month and the percentage of improvement achieved by the fuzzy tuning systems.

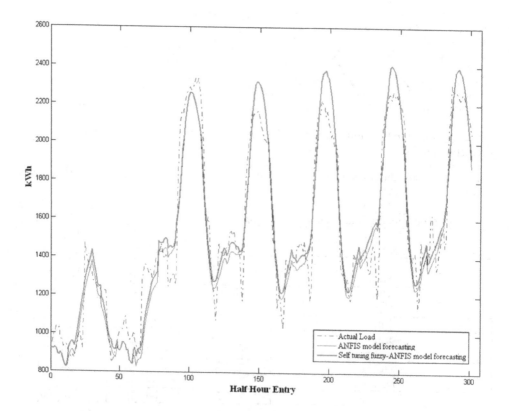

Fig. 10. Self tuning and ANFIS prediction for the 17th to the 21st of January 2009

Month\model	ANFIS ISE	Self-tuning fuzzy-ANFIS ISE	Improvement
January	29030	27230	6.2%
February	23590	22080	6.4%
March	42060	41040	2.5%
April	45300	45160	0.3%
May	27880	27760	0.4%
June	21660	21390	1.2%
July	19100	18760	1.7%
August	25030	24930	0.3%
September	24160	23760	1.6%
October	29260	28920	1.1%
November	27050	25060	7.3%
December	32890	30490	7.2%

Table 5. The amount of ISE in each month with improvement rate made by fuzzy tuning systems

5.2.2 Feedback Self-Tuning Fuzzy System

The Feedback Self-Tuning System FSTF is applied when any external effect variables such as the real load measures are fed to the model to adapt its prediction accuracy. With its adaptation mechanism, it adapts the model prediction to the external effects. The adaptation is developed based on an expert knowledge based system, which achieves successful and safe adaptation when the external effects are applied. The main principle of using this mechanism in our case study is to consider the actual instant demand change pattern change in the next subsequent prediction intervals, which provides flexibility to the model to correct its prediction path. The mechanism is built based on a feedback signal supply to allow the real demand change to enhance the prediction output.

Just like the parallel self-tuning fuzzy system, the adaptation may apply on the main fuzzy parameters e.g. membership function parameters, input-output universe of discourse or the output scale. For simplicity, we aim at utilising the output scale example in this chapter. Fig.11 illustrates the adaptation mechanism for the Feedback Self-Tuning System.

For the twelve different load change patterns in the targeted electric network, twelve different adaptation designs are required. For simplicity, one rule base system could be implemented to cope with twelve-month load change pattern. It is required therefore to tune the FSTFS input-output universe of discourse to fit its output with the load change patterns in every individual month. Out of this adaptation mechanism, different adaptation ranges may come from the twelve-month models. Table 6 illustrates the used rule based system for the proposed FSTFS.

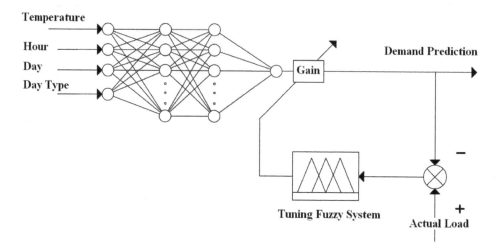

Fig. 11. Feedback Self-Tuning Fuzzy System

Error	Degree of Change
Vvery Low	Vvery High
Very Low	Very High
Low	High
Zero	Normal
High	Low
Very High	Very Low
Vvery High	Vvery Low

Table 6. FSTFS Rule Based System

Fig. 12 illustrates the FSTFS membership function design for the proposed demand prediction model.

The feedback prediction mechanism can be safely utilised in generation scheduling application or any other energy management system applications. For a safe use of prediction output, a safety margin value is added to the prediction results, which allows a flexible utilisation for the predicted demand.

To show the adaptation performance of the investigated systems, a conservative result is shown in Fig. 13, which illustrates the weakest prediction accuracy region throughout the year for the investigated electric power network.

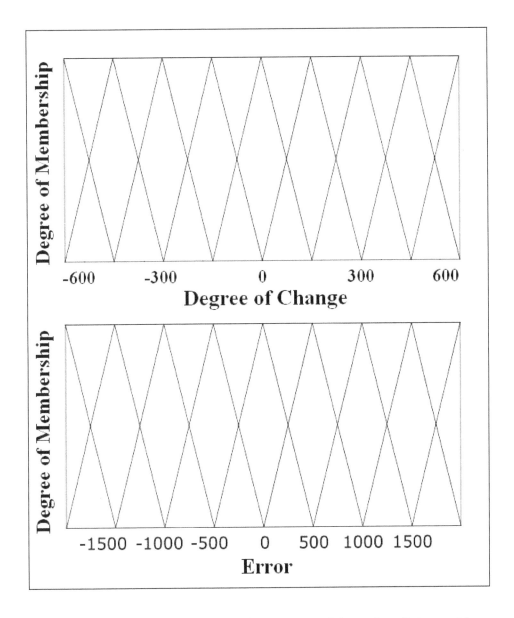

Fig. 12. FSTFS membership function design for the proposed demand prediction model

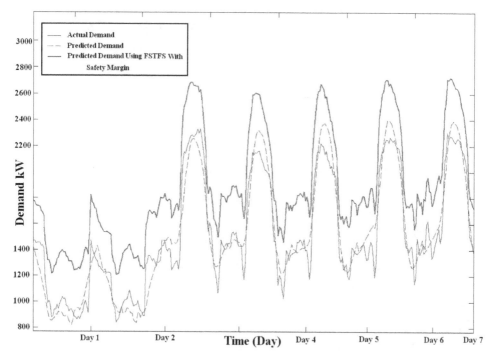

Fig. 13. Actual and Feedback Self-Tuning System Demand Prediction in the ECU Power Network for the 17th to the 21st of January 2009

6. Summary

In this chapter, the art of using FIS in modelling energy demand prediction for a specific electric network has been discussed. The type and the size of the modelled electric network has been comprehensively analysed in terms of the input-output identified effective parameters and their correlation in changing the pattern of the energy use. The identified parameters, however, were used in developing the energy demand prediction models. Fuzzy modelling process has been discussed by looking at its applications and limitations for the selected case study. In our modelling, we have utilised Fuzzy Subtractive Clustering Method to show the tips about its use in modelling, where ANFIS has been applied to develop the zero-order Sugeno fuzzy models. The annual energy demand model for the selected case study has been developed for an individual monthly basis with a specific design applied to deal with the twelve-month patterns. However, certain modifications had to be applied on each month to account for the peculiar conditions to that month.

In addition, two fuzzy tuning mechanisms have been used to improve the fuzzy models prediction accuracy. The first mechanism was used to add the safe operation assumptions to reduce the missing knowledge in the decision making for the developed models. The results from the first mechanism showed that the added fuzzy systems improved the prediction accuracy with different rates throughout the twelve months of the year. In case of the second fuzzy tuning mechanism, a real-time demand change has been added to the main fuzzy models to adapt their prediction to the real-time demand change through tuner fuzzy systems. From the twelve different demand changes throughout the year, different prediction adaptation ranges have been found. As a conclusion for these discussions, the FIS has a wide range of applications in modelling, especially when we deal with highly non-linear multiple input-output systems we have also shown throughout this chapter that several simulation studies have proved the success of using FIS in modelling, which brightens wider its range of mathematical and engineering applications.

7. References

Alireza Khotanzad, E. Z., Hassan Elragal (2002). "A Neuro-Fuzzy Approach to Short-Term Load Forecasting in a Price-Sensitive Environment." *IEEE TRANSACTIONS ON POWER SYSTEMS* 17(4): 10.

Amir-Hamed Mohsenian-Rad, a. A. L.-G. (2010). "Optimal Residential Load Control With Price Prediction in Real-Time Electricity Pricing Environments." *IEEE TRANSACTIONS ON SMART GRID* 1(2): 14.

Chin-Teng Lin, C. S. G. L. (1996). *Neural Fuzzy Systems: A Neuro-Fuzzy Synergism to Intelligent Systems*. New Jersey, Prantice-Hall.

Chiu, S. L. (1994). "Fuzzy Model Indentification Based on Cluster Estimation." *Journal of Intelligent and Fuzzy Systems* 2: 267-278.

Donald, E. G. and C. K. William (1978). *Fuzzy clustering with a fuzzy covariance matrix.* Decision and Control including the 17th Symposium on Adaptive Processes, 1978 IEEE Conference on.

Frank Höppner, F. K., Rudolf Kruse, Thomas Runkler (1999). *Fuzzy Cluster Analysis: Methods for Classification, Data Analysis and Image Recognition.*

Gath, I. and A. B. Geva (1989). "Unsupervised optimal fuzzy clustering." *Pattern Analysis and Machine Intelligence, IEEE Transactions on* 11(7): 773-780.

J. S. R. Jang, C. T. S., and E. Mizutani (1997). *Neuro-Fuzzy and Soft Computing – A Computational Approach to Learning and Machine Intelligence.* Upper Saddle River, NJ, Prentice Hall.

Jang, J. S. R. (1993). "ANFIS: adaptive-network-based fuzzy inference system." *Systems, Man and Cybernetics, IEEE Transactions on* 23(3): 665-685.

Kandel, I., & Langholz, G (1993). *Fuzzy Control Systems*, CRC Press.

Mazumdar, C. M. R. a. M. (2008). "Forecasting the Mean and the Variance of Electricity Prices in Deregulated Markets." *IEEE TRANSACTIONS ON POWER SYSTEMS* 23(1): 8.

McSharry, J. W. T. a. P. E. (2007). "Short-Term Load Forecasting Methods: An Evaluation Based on European Data." *IEEE TRANSACTIONS ON POWER SYSTEMS* 22(4): 7.

Wang, L. X. (1994). *Adaptive fuzzy systems and control: design and stabilityanalysis.* NJ, Prentice-Hall.

Wang, L. X. and J. M. Mendel (1992). *Back-propagation fuzzy system as nonlinear dynamic system identifiers.* Fuzzy Systems, 1992., IEEE International Conference on.

Yager, R. R. and D. P. Filev (1994). "Approximate clustering via the mountain method." *Systems, Man and Cybernetics, IEEE Transactions on* 24(8): 1279-1284.

Section 2

Application to System Modeling and Control Problems

4

System Identification Using Fuzzy Cerebellar Model Articulation Controllers

Cheng-Jian Lin* and Chun-Cheng Peng
National Chin-Yi University of Technology
Taiwan, R. O. C.

1. Introduction

Being an artificial neural network inspired by the cerebellum, the cerebellar model articulation controller (CMAC) was firstly developed in (Albus, 1975a, 1975b). With the advantages such as fast learning speed, high convergence rate, good generalization capability, and easier hardware implementation (Lin & Lee, 2009; Peng & Lin, 2011), the CMAC has been successfully applied to many fields; for example, identification (Lee et al., 2004), image coding (Iiguni, 1996), ultrasonic motors (Leu et al., 2010), grey relational analysis (Chang et al., 2010), pattern recognition (Glanz et al., 1991), robot control (Harmon et al., 2005; Mese, 2003; Miller et al., 1990), signal processing (Kolcz & Allinson, 1994), and diagnosis (Hung & Wang, 2004; Wang & Jiang, 2004). However, there are three main drawbacks of Albus' CMAC, i.e., larger required computing memory (Lee et al., 2007; Leu et al., 2010; Lin et al., 2008)), relatively poor ability of function approximation (Commuri & Lewis, 1997; Guo et al., 2002; Ker et al., 1997), and difficulty of adaptively selecting structural parameters (Hwang & Lin, 1998; Lee et al., 2003).

In order to tackle these disadvantages, several methods, such as online-based clustering (Kasabov & Song, 2002; Tung & Quek, 2002) for the above-mentioned first drawback, B-spline functions (Lane et al., 1992; Wu & Pratt, 1999) and fuzzy concepts (Jou, 1992; Chen, 2001; Guo et al., 2002; Ker et al., 1997; Lai & Wong, 2001; Zhang & Qian, 2000) for the second one, and competitive learning (Chow & Menozzi, 1994), clustering (Hwang & Lin, 1998) and Shannon's entropy and golden-section search (Lee et al., 2003) for the third one, were proposed. Among these approaches, further improvements were implemented by Lin et al. (2008) with self-constructing algorithm and Gaussian basis functions.

The rest of this chapter is organized as follows. Starting from the first CMAC model in 1975 the development processes, related learning algorithms and system identification examples of the fuzzy CMACs are briefly reviewed in section 2. Sections 3 and 4 respectively discuss the self constructing FCMAC (SC-FCMAC) and the powerful parametric FCMAC (P-FCMAC). Lastly, section 5 concludes this chapter, with suggested directions of further researches.

---

* Corresponding Author

2. From CMACs to fuzzy CMAC models

2.1 The traditional CMAC models

As mentioned in the previous section, the traditional CMAC model (Albus, 1975a, 1975b) has fast learning ability and good local generalization capability for approximating nonlinear functions. The basic idea of the CMAC model is to store learned data in overlapping regions in a way that the data can easily be recalled yet use less storage space. The action of storing weight information in the CMAC model is similar to that of the cerebellum in humans. Take a two-dimensional (2-D) input vector, or the so-called two-dimensional CMAC (2-D CMAC), as an example, while its structure is shown as in Fig. 1. The input vector is defined by two input variables, s_1 and s_2, which are quantized into three discrete regions, called blocks. It is noted that the width of the blocks affects the generalization capability of the CMAC. In the first method of quantization, s_1 and s_2 are divided into blocks A, B, and C, and blocks a, b, and c, respectively. The areas Aa, Ab, Ac, Ba, Bb, Bc, Ca, Cb, and Cc formed by quantized regions are called hypercubes. When each block is shifted by a small interval, different hypercubes can be obtained. In Fig. 1, there are 27 hypercubes used to distinguish 49 different states in the 2-D CMAC. For example, let the hypercubes Bb and Ee be addressed by the state $(s_1, s_2) = (2, 2)$. Only these three hypercubes are set to 1, and the others are set to 0.

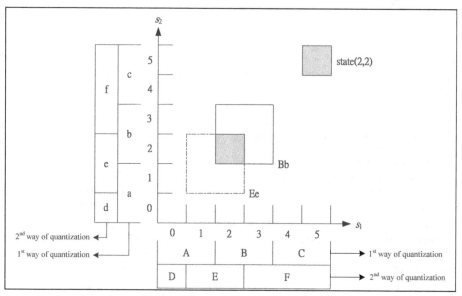

Fig. 1. Structure of a 2-D CMAC

In the work of (Mohajeri et al., 2009a) the hash coding and corresponding comparison with other neural networks for the CMACs were reviewed. There are 13 architectural improvements discussed in (Mohajeri et al., 2009a), including approaches of interpolation, numerous transfer functions (such as sigmoid, basic spline, general basis and wavelet ones), weighted regression, optimized weight smoothing, recurrence and generalization issue. Learning techniques such as neighborhood sequential training and random training were firstly considered, while the developments of other five training schemes (i.e., credit assignment, gray relational, error norm, active deformable and Tikhonov ones) were mentioned as well. In order to reduce relative memory usages, proposed approaches of hierarchical and self-organizing CMACs were reasoned, whereas the fuzzy variation of the self-organizing CMAC will be further presented in the following section of this chapter.

2.2 Fuzzy CMAC models

Many researchers have integrated the fuzzy concept into the CMAC network, such as in (Chen 2001; Dai et al., 2010; Guo et al., 2002; Jou, 1992; Ker et al., 1997; Lai & Wong, 2001; Lee & Lin, 2005; Lee et al., 2007a; Lee et al., 2007b; Lin & Lee, 2008; Lin & Lee, 2009; Lin et al., 2008; Peng & Lin, 2011; Wang, 1994; Zhang & Qian, 2000). In general, they use membership functions rather than basis functions, and the resulting structures are then called fuzzy CMACs (FCMACs).

In addition, the work of (Mohajeri et al., 2009b) provides a review of FCMACs, including over 23 relative aspects such as membership function, memory layered structure, defuzzification and fuzzy systems, was provided. Even FCMACs have originally reduced memory requirement for the CMAC, further discussions of clustering (such as fuzzy C-mean, discrete incremental clustering and Bayesian Ying-Yang) and hierarchical approaches for reducing memory sizes of FCMACs themselves were overviewed in (Mohajeri et al., 2009b) as well. Furthermore, as divided in (Dai et al., 2010), there are two classes of FCMACs architectures, i.e., forward and feedback fuzzy neural networks, which is useful for beginners to have a big picture of the basic concept for the FCMACs.

In the following sections, being the example models in this chapter the self-constructing FCMAC (SC-FCMAC, Lee et al., 2007a) and the powerful parametric FCMAC (P-FCMAC, Lin & Lee, 2009) are reviewed, in order to provide readers the insight knowledge of how these FCMAC work. Companied by their corresponding architectures and learning schemes, illustrative examples of system identification are provided as well.

3. The self-constructing fuzzy CMAC

From relative architectures to learning algorithms this section provides a brief review and discussions of the self-constructing FCMAC (SC-FMAC, Lee et al., 2007a).

3.1 Architecture of the SC-FCMAC model

As illustrated in Fig. 2, the SC-FCMAC model (Lee et al., 2007a) consists of the input space partition, association memory selection, and defuzzification. Similar to the traditional CMAC model, the SC-FCMAC model approximates a nonlinear function $y = f(x)$ by applying the following two primary mappings:

$$S : X \Rightarrow A \tag{1}$$

$$P : A \Rightarrow D \tag{2}$$

where X is an s-dimensional input space, A is an N_A-dimensional association space, and D is a 1-dimensional (1-D) output space. These two mappings are realized by using fuzzy operations. The function $S(x)$ maps each point x in the input space onto an association vector $\alpha = S(x) \in A$ that has N_L nonzero elements ($N_L < N_A$). Here, $\alpha = (\alpha_1, \alpha_2, \ldots, \alpha_{N_A})$, where $0 \leq \alpha \leq 1$ for all components in α is derived from the composition of the receptive field functions and sensory inputs. Different from the traditional CMAC model, several hypercubes are addressed by the input state x. The hypercube values are calculated by product operation through the strength of the receptive field functions for each input state.

In the SC-FCMAC model, we use the Gaussian basis function as the receptive field function and the fuzzy weight function for learning. Some learned information is stored in the fuzzy weight vector. The 1-D Gaussian basis function can be given as follows:

$$\mu(x) = e^{-((x-m)/\sigma)^2} \tag{3}$$

where x represents the specific input state, m represents the corresponding center, and σ represents the corresponding variance.

Let us consider a N_D-dimensional problem. A Gaussian basis function with N_D dimensions is given as follows:

$$\alpha_j = \prod_{i=1}^{N_D} e^{-((x_i - m_{ij})/\sigma_{ij})^2} \tag{4}$$

where Π represents the product operation, α_j represents the j-th element of the association memory selection vector, x_i represents the input value of the i-th dimension for a specific input state x, m_{ij} represents the center of the receptive field functions, σ_{ij} represents the variance of the receptive field functions, and N_D represents the number of the receptive field functions for each input state. The function $P(a)$ computes a scalar output y by projecting the association memory selection vector onto a vector of adjustable fuzzy weights. Each fuzzy weight is inferred to produce a partial fuzzy output using the value of its corresponding association memory selection vector as the input matching degree. The fuzzy weight is considered here so that the partial fuzzy output is defuzzified into a scalar output using standard volume-based centroid defuzzification (Kosko, 1997; Paul & Kumar, 2002). The term volume is used in a general sense to include multi-dimensional functions. For 2-D functions, the volume reduces to the area. If v_j is the volume of the consequent set and ς_j is the weight of the scale α_j, then the general expression for defuzzification is

$$y = \frac{\sum_{j=1}^{N_L} \alpha_j w_j^m v_j \varsigma_j}{\sum_{j=1}^{N_L} \alpha_j v_j \varsigma_j} \tag{5}$$

where w_j^m is the mean value of the fuzzy weights and N_L is the number of hypercube cells. The volume v_j in this case is simply the area of the consequent weights, which are represented by Gaussian fuzzy sets. Therefore, $v_j = w_j^\alpha \sqrt{\pi}$, where w_j^α represents the variance of the fuzzy weights. If the weight ς_j is considered to be one, as in this work, then the actual output y is derived as

$$y = \frac{\sum_{j=1}^{N_L} \alpha_j w_j^m w_j^\alpha}{\sum_{j=1}^{N_L} \alpha_j w_j^\alpha}.$$

(6)

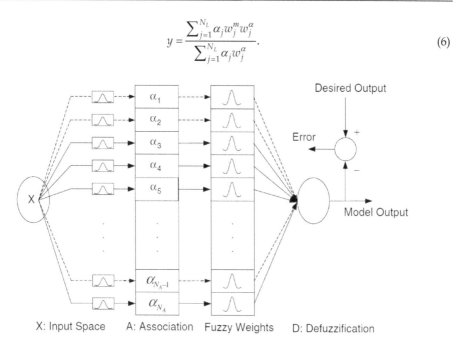

X: Input Space   A: Association   Fuzzy Weights   D: Defuzzification

Fig. 2. Structure of the SC-FCMAC model (Lee et al., 2007)

3.2 Learning Algorithm of the SC-FCMAC

In this section, for completing the SC-FCMAC model (Lee et al., 2007a) the self-constructing learning algorithm, which consists of an input space partition scheme (i.e., scheme 1) and a parameter-learning scheme (i.e., scheme 2), is reviewed. First, the input space partition scheme is used to determine proper input space partitioning and to find the mean and the width of each receptive field function. This scheme is based on the self-clustering method (SCM) to appropriately determine the various distributions of the input training data. Second, the parameter-learning scheme is based on the gradient descent learning algorithm. To minimize a given cost function, the receptive field functions and the fuzzy weights are adjusted using the back-propagation algorithm. According to the requirements of the system, these parameters will be given proper values to represent the memory information. For the initial system, the values of the tuning parameters w_j^m and w_j^σ of the fuzzy weights are generated randomly, and the m and σ of the receptive field functions are generated by the proposed SCM clustering method.

3.2.1 The input space partition scheme

The receptive field functions can map input patterns. Hence, the discriminative ability of these new features is determined by the centers of the receptive field functions. To achieve good classification, centers are best selected based on their ability to provide large class separation.

An input space partition scheme, called the SCM, is used to implement scatter partitioning of the input space. Without any optimization, the proposed SCM is a fast, one-pass algorithm for a dynamic estimation of the number of hypercube cells in a set of data, and for finding the current centers of hypercube cells in the input data space. It is a distance-based connectionist-clustering algorithm. In any hypercube cell, the maximum distance between an example point and the hypercube cell center is less than a threshold value, which has been set as a clustering parameter and which would affect the number of hypercube cells to be estimated.

In the clustering process, the data examples come from a data stream, and the process starts with an empty set of hypercube cells. When a new hypercube cell is created, the hypercube cell center, C, is defined, and its hypercube cell distance and hypercube cell width, Dc and Wd, respectively, are initially set to zero. When more samples are presented one after another, some created hypercube cells will be updated by changing the positions of their centers and increasing the hypercube cell distances and hypercube cell width. Which hypercube cell will be updated and how much it will be changed depends on the position of the current example in the input space. A hypercube cell will not be updated any more when its hypercube cell distance, Dc, reaches the value that is equal to the threshold value D_{thr}.

Figure 3 shows a brief clustering process using the SCM in a two-input space. The detailed clustering process can be found in (Lee et al., 2007a).

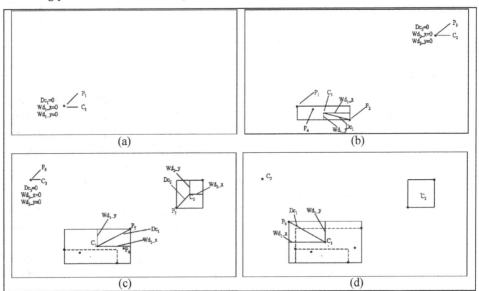

Fig. 3. A brief clustering process using the SCM with samples P_1 to P_9 in a 2-D space. (Notations: P_i for pattern, C_j for hypercube cell center, Dc_j is hypercube cell distance, Wd_{j_x} represents x-dimensions hypercube cell width, and Wd_{j_y} stands for y-dimensions hypercube cell width) (a) The example P_1 causes the SCM to create a new hypercube cell center C_1. (b) P_2: update hypercube cell center C_1, P_3: create a new hypercube cell center C_2, P_4: do nothing. (c) P_5: update hypercube cell C_1, P_6: do nothing, P_7: update hypercube cell center C_2, P_8: create a new hypercube cell C_3. (d) P_9: update hypercube cell C_1.

In this way, the maximum distance from any hypercube cell center to the examples that belong to this hypercube cell is not greater than the threshold value D_{thr}, though the algorithm does not keep any information on passed examples. The center and the jump positions of the receptive field functions are then defined by the following equation:

$$m_j = C_j, \quad j = 1,2,...,n,$$ (7)

$$\theta_j^r = \frac{1}{((n_s+1)/2)} \cdot r \cdot D_j,$$ (8)

where $j = 1,2,...,n$, and $r = 1,2,...,n_s$.

The threshold parameter D_{thr} is an important parameter in the input space partition scheme. A low threshold value leads to the learning of fine clusters (such that many hypercube cells are generated), whereas a high threshold value leads to the learning of coarse clusters (such that fewer hypercube cells are generated). Therefore, the selection of the threshold value D_{thr} critically affects the simulation results, and the threshold value is determined by practical experimentation or trial-and-error

3.2.2 The parameter-learning scheme

In the parameter-learning scheme, there are four adjustable parameters ($m_{ij}, \sigma_{ij}, w_j^m$, and w_j^σ) that need to be tuned. The parameter-learning algorithm of the SC-FCMAC model uses the supervised gradient descent method to modify these parameters. When we consider the single output case for clarity, our goal is to minimize the cost function E, defined as follows:

$$E = \frac{1}{2}\left(y^d(t) - y(t)\right)^2,$$ (9)

where $y^d(t)$ denotes the desired output at time t and $y(t)$ denotes the actual output at time t. The parameter-learning algorithm, based on back-propagation, is defined as follows.

The fuzzy weight cells are updated according to the following equations:

$$w_j^m(t+1) = w_j^m(t) + \Delta w_j^m,$$ (10)

$$w_j^\sigma(t+1) = w_j^\sigma(t) + \Delta w_j^\sigma$$ (11)

where j denotes the j-th fuzzy weight cell for $j=1,2,...N_L$, w_j^m the mean of the fuzzy weights, and w_j^σ the variance of the fuzzy weights. The elements of the fuzzy weights are updated by the amount

$$\Delta w_j^m = \eta \cdot e \cdot \frac{\partial y}{\partial w_j^m} = \eta \cdot e \cdot \frac{\alpha_j w_j^\sigma}{\sum_{j=1}^{N_L} \alpha_j w_j^\sigma}$$ (12)

$$\Delta w_j^\sigma = \eta \cdot e \cdot \frac{\partial y}{\partial w_j^\sigma}$$

$$= \eta \cdot e \cdot \frac{\alpha_j w_j^m \sum_{j=1}^{N_L} \alpha_j w_j^\sigma - \alpha_j \sum_{j=1}^{N_L} \alpha_j w_j^m w_j^\sigma}{\left(\sum_{j=1}^{N_L} \alpha_j w_j^\sigma\right)^2} \tag{13}$$

where η is the learning rate of the mean and the variance for the fuzzy weight functions between 0 and 1, and e is the error between the desired output and the actual output, $e = y^d - y$.

The receptive field functions are updated according to the following equations:

$$m_{ij}(t+1) = m_{ij}(t) + \Delta m_{ij} \tag{14}$$

$$\sigma_{ij}(t+1) = \sigma_{ij}(t) + \Delta \sigma_{ij} \tag{15}$$

where i denotes the ith input dimension for $i=1,2,\ldots,n$, m_{ij} denotes the mean of the receptive field functions, and σ_{ij} denotes the variance of the receptive field functions. The parameters of the receptive field functions are updated by the amount

$$\Delta m_{ij} = \eta \cdot e \cdot \frac{\partial y}{\partial \alpha_j} \cdot \frac{\partial \alpha_j}{\partial m_{ij}}$$

$$= \eta \cdot e \cdot \frac{w_j^m w_j^\sigma \sum_{j=1}^{N_L} \alpha_j w_j^\sigma - w_j^\sigma \sum_{j=1}^{N_L} \alpha_j w_j^m w_j^\sigma}{\left(\sum_{j=1}^{N_L} \alpha_j w_j^\sigma\right)^2} \cdot \alpha_j \cdot \frac{2\left(x_i - m_{ij}\right)}{\sigma_{ij}^2} \tag{16}$$

$$\Delta \sigma_{ij} = \eta \cdot e \cdot \frac{\partial y}{\partial \alpha_j} \cdot \frac{\partial \alpha_j}{\partial \sigma_{ij}}$$

$$= \eta \cdot e \cdot \frac{w_j^m w_j^\sigma \sum_{j=1}^{N_L} \alpha_j w_j^\sigma - w_j^\sigma \sum_{j=1}^{N_L} \alpha_j w_j^m w_j^\sigma}{\left(\sum_{j=1}^{N_L} \alpha_j w_j^\sigma\right)^2} \cdot \alpha_j \cdot \frac{2\left(x_i - m_{ij}\right)^2}{\sigma_{ij}^3} \tag{17}$$

where η is the learning rate of the mean and the variance for the receptive field functions.

3.3 An example: Learning chaotic behaviors

A nonlinear system $y(t)$ with chaotic behaviors (Wang, 1994) is defined by the following equations, i.e.,

$$\dot{x}_1(t) = -x_1(t)x_2^2(t) + 0.999 + 0.42\cos(1.75t) \tag{18}$$

$$\dot{x}_2(t) = x_1(t)x_2^2(t) - x_2(t) \tag{19}$$

$$y(t) = \sin(x_1(t) + x_2(t)) \tag{20}$$

We solved the differential Eqs. (18) and (19) with t from $t=0$ to $t=20$ and with $x_1(0)=1.0$ and $x_2(0)=1.0$. We obtained 107 values of $x_1(t)$ and $x_2(t)$ (the chaotic glycolytic oscillator, Wang, 1994) and 107 values of $y(t)$. Figure 4 shows $y(t)$, which is the desired function to be learned by the SC-FCMAC model.

The input data were $x_1^p(t)$ and $x_2^p(t)$, and the output data was $y^p(t)$, for $p=1,2,...,107$. For this chaotic problem, the initial parameters $\eta=0.1$ and $D_{thr}=1.3$ were chosen. First, using the SCA clustering method, we obtained three hypercube cells. The learning scheme then entered parameter learning using the back-propagation algorithm. The parameter training process continued for 200 epochs, and the final trained rms (root mean square) error was 0.000474. The number of training epochs is determined by practical experimentation or trial-and-error tests.

We compared the SC-FCMAC model with other models (Lin et al., 2004; Lin et al., 2001). Figure 5(a) shows the learning curves of the SC-FCMAC model, the FCMAC model (Lin et al., 2004), and the SCFNN model (Lin et al., 2001). As shown in this figure, the learning curve that resulted from our method has a lower rms error. Trajectories of the desired output $y(t)$ and the SC-FCMAC model's output are shown in Figures 5(b)-5(d). A comparison analysis of the SC-FCMAC model, the FCMAC model (Lin et al., 2004), and the SCFNN model (Lin et al., 2001) is presented in Table 1. It can be concluded that the proposed model obtains better results than some of the other existing models (Lin et al., 2004; Lin et al., 2001).

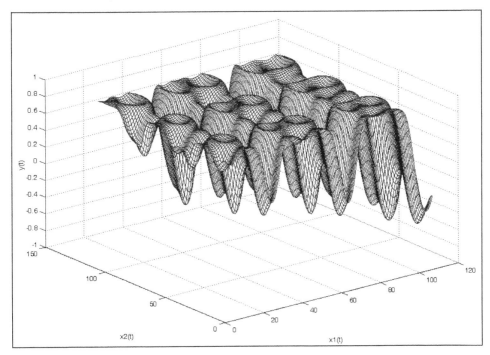

Fig. 4. The nonlinear system: $y(t) = \sin(x_1(t) + x_2(t))$, defined by Eqs. (18)-(20).

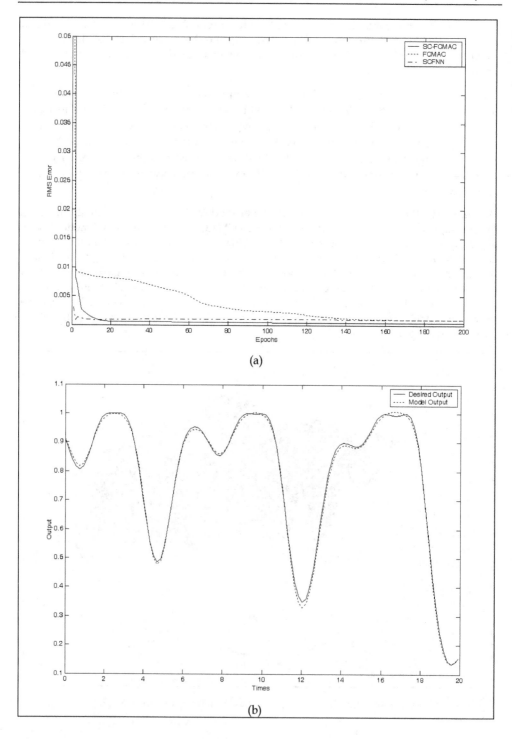

(a)

(b)

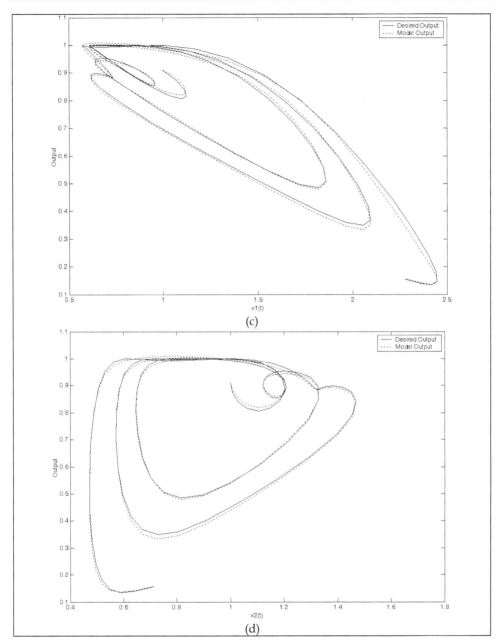

Fig. 5. Simulation results for learning chaotic behaviors. (a) Learning curves of the SC-FCMAC model, the FCMAC model (Lin et al., 2004), and the SCFNN model (Lin et al., 2001). (b) The desired output $y(t)$ and the SC-FCMAC model's output for time t dimension. (c) The desired output $y(t)$ and the SC-FCMAC model's output for $x_1(t)$ dimension. (d) The desired output $y(t)$ and the SC-FCMAC model's output for $x_2(t)$ dimension.

Items \ Models	SC-FCMAC	FCMAC (Lin et al., 2004)	SCFNN (Lin et al., 2001)
Training Steps	200	200	200
Parameters	18	18	20
Hypercube Cells	3	4	N/A
RMS errors	0.000474	0.000885	0.000908

Table 1. Comparisons of the SC-FCMAC model with some existing models for dynamic system identification

4. The parametric fuzzy CMAC (P-FCMAC)

In this section the architecture and learning algorithms of the parametric FCMAC (P-FCMAC, Lin & Lee, 2009) are reviewed, which mainly derived from the traditional CMAC and Takagi-Sugeno-Kang (TSK) parametric fuzzy inference system (Sugeno & Kang, 1988; Takagi & Sugeno, 1985). Since the SCM are inherent in the scheme of input-space partition for the P-FCMAC model, the performance of P-FCMAC is definitional better than the SC-FCMAC. Therefore, another system-identification problem is taken in order to explore the benefit of the P-FCMAC, fully and more fairly.

4.1 Architecture of the P-FCMAC model

As illustrated in Fig. 6, the P-FCMAC model consists of the input space partition, association memory selection, and defuzzification. The P-FCMAC network like the conventional CMAC network that also approximates a nonlinear function $y=f(x)$ by using two primary mappings, $S(x)$ and $P(\alpha)$. These two mappings are realized by fuzzy operations. The function $S(x)$ also maps each point x in the input space onto an association vector $\alpha = S(x) \in A$ that has N_L nonzero elements ($N_L < N_A$). Different from conventional CMAC network, the association vector $\alpha = (\alpha_1, \alpha_2, \cdots, \alpha_{N_A})$, where $0 \leq \alpha \leq 1$ for all components in α, is derived from the composition of the receptive field functions and sensory inputs. Another, several hypercubes is addressed by the input state x that hypercube value is calculated by product operation through the strength of the receptive field functions for each input state. In the P-FCMAC network, we use Gaussian basis function as the receptive field functions and the linear parametric equation of the network input variance as the TSK-type output for learning. Some learned information is stored in the receptive field functions and TSK-type output vectors. A one-dimension Gaussian basis function can be given as defined in Eq. (3). Similar to section 2.2, if a N_D-dimensional problem is considered a Gaussian basis function with N_D dimensions is expressed as Eq. (4) defined.

Each element of the receptive field functions is inferred to produce a partial fuzzy output by applying the value of its corresponding association vector as input matching degree. The partial fuzzy output is defuzzified into a scalar output y by the centroid of area (COA) approach. Then the actual output y is derived as,

$$y = \frac{\sum_{j=1}^{N_L} \alpha_j \left(a_{0j} + \sum_{i=1}^{N_D} a_{ij} x_i \right)}{\sum_{j=1}^{N_L} \alpha_j}$$ (21)

The j-th element of the TSK-type output vectors is described as

$$a_{0j} + \sum_{i=1}^{N_D} a_{ij} x_i \tag{22}$$

where a_{0j} and a_{ij} denote the scalar value, N_D the number of the input dimensions, N_L the number of hypercube cells, and x_i denotes the ith input dimension. Based on the above structure, a learning algorithm will be proposed to determine the proper network structure and its adjustable parameters.

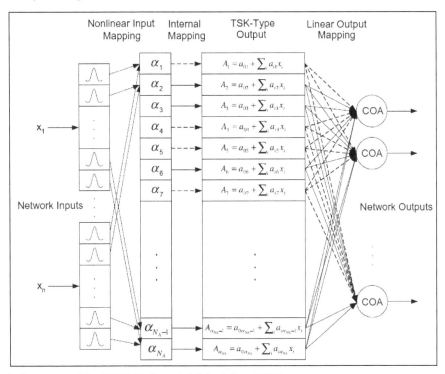

Fig. 6. Structure of the P-FCMAC model (Lin & Lee, 2009)

4.2 Learning algorithm of the P-FCMAC model

Similar to the SC-FCMAC model, the P-FCMAC's learning algorithm consists of an input space partition scheme and a parameter learning scheme. As the same SCM method was applied for input space partition, in the following paragraph the main focus is drawing to the scheme of parameter learning for the P-FCMAC, which is exhibited as in Figure 7.

First, the input space partition scheme (i.e., scheme 1) is used to determine proper input space partitioning and to find the mean and the width of each receptive field function. The input space partition is based on the SCM to appropriately determine the various distributions of the input training data. After the SCM, the number of hypercube cells is determined. That is, we can obtain the initial m and σ of receptive field functions by using SCM. Second, the parameter learning scheme (i.e., scheme 2) is based on supervised learning algorithms. The gradient descent learning algorithm is used to adjust the free parameters. To minimize a given cost function, the m and σ of the receptive field functions and the parameters a_{0j} and a_{ij} of the TSK-type output vector are adjusted using the backpropagation algorithm. According to the requirements of the system, these parameters will be given proper values to represent the memory information. For the initial system, the values of the tuning parameters a_{0j} and a_{ij} of the element of the TSK-type output vector are generated randomly and the m and σ of receptive field functions are generated by the proposed SCM clustering method.

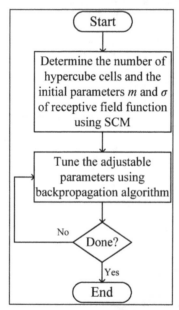

Fig. 7. Flowchart of the P-FCMAC model's learning scheme.

In the parameter learning scheme, there are four parameters need to be tuned, i.e. m_{ij}, σ_{ij}, a_{0j}, and a_{ij}. The total number of tuning parameters for the multi-input single-output P-FCMAC network is $2N_D{}^*N_L+4N_L$, where N_D and N_L denote the number of inputs and hypercube cells, respectively. The parameter learning algorithm of the P-FCMAC network uses the supervised gradient descent method to modify these parameters. When we consider the single output case for clarity, our goal is to minimize the cost function E, defined as in Eq. (9).

Then their parameter learning algorithm, based on backpropagation, is described in detail as follows. The TSK-type outputs are updated according to the following equation:

$$a_{0j}(t+1) = a_{0j}(t) + \Delta a_{0j} \tag{23}$$

$$a_{ij}(t+1) = a_{ij}(t) + \Delta a_{ij} \tag{24}$$

where a_{0j} denotes the proper scalar, a_{ij} the proper scalar coefficient of the i-th input dimension, and j the j-th element of the TSK-type output vector for $j=1,2,\ldots,N_L$. The elements of the TSK-type output vectors are updated by the amounts

$$\Delta a_{0j} = \eta \cdot e \cdot \frac{\partial y}{\partial a_{0j}} = \eta \cdot e \cdot \frac{\alpha_j}{\sum_{j=1}^{N_L} \alpha_j} \tag{25}$$

and

$$\Delta a_{ij} = \eta \cdot e \cdot \frac{\partial y}{\partial a_{ij}} = \eta \cdot e \cdot \frac{x_i \alpha_j}{\sum_{j=1}^{N_L} \alpha_j} \tag{26}$$

where η is the learning rate, between 0 and 1, and e is the error between the desired output and the actual output, $e = y^d - y$.

The receptive field functions are updated according to the following equation:

$$m_{ij}(t+1) = m_{ij}(t) + \Delta m_{ij} \tag{27}$$

$$\sigma_{ij}(t+1) = \sigma_{ij}(t) + \Delta \sigma_{ij} \tag{28}$$

where i denotes the i-th input dimension for $i=1,2,\ldots,n$, m_{ij} the mean of the receptive field functions, and σ_{ij} the variance of the receptive field functions. The parameters of the receptive field functions are updated by the amounts

$$\Delta m_{ij} = \eta \cdot e \cdot \frac{\partial y}{\partial \alpha_j} \cdot \frac{\partial \alpha_j}{\partial m_{ij}}$$
$$= \eta \cdot e \cdot \frac{\left(a_{0j} + \sum_{i=1}^{N_D} a_{ij} x_i\right) \sum_{j=1}^{N_L} \alpha_j - \sum_{j=1}^{N_L} \alpha_j \left(a_{0j} + \sum_{i=1}^{N_D} a_{ij} x_i\right)}{\left(\sum_{j=1}^{N_L} \alpha_j\right)^2} \cdot \alpha_j \cdot \frac{2(x_i - m_{ij})}{\sigma_{ij}^2} \tag{29}$$

and

$$\Delta \sigma_{ij} = \eta \cdot e \cdot \frac{\partial y}{\partial \alpha_j} \cdot \frac{\partial \alpha_j}{\partial \sigma_{ij}}$$
$$= \eta \cdot e \cdot \frac{\left(a_{0j} + \sum_{i=1}^{N_D} a_{ij} x_i\right) \sum_{j=1}^{N_L} \alpha_j - \sum_{j=1}^{N_L} \alpha_j \left(a_{0j} + \sum_{i=1}^{N_D} a_{ij} x_i\right)}{\left(\sum_{j=1}^{N_L} \alpha_j\right)^2} \cdot \alpha_j \cdot \frac{2(x_i - m_{ij})^2}{\sigma_{ij}^3} \tag{30}$$

where η is the learning rate of the mean and the variance for the receptive field functions.

4.3 An example: Identification of a nonlinear system

In this example, a nonlinear system with an unknown nonlinear function, which is approximated by the P-FCMAC network as shown in Figure 8(b), is a model. First, some of training data from the unknown function are collected for an off-line initial learning process of the P-FCMAC network. After off-line learning, the trained P-FCMAC network is applied to the nonlinear system to replace the unknown nonlinear function for on-line test.

Consider a nonlinear system in (Wang, 1994) governed by the difference equation:

$$y(k+1) = 0.3y(k) + 0.6y(k-1) + g[u(k)] \qquad (31)$$

We assume that the unknown nonlinear function has the form:

$$g(u) = 0.6\sin(\pi u) + 0.3\sin(3\pi u) + 0.1\sin(5\pi u) \qquad (32)$$

For off-line learning, twenty-one training data pairs are provided in Table 2 using Eq. (31). The off-line learning configuration of the twenty-one training data points is shown in Figure 12 (a). And the on-line test configuration of the 1000 data points is shown in Figure 12 (b) that using the difference equation is defined as:

$$\hat{y}(k+1) = 0.3y(k) + 0.6y(k-1) + \hat{f}[u(k)] \qquad (33)$$

where $\hat{f}[u(k)]$ is the approximated function for $g[u(k)]$ by the P-FCMAC network and $\alpha_0 = 0.3$, and $\alpha_1 = 0.6$. The error is defined as in Eq. (9)

In this example, the initial threshold value in the SCM is 0.15, and the learning rate is η=0.01. After the SCM clustering process, there are eleven hypercube cells generated. Using the first and second parameter learning schemes, the final trained error of the output approximates 0.00057 and 0.00024 after 300 epochs. The numbers of the adjustable parameters of the trained P-FCMAC network are 66.

For on-line testing, we assume that the series-parallel model shown in Figure 8 (b) is driven by $u(k) = \sin(2\pi k / 250)$. The test results of the P-FCMAC network are shown in Fig. 9(a) and (c) for the scheme-1 and scheme-2 methods. The errors between the desired output and the P-FCMAC network output are shown in Figs. 9(b) and (d) for the scheme-1 and scheme-2 methods. The learning curves of the scheme 1 and scheme 2 methods are shown in Fig. 10. Figures 9 can prove that the P-FCMAC network successfully approximates the unknown nonlinear function.

u	$g(u)$	$\hat{f}(u)$	u	$g(u)$	$\hat{f}(u)$
-1.0000	-0.0000	-0.000357	0.1000	0.5281	0.526161
-0.9000	-0.5281	-0.528020	0.2000	0.6380	0.640683
-0.8000	-0.6380	-0.628281	0.3000	0.4781	0.472271
-0.7000	-0.4781	-0.480252	0.4000	0.3943	0.400248
-0.6000	-0.3943	-0.392093	0.5000	0.4000	0.401699
-0.5000	-0.4000	-0.405011	0.6000	0.3943	0.390031
-0.4000	-0.3943	-0.390852	0.7000	0.4781	0.471195
-0.3000	-0.4781	-0.481167	0.8000	0.6380	0.648287
-0.2000	-0.6380	-0.635818	0.9000	0.5281	0.516553
-0.1000	-0.5281	-0.531204	1.0000	0.0000	0.007459
0.0000	0.0000	0.002119			

Table 2. Training data and approximated data obtained using the P-FCMAC network for 300 epochs

Table 3 shows the comparison the learning result among various models. The previous results were taken from (Wan & Li, 2003; Wang et al., 1995; Farag et al., 1998; Juang et al., 2000). The performance of the very compact fuzzy system obtained by the P-FCMAC network is better than all previous works.

Methods	Error	Methods	Error
P-FCMAC	0.00057 (Scheme 1) 0.00024 (Scheme 2)	Gradient Descent (Wang et al., 1995)	0.2841
SGA-SSCP (Wan & Li, 2003)	0.00028	MRDGA (Farag et al., 1998)	0.5221
Symbiotic Evolution (Juang et al., 2000)	0.1997	Genetic Algorithm et al. (Karr 1991)	0.67243

Table 3. Comparison results of the twenty-one training data for off-line learning.

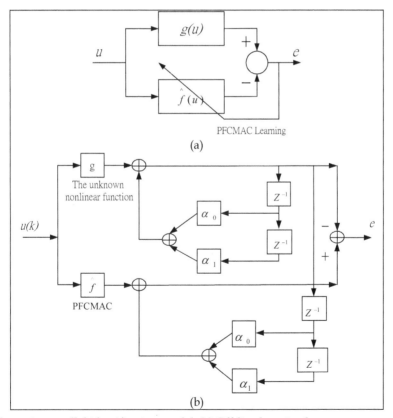

Fig. 8. The series-parallel identification model. (a) Off-line learning by twenty-one training data in Table IV; (b) On-line testing for real $u(k) = \sin(2\pi k / 250)$

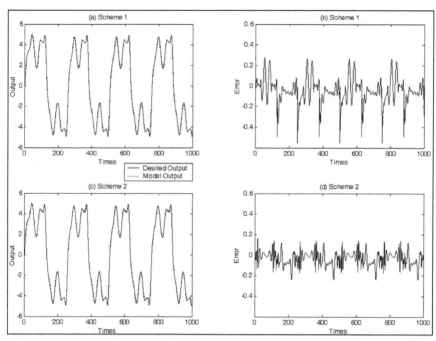

Fig. 9. Comparison of simulation results. (a) Outputs of the nonlinear system (solid line) and the identification model using the proposed network (dotted line) for the scheme 1 method. (b) Identification error of the approximated model for the scheme 1 method. (c) Outputs of the nonlinear system (solid line) and the identification model using the proposed network (dotted line) for the scheme 2 method. (d) Identification error of the approximated model for the scheme 2 method.

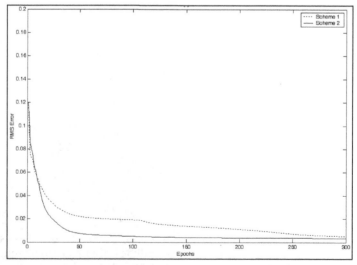

Fig. 10. Learning curves for the scheme 1 and scheme 2 parameter learning methods.

5. Conclusions

In this paper, starting from the discussion of traditional CMAC approach, two novel and latest developed fuzzy CMACs are reviewed. By summarizing the drawbacks of the CMAC model, relative improvement made in the literature have been addressed and presented. Via the exhibited self-constructing FCMAC (SC-FCMAC) and parametric FCMAC (P-FCMAC), not only the inference ability of FCMAC is demonstrated, but also presented the state-of-the art in the field of fuzzy inference systems.

6. References

Albus, J.S. (1975a). A new approach to manipulator control: The Cerebellar Model Articulation Controller (CMAC). *Transactions of the ASME: Journal of Dynamic Systems Measurement and Control*, Vol. 97, (September 1975), pp. 220-227, ISSN 0022-0434

Albus, J. S. (1975b). Data Storage in the Cerebellar Model Articulation Controller (CMAC). *Transactions of the ASME: Journal of Dynamic Systems Measurement and Control*, Vol. 97, (September 1975), pp. 228-233, ISSN 0022-0434

Chang, P.-L.; Yang, Y.-K.; Shieh, H.-L.; Hsieh, F.-H. & Jeng, M.-D. (2010). Grey Relational Analysis based Approach for CMAC Learning. *International Journal of Innovative Computing, Information and Control*, Vol.6, No.9, (September 2010), pp. 4001-4018, ISSN 1349-4198

Chen, J.Y. (2001). A VSS-type FCMAC Controller, *Proceedings of IEEE International Conference on Fuzzy Systems*, vol. 1, pp. 872-875, ISBN 0-7803-7293-X, December 2-5, 2001

Chow, M.Y. & Menozzi, A. (1994). A Self-organized CMAC Controller, *Proceedings of the IEEE International Conference on Industrial Technology*, pp. 68-72, ISBN 0-7803-1978-8, Guangzhou, China, December 5-9, 1994

Commuri, S. & Lewis, F.L. (1997). CMAC Neural networks for Control of Nonlinear Dynamical Systems: Structure, Stability, and Passivity. *Automatica*, Vol.33, No.4, (April 1997), pp. 635-641, ISSN 0005-1098

Dai, Y.; Liu, L. & Zhao, X. (2010) Modeling Of Nonlinear Parameters on Ship with Fuzzy CMAC Neural Networks, *Proceedings of IEEE International Conference on Information and Automation*, pp. 2070-2075, ISBN 978-1-4244-5701-4, June 20-23, Harbin, China, 2010.

Farag, W.A.; Quintana, V.H. & Lambert-Torres, G. (1998). A Genetic-Based Neuro-fuzzy Approach for Modeling and Control of Dynamical Systems. *IEEE Transactions on Neural Networks*, Vol.9, No.5, (September 1998), pp. 756–767, ISSN 1045-9227

Glanz, F.H.; Miller, W.T. & Graft, L. G. (1991). An Overview of the CMAC Neural Network, *Proceedings of IEEE Conference on Neural Networks for Ocean Engineering*, pp. 301-308, ISBN 0-7803-0205-2, Washington, DC, USA, August 15-17, 1991

Guo, C.; Ye, Z.; Sun, Z.; Sarkar, P. & Jamshidi, M. (2002). A Hybrid Fuzzy Cerebellar Model Articulation Controller Based Autonomous Controller. *Computers & Electrical Engineering: an International Journal*, (January 2002), Vol.28, pp.1-16, ISSN 0045-7906

Harmon, F.G.; Frank, A.A. & Joshi, S.S. (2005). The Control of a Parallel Hybrid-electric Propulsion System for a Small Unmanned Aerial Vehicle Using a CMAC Neural Network. *Neural Networks*, Vol.18, No.5-6, (June-July 2005), pp. 772-780. ISSN 0893-6080

Hung, C.P. & Wang, M.H. (2004). Diagnosis of Incipient Faults in Power Transformers Using CMAC Neural Network Approach. *Electric Power Systems Research*, Vol.71, No.3, (November 2004), pp. 235-244, ISSN 378-7796

Hwang, K.S. & Lin, C.S. (1998). Smooth Trajectory Tracking of Three-link Robot: a Self-Organizing CMAC Approach. *IEEE Transactions on Systems, Man, and Cybernetics, Part B: Cybernetics*, Vol.28, No.5, (October 1998), pp.680-692, ISSN 1083-4419

Iiguni, Y. (1996). Hierarchical Image Coding via Cerebellar Model Arithmetic Computers. *IEEE Transactions on Image Processing*, Vol.5, No.10, (October 1996), pp. 1393-1401, ISSN 1057-7149

Jou, C.C. (1992). A Fuzzy Cerebellar Model Articulation Controller, *Proceedings of IEEE International Conference on Fuzzy Systems*, pp. 1171-1178, ISBN 0-7803-0236-2, San Diego, CA, USA, March 8-12, 1992

Juang, C.F.; Lin, J.Y. & Lin, C.T. (2000). Genetic Reinforcement Learning through Symbiotic Evolution for Fuzzy Controller Design. *IEEE Transactions on Systems, Man, and Cybernetics, Part B: Cybernetics*, Vol.30, No.2, (Apr. 2000), pp. 290-302, ISSN 1083-4419

Karr, C.L. (1991) Design of an Adaptive Fuzzy Logic Controller Using a Genetic Algorithm, *Proceedings of the 4th International Conference on Genetic Algorithms*, ISBN 1-55860-208-9, pp. 450-457, San Diego, CA, USA, July 1991

Kasabov, N.K. & Song, Q. (2002). DENFIS: Dynamic Evolving Neural-Fuzzy Inference System and Its Application for Time-Series Prediction. *IEEE Transactions on Fuzzy Systems*, Vol.10, No.2, (April 2002), pp. 144-154, ISSN 1063-6706

Ker, J.S.; Hsu, C.C.; Huo, Y.H. & Liu, B.D. (1997). A Fuzzy CMAC Model for Color Reproduction. *Fuzzy Sets and Systems*, Vol.91, No.1, (October 1997), pp.53-68, ISSN 0165-0114

Kolcz, A. & Allinson, N.M. (1994). Application of the CMAC Input Encoding Scheme in the N-tuple Approximation Network, *IEE Proceedings of Computers and Digital Techniques*, Vol.141, No.3, (May 1994), pp. 177-183, ISSN 1350-2387

Kosko, B. (1997). *Fuzzy Engineering*, Prentice-Hall, ISBN 0-1312-4991-6, Englewood Cliffs, NJ.

Lai, H.R. & Wong, C.C. (2001). A Fuzzy CMAC Structure and Learning Method for Function Approximation, *Proceedings of IEEE International Conference on Fuzzy Systems*, Vol.1, pp. 436-439, ISBN 0-7803-7293-X, Melbourne, Australia, December 2-5, 2001

Lane, S. H., Handelman, D. A., & Gelfand, J. J. (1992). Theory and Development of Higher-Order CMAC Neural Networks. *IEEE Control Systems Magazine*, Vol.12, No.2, (April 1992), pp. 23-30, ISSN 1066-033X

Lee, C.-Y. & Lin, C.-J. (2005). A Self-Constructing Fuzzy CMAC Model for Learning Chaotic Behaviors. *GEST International Transactions on Computer Science and Engineering*, Vol.15, No.1, (July 2005), pp. 9-20, ISSN 1738-6438

Lee, C.-Y.; Lin, C.-J. & Chen, H.-J. (2007a). A Self-constructing Fuzzy CMAC Model and Its Applications. *Information Sciences: An International Journal*, Vol.177, No.1, (January 2007), pp. 264-280, ISSN 0020-0255

Lee, C.-Y.; Lin, C.-J. & Hsu, Y.-C. (2007b). A Parametric Fuzzy CMAC Model with Hybrid Evolutionary Learning Algorithms. *Journal of Multiple-Valued Logic and Soft Computing*, Vol.13, No.1-2, (February 2007), pp. 89-114, ISSN 1542-3980

Lee, H.M.; Chen, C.M. & Lu, Y.F. (2003). A Self-Organizing HCMAC Neural-Network Classifier. *IEEE Transactions on Neural Networks*, Vol.14, No.1, (January 2003), pp.15-27, ISSN 1045-9227

Lee, Z.J.; Wang, Y.P. & Su, S.F. (2004). A Genetic Algorithm based Robust Learning Credit Assignment Cerebellar Model Articulation Controller. *Applied Soft Computing*, Vol.4, No.4, (September 2004), pp. 357-367, ISSN 1568-4946

Leu, Y.-G.; Hong, C.-M.; Chen, Z.-R. & Liao, J.-H. (2010). Compact Cerebellar Model Articulation Controller for Ultrasonic Motors. *International Journal of Innovative Computing, Information and Control*, vol.6, No.12, (December 2010), pp. 5539-5552, ISSN 1349-4198

Lin, C.-J. & Lee, C.-Y. (2008). A Self-Organizing Recurrent Fuzzy CMAC Model for Dynamic System Identification. *International Journal of Intelligent Systems*, Vol.23, No.3, (March 2008), pp. 384-396, ISSN 1098-111X

Lin, C.-J. & Lee, C.-Y. (2009). A Novel Parametric Fuzzy CMAC Network and Its Applications. *Journal of Applied Soft Computing*, Vol.9, No.2, (March 2009), pp. 775-785, ISSN 1568-4946

Lin, C.-J.; Lee, C.-H. & Lee, C.-Y. (2008). A Novel Hybrid Learning Algorithm for Parametric Fuzzy CMAC Networks and Its Classification Applications. *Expert Systems with Applications*, Vol.35, No.4, (Nov. 2008), pp. 1711-1720, ISSN 0957-4174

Mese, E. (2003). A Rotor Position Estimator for Switched Reluctance Motors using CMAC. *Energy Conversion and Management*, Vol.44, No.8, (May 2003), pp. 1229-1245, ISSN 0196-8904

Miller, W.T.; Hewes, R.P.; Glanz, F.H. & Graft, L.G. (1990). Real-time Dynamic Control of an Industrial Manipulator using a Neural-Network Based Learning Controller. *IEEE Transactions on Robotics and Automation*, Vol.6, No.1, (February 1990), pp. 1-9, ISSN 1042-296X

Mohajeri, K.; Pishehvar, G. & Seifi, M. (2009a). CMAC Neural Networks Structures, *Proceedings of IEEE International Symposium on Computational Intelligence in Robotics and Automation*, pp. 39-45, ISBN 978-1-4244-4808-1, Daejeon, December 15-18, 2009

Mohajeri, K.; Zakizadeh, M.; Moaveni, B. & Teshnehlab, M. (2009b). Fuzzy CMAC Structures, *Proceedings of IEEE International Conference on Fuzzy Systems*, pp. 2126-2131, ISBN 978-1-4244-3596-8, August 20-24, Jeju Island, Korea, 2009

Paul, S. & Kumar, S. (2002). Subsethood-Product Fuzzy Neural Inference System (SuPFuNIS). *IEEE Transactions on Neural Networks*, Vol.13, No.3, (May 2002), pp. 578-599, ISSN 1045-9227

Peng, C.-C. & Lin, C.-J. (2011). A Self-Organizing Fuzzy CMAC Model for Classification Applications. *Innovative Computing, Information and Control Express Letters*, Vol.5, No.7, (July 2011), pp. 2389-2394, ISSN 1881-803X

Sugeno, M. & Kang, G.T. (1988). Structure Identification of a Fuzzy Model. *Fuzzy Sets and Systems*, Vol.28, No.1, (October 1988), pp. 15-33, ISSN 0165-0114

Takagi, T. & Segeno, M. (1985). Fuzzy Identification of Systems and Its Applications to Modeling and Control. *IEEE Transactions on Systems, Man, and Cybernetics, Part B: Cybernetics*, Vol.SMC-15, (January/Feburary 1985), pp. 116-132, ISSN 1083-4419

Tung, W.L. & Quek, C. (2002). GenSoFNN: A Generic Self-Organizing Fuzzy Neural Network. *IEEE Transactions on Neural Networks*, Vol.13, No.5, (September 2002), pp. 1075-1086, ISSN 1045-9227

Wan, W.Y. & Li, Y.H. (2003). Evolutionary Learning of BMF Fuzzy-Neural Networks Using a Reduced-Form Genetic Algorithm. *IEEE Transactions on Systems, Man, and Cybernetics, Part B: Cybernetics*, Vol.33, No.6, (December 2003), pp. 966–976, ISSN 1083-4419

Wang, C.H.; Wang, W.Y.; Lee, T.T. & Tseng, P.S. (1995). Fuzzy B-Spline membership Function (BMF) and Its Applications in Fuzzy-Neural Control. *IEEE Transactions on Systems, Man, and Cybernetics*, Vol.25, No.5, (May 1995), pp. 841–851, ISSN 0018-9472

Wang, D.-Y.; Lin, C.-J. & Lee, C.-Y. (2008). A New Pseudo-Gaussian-Based Recurrent Fuzzy CMAC Model for Dynamic Systems Processing. *International Journal of Systems Science*, Vol.39, No.3, (March 2008), pp. 289-304, ISSN 0020-7721

Wang, L.X. (1994). *Adaptive Fuzzy Systems and Control: Design and Stability Analysis*, Prentice-Hall, ISBN 0-1309-9631-9, Englewood Cliffs, NJ.

Wang, S. & Jiang, Z. (2004). Valve Fault Detection and Diagnosis Based on CMAC Neural Networks. *Energy and Buildings*, Vol.36, No.6, (June 2004), pp. 599-610, ISSN 0378-7788

Wu, J. & Pratt, F. (1999). Self-Organizing CMAC Neural Networks and Adaptive Dynamic Control, *Proceedings of IEEE International Symposium on Intelligent Control/Intelligent Systems and Semiotics*, pp. 259-265, ISBN 0-7803-5665-9, Cambridge, MA, USA, September 15-17, 1999

Zhang, K. & Qian, F. (2000). Fuzzy CMAC and Its Application, *Proceedings of the 3rd World Congress on Intelligent Control and Automation*, pp. 944-947, ISBN 0-7803-5995-X, Hefei, China, June 28-July 2, 2000

5

An Evolutionary Fuzzy Hybrid System for Educational Purposes

Ahmed Ali Abadalla Esmin[1], Marcos Alberto de Carvalho[2],
Carlos Henrique Valério de Moraes[3] and Germano Lambert-Torres[3]
[1]Lavras Federal University
[2]José do Rosário Vellano University
[3]Itajuba Federal University
Brazil

1. Introduction

When the Fuzzy Set Theory was proposed by Lotfi Zadeh in a seminal paper published in 1965, he noted that the technological resources available until then were not able to automate the activities related to industrial, biological or chemical problems. These activities use typically analog data which are inappropriate to be handled in a digital computer that works with well-defined numerical data, i.e. , discrete values.

Using this idea, Fuzzy Logic can be defined as a way to use data from typical analog processes that move through a continuous track in a digital computer that works with discrete values. The use of Fuzzy Logic for solving control problems has tremendously increased over the last few years. Recently the Fuzzy Logic has been used in industrial process control electronic equipment, entertainment devices, diagnose systems and even to control appliances. Thus, the teaching of fuzzy control in engineering courses is becoming a necessity. In a previous work, it has been presented a computational package for students' self-training on fuzzy control theory. The package contains all required instructions for the users to gain the understanding of fuzzy control principles. The training instructions are presented via a practical example.

Although this approach has proven to be convenient in giving to students an opportunity to appreciate real life like situations, it suffers a serious disadvantage: the type of learning. In fact, students often go through a "trial-and-error" method to select an appropriate control action, such as rule definitions or membership fitting. The problem of this type of learning is a tendency from students to get the erroneous concept that corrective actions are much a matter of guess. The purpose of this chapter is to present a strategy for an automatic membership function fitting using three different evolutionary algorithms, namely: modified genetic algorithms (MGA), particle swarm optimization (PSO) and hybrid particle swarm optimization (HPSO).

The proposed strategies are applied in a computational package for fuzzy logic learning. This computer program was developed for self-training in engineering students in the theory of fuzzy control. The program contains all necessary instructions for users to understand the principles of diffuse control. In this package the main goal is to park a vehicle in a garage, starting from any starting position. The user must first develop a set of fuzzy control rules and functions of relevance that will shape the trajectory of the vehicle. The processes of fuzzification and defuzzification variables are performed by the program without user interference.

2. Description of the main features of the training package

The computational package has as main objective to park a vehicle in a garage, starting from any starting point within a pre-defined area. To this goal, the user should design a set of fuzzy control rules and also the functions of relevance that will control the trajectory of the vehicle. To set these rules, the program offers various menus with Windows and numerical routines. The processes of fuzzification and defuzzification variables are made by the program without user interference (Park et al., 1994).

Figure 1 shows the main screen to represent the problem of parking of a vehicle. This window shows the position of the garage, the existing limits (the walls) and the values of coordinated limits. Also this window presents the input variables (x, y) measured from the center point of the rear of the vehicle and finally, the car angle (ϕ).

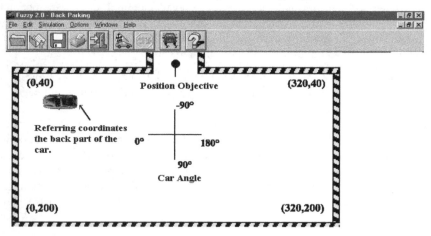

Fig. 1. Main screen of the program

For parking the vehicle, some conditions are established, and belong to two types: computational package related and linked to logical. The conditions attaching to the package represent the physical limitations, they are:

a.   limits of input variables:
-    position (x, y): $0 < x < 32$ and $0 < y < 20$ (in meters - parking dimensions);
-    car angle of $-90° \leq \phi \leq 270°$;
-    sense of the vehicle: forward or backward.
b.   limit of the output variable:
-    vehicle wheel angle $-30° \leq \theta \leq 30°$ (limitation of the real model).

With respect to logical limitations, they may vary according to the types of strategies employed. Some examples of these strategies can be, among others:

-   minimization of the number of changes of vehicle direction (forward or backward);
-   minimizing the space traversed by vehicle to the garage;
-   the restriction of parts of garage for parking.

For the movement of the vehicle shall be laid down the following conditions: Acceleration equal to 1 (m/s²) and maximum speed 1 (m/s). These two values are used as reference for all movements. To reverse the direction of motion of the vehicle there are three possibilities, which are:

a. shock against the wall: when the system verifies that the vehicle will collide against the wall in the next step;
b. rule that forces the inversion: when the reverse order is used as a result of a rule; or,
c. lack of outputs: when no rule is used by the control, i.e., if the output is zero.

The user of this computational package can define a new system by creating the roles of relevance and control rules. Initially, the user sets the number of functions of relevance for each variable. When the functions are created, they are equally spaced on the surface of the control variable. The user can modify these functions of belongingness by Fuzzy Sets Edition window. Figure 2 presents an example of editing for the x input variable.

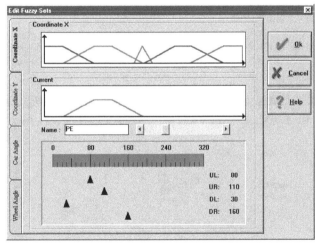

Fig. 2. Fuzzy Sets Edition window

To set the rules for the control, i.e., how the functions of relevance will be grouped, there is the Fuzzy Rules Edition window. In Figure 3, one can find two regions of interest. The first where there is the possibility of selecting the direction (forward or reverse) and coordinated corresponding to the angle of the car. The second region of interest contains the padding of the conclusion of the rule. This can be done by selecting one of the output values (or none for a rule does not set or reverse). For instance for x = LE (left), y = YT (small values), car angle = RB (right big angle) and direction = ahead (forward) values was selected as NB (negative big angle) to wheel angle, which corresponds to rule:

"IF *x* is **and** LE *y* **and** is YT **and** *car angle* is RB **and** direction of movement is *forward (ahead)* THEN wheel angle is NB."

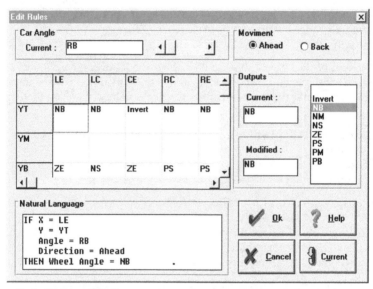

Fig. 3. Fuzzy Rules Edition window

Through the initial position of the Edition menu option the user can set a start position (x-y coordinates and car angle ϕ) to the vehicle. The simulation is started through the Start menu simulation. Figure 4 shows three possible initial positions.

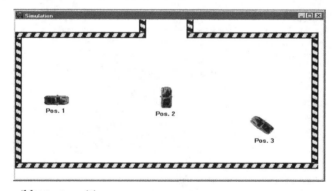

Fig. 4. Three possible start positions

In the examples of simulation in Figure 5, you can check the trail left by the vehicle during its trajectory. Each point means iteration (i.e. a full pass on the set of rules) and the count is recorded in the variables window. The first example, shown in Figure 5 (a), has produced 628 iterations; while, in the second, in Figure 5(b), for another set of rules was queried by 224 times, for the same start position. It is easy to see that the second set of rules has a batter performance than the first one for this start position.

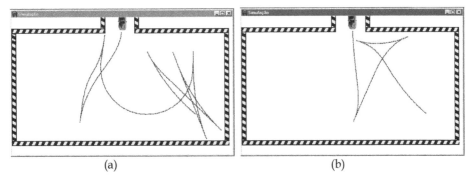

(a)   (b)

Fig. 5. Examples of computational simulation package

The computational package has features that allow you to vary the size of the car between: small, medium or large. This variation creates the opportunity to verify the behavior of the control system for an outfit that has changed some of its grandeur. The computational package also has three methods of defuzzification, which are: the centroid (center of gravity), average of the areas and average of maximum values (Kandel & Langholz, 1993).

In the first version of the computational package, the learning process used is by trial and error. The user creates the functions of relevance, provides a set of rules and then performs several tests to verify the quality of control. It is known that this learning process (by trial and error) may not bring the expected results because several errors of interpretation can occur (da Silva et al., 2010).

3. Description of the evolutionary methods used in the hybrid system

The whole task of search and the optimization has several components, including: the search space, where they are considered all possibilities of solution of a given problem and the evaluation function (or function), a way to evaluate members of the search space. There are many methods of search and evaluation functions.

Search optimization techniques and traditional begin with a single candidate, iteratively, is manipulated using some heuristics (static) directly associated with the problem to be solved. Generally, these processes are not heuristic algorithmic and its simulation in computers can be very complex. Despite these methods were not sufficiently robust, this does not imply they are useless. In practice, they are widely used, successfully, in innumerable applications (Ross, 2010).

On the other hand, the evolutionary computation techniques operate on a population of candidates in parallel. Thus, they can search in different areas of the solution space, allocating an appropriate number of members to search in multiple regions.

Meta-heuristic methods differ from traditional methods of search and optimization, mainly in four aspects (Esmin et al., 2005; Medsker, 2005):

1. Meta-heuristic methods work with an encoding of the set of parameters and not with their own parameters.
2. Meta-heuristic methods work with a population and not with a single point.

3. Meta-heuristic methods use cost information or reward and not derived or other auxiliary knowledge.
4. Meta-heuristic methods use probabilistic transition rules and not deterministic.

In addition to being a strategy to generate-and-test very elegant, because they are based on social organization or biological evolution, are able to identify and explore environmental factors and converge to optimal solutions, or approximately optimal in overall levels. The better a person adapt to their environment, the greater your chance of surviving and generate descendants: this is the basic concept of social organization or biological genetic evolution. The biological area more closely linked to genetic algorithms is the genetics, and the social area is particle swarm optimization.

3.1 Genetic algorithms

In the years 50 and 60, many biologists began to develop computational simulations of genetic systems. However, it was John Holland who began, in earnest, developing the first researches in the theme. Holland was gradually refining their ideas and in 1975 published his book "Adaptation in Natural and Artificial Systems" (Holland, 1975), now considered the bible of genetic algorithms. Since then, these algorithms are being applied with success in the most diverse problems of optimization and machine learning.

Genetic algorithms are global optimization algorithms, based on the mechanisms of natural selection and genetics. They employ a parallel search strategy and structured, but random, which is geared toward enhancing search of "high fitness" points, i.e. points where the function to be minimized (or maximized) has values relatively low (or high).

Although they are not random, random walks, directed not because explore historical information to find new points of search where are expected best performances. This is done through iterative processes, where each iteration is called generation.

During each iteration, the principles of selection and reproduction are applied to a population of candidates that can vary, depending on the complexity of the problem and the computational resources available. Through the selection, if determines which individuals will be able to reproduce, generating a particular number of descendants for the next generation, with a probability given by its index of fitness. In other words, individuals with greater relative adaptation have greater chances of reproducing.

The starting point for the use of genetic algorithms, as a tool for troubleshooting is the representation of these problems in a way that the genetic algorithms to work properly on them. Most representations are genotype, use vectors of finite size in a finite alphabet.

Traditionally, individuals are represented by binary vectors, where each element of a vector (1) denotes the presence or absence (0) of a particular characteristic. However, there are applications where it is more convenient to use representations for integers as shown later in this work.

The basic principle of operation of AGs is that a selection criterion will do with that, after many generations, the initial set of individuals generates another set of individuals more able. Most methods are designed to check individuals preferentially choose majors with fitness, although not exclusively, in order to maintain the diversity of the population. A selection method used is the method of roulette, where individuals of one generation are chosen to be part of the next generation, through a raffle of roulette. Figure 6 shows the representation of the roulette to a population of 4 individuals.

I	Individual x_i	$f(x)$ Fitness Function (x^2)	Relative Values of Fitness Function
1	00101	25	0.04
2	00010	4	0.01
3	10110	484	0.81
4	01001	81	0.14
Total		594	1.00

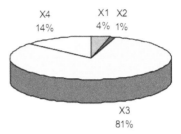

Fig. 6. Individuals of a population and its corresponding check roulette

In this method, each individual of the population is represented in roulette in proportion to its index of fitness. Thus, individuals with high fitness are given a greater portion of the wheel, while the lowest fitness is given a relatively smaller portion of roulette. Finally, the roulette wheel is rotated a certain number of times, depending on the size of the population, and are chosen, as individuals who will participate in the next generation, those drawn in roulette.

A set of operations is necessary so that, given a population, to generate successive populations that (hopefully) improve your fitness with time. These operators are: crossover (crossover) and mutation. They are used to ensure that the new generation is entirely new, but has in some way, characteristics of their parents, i.e. the population diversifies and maintains adaptation characteristics acquired by previous generations. To prevent the best individuals does not disappear from the population by manipulating the genetic operators; they can be automatically placed on the next generation via playing elitist.

This cycle is repeated a specified number of times. The following is an example of genetic algorithm. During this process, the best individuals, as well as some statistical data, can be collected and stored for evaluation.

Procedure AG
{g = 0;
inicial_population (P, g)
evaluation (P, g);
Repeat until (g = t)
{g = g +1;
    Father_selection (P, g);
recombination (P, g);
mutation (P, g);
evaluation (P, g);
    }
}

Where g is the current generation; t is the number of generations to terminate the algorithm; and P is the population.

These algorithms are computationally very simple, are quite powerful. In addition, they are not limited by assumptions about the search space, for continuity, existence of derivatives, and so on.

3.1.1 Genetic operators

The basic principle of genetic operators is to transform the population through successive generations, extending the search until you reach a satisfactory outcome. Genetic operators are needed to enable the population to diversify and keep adaptation characteristics acquired by previous generations.

The operator mutation is necessary for the introduction and maintenance of genetic diversity of the population, arbitrarily changing one or more components of a structure chosen, as is illustrated in Figure 7, thus providing the means for introduction of new elements in the population. Thus, the mutation ensures that the probability of reaching any point in the search space will never be zero, in addition to circumvent the problem of local minima, because with this mechanism, slightly changes the search direction. The mutation operator is applied to individuals with a probability given by the mutation rate Pm; usually uses a small mutation rate, because it is a genetic operator secondary.

Before the mutation	0 1 0 0 0
After the mutation	0 1 1 0 0

Fig. 7. Example of mutation

The crossing is the operator responsible for the recombination of traits of parents during play, allowing future generations to inherit these traits. It is considered the predominant genetic operator, so it is applied with probability given by the crossover rate Pc, which must be greater than the rate of mutation.

This operator can also be used in several ways; the most commonly used are:

a. One-point: a crossover point is chosen and from this point the parental genetic information will be exchanged. The information prior to this point in one of the parents is related to information subsequent to this point in the other parent, as shown in the example in Figure 8.

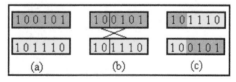

Fig. 8. Example of crossover from one-point: (a) two individuals are chosen; (b) a crossover point (2) is chosen; (c) the characteristics are recombined, generating two new individuals

b. Multi-points: is a generalization of this idea of an exchange of genetic material through points, where many crossing points can be used.
c. Uniform: don't use crossing points, but determines, through a global parameter, which the probability of each variable be exchanged between parents.

3.1.2 Genetic parameters

It is also important to analyze how some parameters influence the behavior of genetic algorithms in order to establish them as the needs of the problem and available resources.

Population size. The size of the population affects the overall performance and efficiency of AGs. With a small population performance may fall, because this way the population provides a small coverage of the search space of the problem. A large population typically provides a representative coverage of the problem domain, and preventing premature convergence solutions to local rather than global. However, for working with large populations, larger computational resources are required, or that the algorithm works by a much longer time period.

Passing Rate. The higher this ratio, the faster new structures will be introduced in the population. But if this is too high, the majority of the population will be replaced and can be lost high fitness structures. With a low value, the algorithm can become very slow.

Mutation rate. A low mutation rate prevents a given position stay stagnant in a value, and allow to reach anywhere in the search space. With a very high search becomes essentially random.

3.2 Particle Swarm Optimization

The optimization method called Particle Swarm Optimization (PSO) as other meta-heuristics recently developed, simulates the behavior of systems making the analogy with social behaviors. PSO was originally inspired by biological partner behavior associated with group of birds (Goldberg, 1989). This topic will be discussed in more detail after the basic algorithm is described.

The PSO was first proposed by John Kennedy and Russell Eberhart (1995a, 1995b). Some of the interesting features of PSO include ease of implementation and the fact that no gradient information is required. It can be used to solve a range of different optimization problems, including most of the problems can be solved through genetic algorithms; one can cite as an example some of the applications, such as neural network training (Lee & El-Sharkawi, 2008) and to minimize various types of functions (Eberhart et al., 1996).

Many popular optimizations algorithms are deterministic, as the gradient-based algorithms. The PSO, like its similar, belonging to the family of Evolutionary Algorithm is an algorithm of stochastic type that needs no gradient information derived from error function. This allows the use of PSO in functions where the gradient is unavailable or the production of which is associated with a high computational cost.

3.2.1 The PSO algorithm

The algorithm maintains a population of particles, where each particle represents a potential solution to an optimization problem. S assumed as being the size of the swarm. I each particle can be represented as an object with various features. These characteristics are as follows:

x_i: the current position of the particle;
v_i: the current speed of the particle;
y_i: the best personal position achieved by the particle.

The best personal position i particle represents the best position that the particle has visited and where he obtained the best evaluation. In the case of a task of minimizing, for example, a position that earned the lowest function value is considered to be the best position or with highest fitness assessment. F symbol is used to denote the objective function being minimized. The update equation for the best staff position is given by equation (1) using t time explicitly.

$$y_i(t+1) = \begin{cases} y_i(t) & if & f(y_i(t) \le f(x_i(t+1))) \\ x_i(t+1) & if & f(y_i(t) > f(x_i(t+1))) \end{cases} \tag{1}$$

There are two versions of PSO, calls *gbest* templates and *lbest* *(the global best and the best place)* (Goldberg, 1989). The difference between the two algorithms is based directly in the way that a particular particle interacts with its set of particles. To represent this interaction will be used the symbol $\hat{y}$. The details of the two models will be discussed in full later. The definition of $\hat{y}$ as used in *gbest* model, is shown by equation (2).

$$\hat{y}(t) \in \{y_0(t), y_1(t), \ldots, y_s(t)\} \mid f(\hat{y}(t))$$
$$= \min\{f(y_0(t)), f(y_1(t)), \ldots, f(y_s(t))\} \tag{2}$$

Note that this definition shows that $\hat{y}$ is the best position until then found by all particles in the swarm S size.

The PSO algorithm makes use of two independent random sequences $r_1 \sim U(0,1)$ and $r_2 \sim U(0,1)$. These strings are used to give nature to stochastic algorithm, as shown below in the equation (3). The values of r_1 and r_2 are scaled through constant $c_1 > 0$ and $c_2 \le 2$. These constants are called *acceleration coefficients*, and they exert influence on the maximum size of a particle can give in a single iteration. The speed that updates the step is specified separately for each dimension $j \in 1 \ldots n$, so that $v_{i,j}$ denotes the dimension j vector associated with the particle speed i. The update speed is given by the following equation:

$$v_{i,j}(t+1) = v_{i,j}(t) + c_1 r_{1,j}(t)[y_{i,j}(t) - x_{i,j}(t)] +$$
$$c_2 r_{2,j}(t)[\hat{y}_j(t) - x_{i,j}(t)] \tag{3}$$

In the definition of the equation, the constant speed update c_2 regulates clearly the maximum size of the step in the direction of better global particle, and the constant c_1 adjusts the size of the step in the direction of better personal position of the particle. The value of $v_{i,j}$ is maintained within the range of $[-v_{max}, v_{max}]$ by reducing the probability that a particle can exit the search space. If the search space is defined by the interval $[-x_{max}, x_{max}]$, then the value of v_{max} is calculated as follows:

$$v_{max} = k \ X \ x_{max} \quad where \quad 0.1 \le k \ge 1.0$$

The position of each particle is updated using your new velocity vector:

$$x_i(t+1) = x_i(t) + v_i(t+1) \tag{4}$$

The algorithm consists of repeated application of the equations above update. Below the basic PSO algorithm code is shown.

Create and initialize:
i – current particle;
s – PSO of n-dimensions:

repeat:
  for each *particle i = [1 .. s]*
    If f ($S_ix.x$) < f ($S_i.y$)
      then S_i y = x_i S.
    If f ($S_i.y$) < f (s. $\hat{y}$)
      then *S. $\hat{y}$ = Y_i S.*
  end loop
Update S using the equations (3) and (4)
until *the stopping condition is* **True**
end

The startup mentioned in the first step of the algorithm consists of the following:

1. initialize each coordinated $x_{i,j}$ with a random value in the range [-x_{max}, x_{max}], for the entire $i \in 1 \ldots s$ and $j \in 1 \ldots n$. This distributes the initial positions of the particles along the search space. Select a good random distribution algorithm to obtain a uniform distribution in the search space.

2. initialize each $v_{i,j}$ with a value taken from the range [-v_{max}, v_{max}] for the entire $i \in 1 \ldots s$ and $j \in 1 \ldots n$. Alternatively, the velocities of particles may be initialized with 0 (zero), provided that the initial positions are initialized in a random fashion.

The stopping criterion mentioned in the algorithm depends on the type of problem to be solved. Typically the algorithm is run for a predetermined and fixed number of iterations (a fixed number of function evaluation) or until it reaches a specific value of error. It is important to realize that the term speed models the rate of change in the position of the particle. The changes induced by speed update equation (3) represent acceleration, which explains why the constants c_1 and c_2 are called acceleration coefficients.

A brief description of how the algorithm works is given as follows: Initially, a particle any is identified as being the best particle in the group, based on his ability using the objective function. Then, all particles will be accelerated in the direction of this particle, and at the same time in the direction of own best positions previously found. Occasionally particles explore the search space around the current best particle. This way, all particles will have the opportunity to change their direction and seek a new 'best' particle. Whereas most functions have some form of continuity, chances are good to find the best solutions in the space that surrounds the best particle. Approximation of the particles coming from different directions in the search space towards the best solution increases the chances of finding the best solutions that are in the area nearby the best particle.

3.2.2 The behavior of the PSO

Many interpretations have been suggested regarding the operation and behavior of the PSO. Kennedy, in his research strengthened biological vision partner-PSO, performing experiments to investigate the roles of the different components of the velocity update equation (Kennedy & Eberhart, 1995). The task of training a neural network was used to compare performance of different models. Kennedy made use of *lbest* model (see *lbest* section for a complete description of this template), instead *gbest* model.

For this update equations developed two speed, the first by using just the experience of the particle, called the *component of cognition*, and the second, using only the interaction between the particles and called *social component*.

Consider the equation speed update (3) presented earlier. The term $c_1r_{1,j}(t)[y_{i,j}(t) - x_{i,j}(t)]$ is associated only with the cognition, where it takes into account only the experiences of the particle itself. If an OSP is built using only the cognitive component, the upgrade speed equation becomes:

$$v_{i,j}(t+1) = v_{i,j}(t) + c_1r_{1,j}(t)[y_{i,j}(t) - x_{i,j}(t)]$$

Kennedy found that the performance of this model of "only with cognition" was less than the original PSO's performance. One of the reasons of bad performance is attributed to total absence of interaction between the different particles.

The third term in the equation, speed update $c_2r_{2,j}(t)[\hat{y}_j(t) - x_{i,j}(t)]$, represents the social interaction between the particles. A version of PSO with just the social component can be constructed using the following equation: speed update

$$v_{i,j}(t+1) = v_{i,j}(t) + c_2r_{2,j}(t)[\hat{y}_j(t) - x_{i,j}(t)]$$

It was observed that in the specific problems that Kennedy, investigated the performance of this model was superior to the original PSO.

In summary, the term speed of PSO update consists of two components, the component of cognition and the social component. Currently, little is known about the relative importance of them, although initial results indicate that the social component is more important in most of the problems studied. This social interaction between the particles develops cooperation between them to resolve the problem.

3.2.3 Model of the best global (*gbest*)

The model allows *gbest* a faster rate of convergence at the expense of robustness. This model keeps only a single "best solution", called the *best global particle*, between all particles in the swarm. This particle acts as an attractor, pulling all particles to it. Eventually, all particles will converge to this position. If it is not updated regularly, the swarm can converge prematurely. The equations for update $\hat{y}$ and x_i are the same as shown above:

$$\hat{y}(t) \in \{y_0(t), y_1(t), ..., y_s(t)\} \mid f(\hat{y}(t))$$
$$= \min\{f(y_0(t)), f(y_1(t)), ..., f(y_s(t))\} \tag{5}$$

$$v_{i,j}(t+1) = v_{i,j}(t) + c_1r_{1,j}(t)[y_{i,j}(t) - x_{i,j}(t)] +$$
$$c_2r_{2,j}(t)[\hat{y}_j(t) - x_{i,j}(t)] \tag{6}$$

Note that $\hat{y}$ is called *the best overall position*, and belongs to the particle called *the best global particle*.

3.2.4 The model of the best location (*lbest*)

The *lbest* model tries to prevent premature convergence keeping multiple attractors. A subset of particles is defined for each particle of which is selected *the best local particle*, $\hat{y}_i$. The symbol $\hat{y}_i$ is called *the best local position* or *better in the vicinity (the local best position or the neighborhood best)*. Assuming that the indexes of the particles are around space s, the equations of *lbest* update for a neighborhood size l are as follows:

$$N_i = \{y_{i-l}(t), y_{i-l+1}(t), \ldots, y_{i-1}(t), y_i(t), \tag{7}$$
$$y_{i+1}(t), \ldots, y_{i+l}(t)\}$$

$$\hat{y}_i(t+1) \in N_i \ \left| f(\hat{y}_i(t+1)) = \min\{f(a)\}, \forall a \in N_i \right. \tag{8}$$

$$v_{i,j}(t+1) = v_{i,j}(t) + c_1 r_{1,j}(t)[y_{i,j}(t) - x_{i,j}(t)] + \tag{9}$$
$$c_2 r_{2,j}(t)[\hat{y}_j(t) - x_{i,j}(t)]$$

Note that the particles are selected in the subset N_i and they have no relation with the other particles within the domain of the search space; the selection is based solely on the index of the particle. This is done for two main reasons: the computational cost is lower, by not requiring grouping, and this also helps to promote the expansion of information on good solutions for all particles, although these are local search.

Finally, you can observe that the *gbest* model is in fact a special case of *lbest* model, when the $l = s$, i.e. when the selected set encompasses the entire swarm.

3.2.5 Considerations about the similarity between PSO and EAs

There is a clear relationship of PSO with the evolutionary algorithms (EAs). To some authors, the PSO maintains a population of individuals who represent potential solutions, one of the features found in all EAs. If the best personal positions (y_i) are treated as part of the population, then clearly there is a weak check (Lee & El-Sharkawi, 2008). In some algorithms of ES, the descendants (*offspring*), parents compete, replacing them if they are more suited. The equation (1) resembles this mechanism, with the difference that the best staff position (the father) can only be replaced by your own current position (descending), provided that the current position is more adapted to the best old staff position. Therefore, it seems to be some weak form check this on the PSO.

The speed update equation resembles arithmetic crossover operator (*crossover*) found in AGs. Typically, the intersection arithmetic produces two descendants that are results of mixing both parents involved in the crossing. The equation of speed update, PSO without term $v_{i,j}$ (see equation 3), can be interpreted as a form of arithmetic crossover involving two parents, returning only one descendant. Alternatively, the update equation of speed, without the term $v_{i,j}$. It can be seen as changing operator.

The best way to analyze the term $v_{i,j}$ is not to think of each iteration as a population replacement process by a new engine (birth and death), but as a process of continuous adaptation (Eberhart and J. Kennedy, 2001). This way the values of x_i are not replaced, but continually adapted using vectors speed v_i. This makes the difference between the OSP and the other EAs clearer: the PSO maintains information on the position and velocity (changes in position); In contrast, traditional EAs only keep information on the position.

In spite of the opinion that there is some degree of similarity between the PSO and the majority of other EAs, the PSO has a few features that currently are not present in any other EAs, especially the fact that the PSO models the speed of the particles as well as their positions.

3.3 Hybrid Particle Swarm optimization

The Hybrid Particle Swarm algorithm with Mutation (HPSOM) incorporates the mutation process often used in genetic algorithm in PSO (Esmin et al., 2005). This process will allow the particles can escape a local optimum point and perform searches in different area in the search space. This process starts by random choice in Particle Swarm and move to a new different position within the search space. The process of mutation used is given by the following equation:

$$mut(p[k]) = p([k]^* - 1) + \omega \tag{10}$$

Where the $p[k]$ is the randomly chosen particle swarm of and ω is also obtained from a random order within the following scale: $[0, 0.1(x_{max} - x_{min})]$ representing 0.1 times the length of the search space. The HPSOM algorithm has the following pseudocode.

begin
Create and initialise:
While (stop condition is **false)**
begin
evalaute
update velocity and position
mutation
  end
 end

4. Integration of meta-heuristic methods with fuzzy control

4.1 Advantages of hybrid systems

The integration of fuzzy systems with meta-heuristics methods has some characteristics in common and others that complement each other, as shown in Table 1. The junction of these two techniques forms a proper way to deal with non-linear systems and data. Systems that use these techniques have improved their performance in terms of efficiency and speed of execution.

Fuzzy systems have the advantage of storing knowledge. This is a feature of expert systems so that rules, for example, are easy to modify. Fuzzy systems are an effective and convenient alternative to represent the troubleshooting when the states are well defined. However, for large and complicated systems, fuzzy systems become difficult to adjust, depending on manual methods that involve trial and error. The fuzzy relation matrix representing the relationships between concepts and actions can be unwieldy, and the best values for the parameters needed to describe the functions of relevance may be difficult to determine. The performance of a diffuse system can be very sensitive to specific values of the parameters.

	Knowledge Saving	Learning	Optimizing	Speed	Non-Linear Systems
Fuzzy Systems	✓			✓	✓
Meta-heuristic Methods		✓	✓	✓	✓

Table 1. Comparison of characteristics of fuzzy logic with meta-heuristic techniques

In general, meta-heuristic methods offer distinct advantages of optimization of functions of relevance and even learning fuzzy rules. The meta-heuristic methods result in a more comprehensive search, reducing the chance of finishing in a local minimum, through sampling of several solutions sets simultaneously. Fuzzy logic contributes with the evaluation function, stage of genetic algorithm where the adjustment is determined.

There are several possible ways to use meta-heuristic methods with fuzzy systems. A type of hybrid system involves the use of separate modules as part of a global system. The modules based on meta-heuristic methods and fuzzy logic can be grouped singly or with other subsystems of computational intelligent or conventional programs that form an application system.

Another use is the design of systems that are primarily of applications with fuzzy logic. The use of genetic algorithms aims to improve the design process and the performance of the operating system based on fuzzy system. The meta-heuristic methods can be used to discover the best values for functions of relevance when the manual selection of values is difficult or takes a long time.

There are different types of meta-heuristic methods. Among them, genetic algorithms (GA) and particle swarm optimization (PSO), which are used in this chapter. These two methods, more another variation of the PSO, called hybrid PSO (HPSO), are chosen due to their features for integration with other systems. The general procedure for using the meta-heuristic methods with fuzzy systems is shown in Figure 6. For example, a possible solution (represented by a chromosome or a bird) can be defined as a concatenation of the values of all functions of relevance. When the triangular functions are used to represent the functions of relevance, the parameters are the centers for each set widths and fuzzy. An initial range of possible parameter values, the fuzzy system is rotated to determine how much it works well. This information is used to determine the fit of each solution and to establish a new population. The cycle is repeated until you found the best set of values for the parameters of the functions of relevance.

This process can be expanded to use the population that includes information about the conditions and actions corresponding to fuzzy rules. Include them in meta-heuristic treatment allows the system to learn or refine the fuzzy rules.

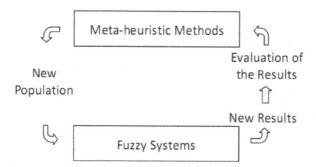

Fig. 9. Overall process for using a meta-heuristic method to improve the performance of a fuzzy system

4.2 Description of the training module

The integration of meta-heuristic methods with the fuzzy control has been implemented as follows:

a. the chromosome (or particle) was defined as the concatenation of the adjustment values of the functions of relevance
b. parameters are the centers and the widths of each fuzzy sets. The genes of chromosome (or the particles) are composed by these parameters.
c. a range of possible parameter values, the fuzzy system is rotated to determine how much it works well
d. this information is used to determine the fit of each chromosome or particle (adaptability) and establish a new population, and
e. the cycle is repeated until the number of user-defined generations (or iterations). Each generation (or iteration) is found the best set of values for the parameters of the functions of relevance.

For the meta-heuristic training, many initial positions that the vehicle will start from are defined by the user. Each initial position assesses a sub-population of the chromosomes (or particles) that represents the set of values for the parameters of the functions of relevance, seeking thus an optimization of the control not only over a single trajectory, but all possible starting positions of if from the vehicle to the parking.

After the settings makes by the user, such as number of population, number of generations (or iterations), GA values (rates of crossover, mutation, and son), and PSO values (values of r_1, r_2, c_1, c_2, and so on), the adjustment of the fuzzy membership functions starts.

The main idea behind the training is to establish the value of adjustment to the fuzzy membership functions of relevance that is how the function shifted to the left or right and how much it will shrink or expand. It is made by 2 parameters for each membership function, denoted by k_i and w_i, for the fuzzy membership function i. The value k makes a shift in the membership function, if with negative value to left or if with positive value to right; while the value of w shrink the function for negative values and expand the function for positive values. These values are included in the functions in the following way.

To describe each function of relevance of fuzzy controller are defined four parameters, they are: LL (lower left), LR (lower right), UL (upper left) and UR (upper right). In this case, all functions are trapezoids. Figure 10(a) shows the position of each these values. For setting the functions the following equations are used:

$$LL_{New} = (LL_{Old} + k_i) - w_i$$
$$LR_{New} = (LR_{Old} + k_i) + w_i$$
$$UL_{New} = (UL_{Old} + k_i)$$
$$UR_{New} = (UR_{Old} + k_i)$$

(11)

Figure 10(b) shows an example of shifting membership to the following values: $k = -8$ and $w = 2$.

$$LL_{New} = (LL_{Old} - 8) - 2$$
$$LR_{New} = (LR_{Old} - 8) + 2$$
$$UL_{New} = (UL_{Old} - 8)$$
$$UR_{New} = (UR_{Old} - 8)$$

(12)

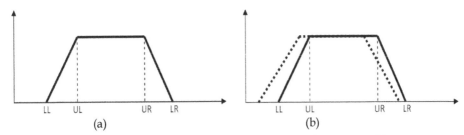

(a)   (b)

Fig. 10. Typical fuzzy membership function: (a) parameters of relevance, (b) training parameters

Meta-heuristic methods are used to find the optimal values, according to the strategy and starting points used, for k_i and w_i to the functions of relevance.

Usually a viable solution to a problem is associated with an individual (chromosome or particle) p in the form of a m vector with positions $p = \{x_1, x_2, x_3, ..., x_m\}$ where each component x_i represents a gene. Among the types of representation of individuals, the best known are: the binary representation and representation for integers. The binary representation is the classic, as proposed by John Holland (1992). However, for this development the integer code is used to represent each part of the individuals, i.e., each individual is composed by the adjustment coefficients k_i and w_i which are integer values.

With respect to the size of the chromosome, the size of each individual depends on the number of user-defined relevance functions. For a fuzzy control with a group of 18 functions of relevance for example, an individual with 36 variables (k_i and w_i where $i = 1, ..., 18$) is composed.

The population is initialized by setting each part of all individuals to zero (functions given by the user, the coefficients are equal to zero) and the other individuals are initialized with a string of positive or negative integers in a random procedure taken into a range [-10, 10].

The evaluation function has the role to assess the level of fitness (adaptation) of each chromosome generated by algorithms. The problem goal is to minimize the trajectory of the vehicle to be parked. In case the evaluation function is given by:

$$f = \frac{1}{1+I} \tag{13}$$

where I is the total number of iterations until the final position into the park lot. According to the fitness function, the fitness of each chromosome is inversely proportional to the number of iterations.

The integration of meta-heuristic training algorithms with fuzzy model has made as follow:

1.   The individual is defined as a link of the membership functions adjustment values.
2.   The parameters are the centers and widths of each fuzzy set. These parameters compose the individual.
3.   To check the performance of the fuzzy system it is rolled up from an initial set of possible parameters.
4.   This information is used for set up each individual adjustment (adaptability) and the making of the evolution of the particle.
5.   The cycle repetition is made up to complete the defined meta-heuristic method iteration number made by the user. To each meta-heuristic method iteration the best values set for the membership functions parameters is found.

5. Illustrative training examples of fuzzy control

5.1 Fuzzy control

This section presents the tests with fuzzy controls that have had their relevance adjusted using meta-heuristic methods. These tests demonstrate the efficiency of such mechanisms, allowing an objective assessment of results found. The original relevance functions are shown in Figure 11. This control has 148 rules, 15 functions relevant for the x and y input variables and car angle, and 7 output functions of angle of the wheel.

Table 2 shows the training results for the fuzzy functions shown in Fig. 11. Three initial positions have been used in this test. This table has the number of iterations that are generated by the vehicle to park using the original relevance functions.

Position	X	Y	Angle of the car	Iterations without training
1	2.5	12.0	180	330
2	16.0	13.0	-90	888
3	27.5	16.0	-40	655

Table 2. Initial positions for training and number of iterations

Figure 12 shows the vehicle in each of the initial positions. These positions were chosen according to the points where the vehicle doesn't develop a good trajectory until park and therefore generating an excessive number of iterations. The main idea is setting several initial positions will not only minimize the trajectories for these points, but as well as for other points, thus achieving a global minimization of space covered. Figures 13 show the trajectories for each initial position.

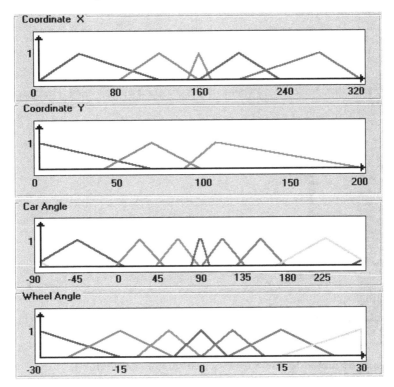

Fig. 11. Original relevance functions

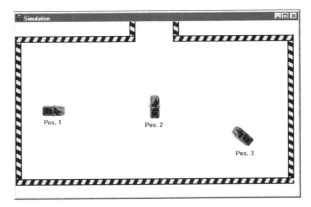

Fig. 12. Initial positions training

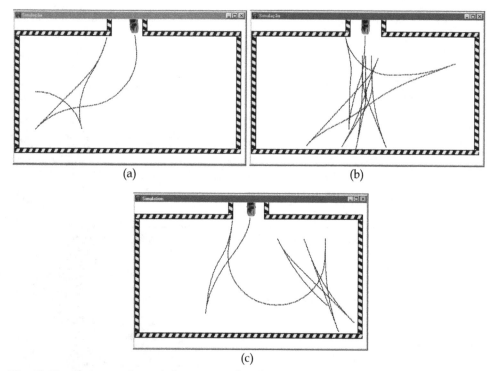

(a)   (b)

(c)

Fig. 13. Simulation results with fuzzy control without training for the following initial position: (a) position 1, (b) position 2, (c) position3

5.2 Meta-heuristic methods training fuzzy control memberships

The definition of several initial positions will not only minimize the routes referred to these points but also for other points, resulting a global minimization of traveled space. The defined GA and PSO parameters for the training are shown in Tables 3 and 4.

Population Size	14
Generations Number	30
Crossover Probability	90%
Mutation Probability	1%

Table 3. GA parameters

Size of Population	14
Number of Iterations	30
Vmax	10

Table 4. PSO parameters

After the training if the algorithm described in Section 4.2 with the fuzzy membership functions presented in Figure 11 and for three initial positions presented in Table 2, three sets of fuzzy membership are computed one for each meta-heuristic method of training (GA, PSO and HPSO). For example, the resultant GA fuzzy membership functions after adjustment are shown in Figure 14.

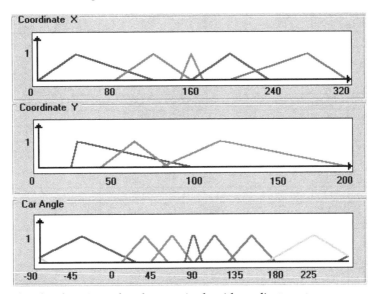

Fig. 14. Membership functions after the genetic algorithm adjustment

The generated results by meta-heuristic methods are shown in Table 5. The reduction of 941 iterations (50,2%) for GA training, 1116 iterations (59,6%) for PSO training, and 930 iterations (49,6%) were made for parking the vehicle starting from the three initial positions. These results are not optimal. Other control setups could be chosen in oder to get better results from these three initila start positions. The idea of theses simulations is presented possible adjustements of the fuzzy memberships. Also, ohter silmulations with other initial positions could create other fuzzy membership functions.

Other kind of possible simulation is to verify the quality of the resultant fuzzy membership for other initial position different from the initial position used in the training. Table 6 presents results of simulations results made starting from initial positions not used in the training for 4 types of adjustments of the fuzzy functions: human setting, and GA, PSO and HPSO trainning methods (from the functions setting by the human). The average of results of meta-heuristic methods are able to improve the better chose of the human being.

Position	Iterations without training	Iterations with GA training	Iterations with PSO training	Iterations with HPSO training
1	330	280	285	278
2	888	384	592	402
3	655	277	239	250
Total	1873	941	1116	930
Average	624,33	331.67	372	310

Table 5. Iterations after the meta-heuristic training

Case	X	Y	Car Angle	Iterations generated by Fuzzy Controls			
				Human Setting	GA Trained	PSO Trained	HPSO Trained
1	1	126	182	450	329	529	445
2	6	46	132	167	154	284	303
3	8	41	190	1000	1000	1000	1000
4	10	187	228	453	328	303	291
5	15	70	-90	318	162	282	313
6	51	112	48	278	130	128	120
7	51	112	54	280	132	126	120
8	70	95	-40	275	261	465	257
9	74	69	190	164	164	162	162
10	76	193	232	605	363	663	363
11	88	46	44	283	305	475	289
12	115	120	0	182	280	180	182
13	120	90	45	182	156	150	146
14	131	140	-72	457	292	592	512
15	141	69	-28	342	314	314	225
16	154	166	-80	863	436	980	420
17	160	135	268	1101	545	545	445
18	161	191	178	315	286	270	266
19	173	140	-72	762	590	580	544
20	208	143	244	363	310	321	312
21	217	66	-50	684	325	725	506
22	228	194	-48	830	655	855	476
23	246	169	154	312	307	507	320
24	250	180	-40	739	800	800	489
25	265	170	-40	672	329	629	483
26	290	95	-40	280	190	189	192
27	300	124	258	317	306	326	319
28	305	156	-90	350	346	340	320
29	314	73	-46	235	355	223	210
30	314	194	-44	513	744	402	388
Average				459.07	363.13	444,83	347,27

Table 6. Results of simulations for different initial position from the used to training

6. Conclusion

The fuzzy systems are a convenient and efficient alternative for solution of problems where the fuzzy statements are well defined. Nevertheless, the project of a fuzzy system may became difficult for large and complex systems, when the control quality depends of "try-and-error" methods for defining the best membership functions to solve the problem.

The meta-heuristic method training modulus provides an automatic way for the adjustment of the membership functions parameters. These techniques show that the performance of a fuzzy control may be improved through the genetic algorithms, the particle swarm optimization or the hybrid particle swarm optimization, substituting for the "try-and-error" method, as used before by students for this purpose, with no good results.

The meta-heuristic methods provided distinctive advantages for the optimization of membership functions, resulting in a global survey, reducing the chances of ending into a local minimum, once it uses several sets of simultaneous solutions. The fuzzy logic supplied the evaluation function, a stage of the meta-heuristic methods where the adjustment is settled.

7. Acknowledgment

The authors would like to express their thanks to the financial support of this work given by the Brazilian research agencies: CNPq, CAPES, and FAPEMIG.

8. References

da Silva Filho, J.I. ; Lambert-Torres, G. & Abe, J.M. (2010). *Uncertainty Treatment using Paraconsistent Logic*, IOS Press, ISBN 978-1-60750-557-0, Amsterdam, The Netherlands.

Eberhart, R. C. & Kennedy, J. (2001). *Swarm Intelligence*, ISBN 1558605959, Morgan Kaufmann, San Francisco, USA.

Eberhart, R. C. ; Simpson, P. & Dobbins, R. (1996). *Computational Intelligence PC Tools*, ISBN 0122286308, Academic Press Professional, Amsterdam, The Netherlands.

Eberhart, R.C. & Kennedy, J. (1995a). A New Optimizer using Particle Swarm Theory, *Proceedings of the Sixth International Symposium on Micro Machine and Human Science*, pp. 39-43, ISBN 0-7803-2676-8, Nagoya, Japan, Oct. 4-6, 1995.

Esmin, A.A.; Lambert-Torres, G. & Souza, A.C.Z. (2005). A Hybrid Particle Swarm Optimization Applied to Loss Power Minimization. *IEEE Transactions on Power Systems*, Vol.20, No.2, (May 2005), pp. 859-866, ISSN 0885-8950.

Goldberg, D.E. (1989). *Genetic Algorithms in Search, Optimization and Machine Learning*, ISBN 0201157675, Addison Wesley, Boston, USA.

Holland, J.H. (1975). *Adaptation in Natural and Artificial Systems*, The University of Michigam Press, ISBN 0-262-58111-6, Ann Arbor, USA.

Kandel A. & Langholz, G. (1993). *Fuzzy Control Systems*, CRC Press, ISBN 9780849344961, Boca Raton, USA.

Kennedy, J. & Eberhart, R.C. (1995b). Particle Swarm Optimization, *Proceedings of IEEE International Conference on Neural Networks*, Vol.IV, pp. 1942-1948, ISBN 0852966415, Perth, Australia, June 26-28, 1995.

Lee, K.Y. & El-Sharkawi, M.A. (2008). *Modern Heuristic Optimization Techniques: Applications to Power Systems*, Wiley – IEEE Press, ISBN 0-471-45711-6, Hoboken, USA.

Medsker, L.R. (1995). *Hybrid Intelligent Systems*, Kulwer Academic Pub., ISBN 0792395883, Boston, USA.

Park, D. ; Kandel, A. & Langholz, G. (1994). Genetic-Based New Fuzzy Reasoning Models with Application to Fuzzy Control. *IEEE Transactions on System, Man and Cybernetics*, Vol.24, No.1, (January 1994), pp. 39-47, ISSN 0018-9472.

Ross, T.J. (2010). *Fuzzy Logic with Engineering Applications*, John Wiley and Sons, ISBN 9780470743768, West Sussex, United Kingdom.

6

Control Application Using Fuzzy Logic: Design of a Fuzzy Temperature Controller

R.M. Aguilar, V. Muñoz and Y. Callero
University of La Laguna
Spain

1. Introduction

The reason for using fuzzy logic in control applications stems from the idea of modeling uncertainties in the knowledge of a system's behavior through fuzzy sets and rules that are vaguely or ambiguously specified. By defining a system's variables as linguistic variables such that the values they can take are also linguistic terms (modeled as fuzzy sets), and by establishing the rules based on said variables, a general method can be devised to control these systems: Fuzzy Control (Babuška, 1998; Chen, 2009). Fuzzy control is a class of control methodology that utilizes fuzzy set theory (Pedrycz, 1993). The advantages of fuzzy control are twofold. First, fuzzy control offers a novel mechanism for implementing control laws that are often based on knowledge or on linguistic descriptions. Second, fuzzy control provides an alternative methodology for facilitating the design of non-linear controllers for plants that rely on generally uncertain control that is very difficult to relate to the conventional theory of non-linear control (Li & Tong, 2003; A. Sala et al., 2005).

Every day we mindlessly perform complex tasks: parking, driving, recognizing faces, packing the groceries at the supermarket, moving delicate objects, etc. To solve these tasks (overcome an obstacle), we gather all the information necessary for the situation (topology of the terrain, characteristics of the obstacle such as speed, size, …). With this information and by relying on our experience, we can carry out a series of control actions that, thanks to the feedback present between the system under control and our bodies, can achieve the desired goal.

The controller receives the performance indices (reference) and the system output. To replace the human in a control process, a controller must be added. The controller is a mathematical element, and as such all of the tasks that it is able to perform must be perfectly defined. This control link is studied in Control Theory and is based on two principles:

1. The system to be controlled must be known so that its response to a given input can be predicted. This prediction task requires having a complete model of the system. This identification phase is essential to the performance of the control algorithm.
2. The objective of the control must be specified in terms of concise mathematical formulas directly related to the system's variables (performance index).

When a system's complexity increases, mathematics cannot be used to define the aforementioned points. The model cannot be defined due to non-linearities, to its non-stationary nature, to the lack of information regarding the model, and so on.

We are, however, living in rapidly evolving times where the main goal is to break the limitations that exist in our use of machines in an effort to increase productivity. The use of and advances in intelligent machines will fundamentally change the way we work and live.

To this end, we are building autonomous control systems that are designed to work properly for long periods of time under given uncertainties in the system and the environment. These systems must be capable of compensating for faults in the system without any outside intervention. Intelligent autonomous control systems use techniques from the field of Artificial Intelligence (AI) to achieve autonomy. These control systems consist of conventional control systems that have been augmented using intelligent components, meaning their development requires interdisciplinary research (Jang et al., 1997).

The emergence and development of Artificial Intelligence is of great importance. AI can be defined as that part of computer science that is charged with the design of intelligent computers, meaning systems that exhibit those characteristics that we associate with intelligent human behavior, such as understanding, learning, reasoning, problem solving, etc. Fuzzy Control is one of the new techniques in Intelligent Control, one that aims to imitate the procedure we humans use when dealing with systems (Cai, 1997). For example, when operating a water tap, if we want to obtain the desired flow rate, we reason using terms such as:

"If the flow is low, turn the handle all the way left"

"If the flow is high, turn the handle right a little bit", etc.

Precise quantities such as "2 liters/second" of "65 degrees counterclockwise" do not appear in these rules, and yet we manage to achieve the desired flow rate.

We also apply this form of reasoning to more complex situations, from regulating not only the flow rate but the water temperature, and even when driving a car. In none of these cases do we know precise values; rather, vague magnitudes suffice, such as "very hot", "near", "fast", etc.

Another important consideration is that the control can be expressed as a set of rules of the type: "For certain conditions with some variables, do these actions in others". In this structure, the conditions are called antecedents and the actions consequents.

We may conclude that human reasoning in these situations involves applying logic to uncertain magnitudes. If we want to implement this control artificially, the most convenient course of action is to use a tool that models uncertain magnitudes, this being Fuzzy Set Theory, and apply a logic to these magnitudes, this being Fuzzy Logic (Klir & Yuan, 1995). Both elements belong to a new field in the symbolic branch of Artificial Intelligence that has found in Fuzzy Control one of its main applications, even above other, more formal applications such as expert systems. The fact that it mirrors the process of human reasoning justifies the success of this new method, due to its ease of use and understanding. In a few years AI has blossomed and experienced great commercial success, eclipsing even that of expert systems.

In this chapter we will consider the fuzzy control of a liquid's temperature. This is a very simple academic problem that can be solved using various techniques, such as a classic PI control scheme (Horváth & Rudas, 2004). We will use it in this text, however, to illustrate the design and operation of a fuzzy controller.

An introduction to fuzzy control is presented first, followed by a description of the general outline. In subsequent sections we describe each of the steps in the design of the fuzzy controller: choice of inputs and outputs, rule base, fuzzy quantification, and fuzzification, inference and defuzzification mechanisms. We conclude with a simulation of the proposed temperature controller.

2. Fuzzy logic applied to control: Fuzzy control of temperature

The use of the Fuzzy Logic methodology in real systems is immediately applicable to those systems whose behavior is known based on imprecisely defined rules. This imprecision arises from the complexity of the system itself. The way to approach such a problem is to reduce the complexity by increasing the uncertainty of the variables (J. Sala et al., 2000; Yager & Filev, 1994). Thus, in problems that present non-linearities, and to which classical control techniques are hardest to apply, these techniques are very useful and easy to use (Takana & Sugeno, 1992; Tanaka & Wang, 2001; Wang, 1994).

In the vast majority of systems, be they highly complex or not, the systems' behavior can be given by a set of rules that are often imprecise, or that rely on linguistic terms laden with uncertainty. This results in rules of the type "If the volume is large, the pressure is small", which define the behavior of a system. If we focus on the rules that are defined to control the system, we can formulate different rules of the type "If the cost is small and the quality is good, make a large investment".

This last rule type is the most frequently seen in daily life. For example, to regulate water flow from a faucet, we need only apply rules of the type "If the flow is excessive, close the tap a lot", or "If the flow is low, open the tap a little" in order to carry out the desired action. Using precise magnitudes such as "flow rate of 1.2 gallons/minute" or "turn 45° clockwise" is unnecessary.

Therefore, a general knowledge base for the system is available; that is, a set of rules that aim to model the actions to be carried out on the system so as to achieve the desired action. Said rules are provided by an expert, one whose experience with handling the system provides him with knowledge of how the system behaves.

The Mandani fuzzy inference mechanism is very useful when applying Fuzzy Logic to the control of systems (Passino, 1998). If we consider a classic feedback scheme, the controller has enough information about the system to determine the command that must be applied to said system so as to achieve a desired setpoint. The idea, put forth by Zadeh, for using Fuzzy Control algorithms relies on introducing the knowledge base into the controller such that its output is determined by the control rules proposed by the expert. Said rules contain fuzzy sets (linguistic terms) in the antecedents and in the consequents, and hence they are referred to as a whole as a fuzzy control rule base.

If we wish to apply this control scheme to a real system, the fuzzy controller must be adjusted to existing sensor and actuator technology, which relies on precise magnitudes (Jantzen, 2007). The exact values provided by a sensor must therefore be converted into the fuzzy values that comprise the variables of the antecedent in the rule base. Likewise, the fuzzy values inferred from the rules must be transformed into exact values for use in the actuators. A diagram of this process is shown in Figure 1.

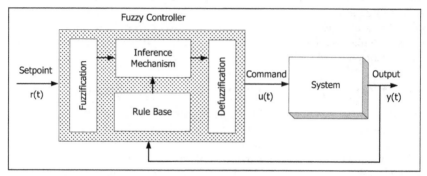

Fig. 1. Fuzzy controller

A block diagram for a fuzzy control system is given in Figure 1. The fuzzy controller consists of the following four components:

1. Rule base: set of fuzzy rules of the type "if-then" which use fuzzy logic to quantify the expert's linguistic descriptions regarding how to control the plant.
2. Inference mechanism: emulates the expert's decision-making process by interpreting and applying existing knowledge to determine the best control to apply in a given situation.
3. Fuzzification interface: converts the controller inputs into fuzzy information that the inference process can easily use to activate and trigger the corresponding rules.
4. Defuzzification interface: converts the inference mechanism's conclusions into exact inputs for the system to be controlled.

We shall now present a simple temperature control example, shown in Figure 2, to introduce each of the fuzzy controller components.

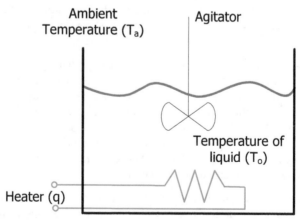

Fig. 2. Temperature controller.

Consider the system shown in Figure 2, where T_o is the temperature of the liquid that we wish to control and T_a is the ambient temperature. The input produced by the heating element is denoted with the letter q, and the desired temperature is T_d. The model for the system, keeping in mind that there are two energy sources (one generated by the heating element and one from the environment), is given by the transfer matrix that results when each of the inputs is considered separately. The expression shown in Equation 1 yields $G_1(s)$ and $G_2(s)$, given in Equations 2 and 3, respectively.

$$\frac{T_o(s)}{Q(s)} = G_1(s) * G_2(s) \tag{1}$$

$$G_1(s) = \frac{T_a(s)}{Q(s)} = \frac{\frac{1}{\mu A}}{\frac{MC_e}{\mu A}s + 1} \tag{2}$$

$$G_2(s) = \frac{T_o(s)}{T_a(s)} = \frac{1}{\frac{MC_e}{\mu A}s + 1} \tag{3}$$

where:

1. M: Mass of liquid
2. C_e: Specific heat
3. μ: heat transfer coefficient between the tank and the environment
4. A: heat transfer area
5. T_o: temperature of liquid
6. T_a: ambient temperature
7. Q: heat input

This is a simple academic problem and many techniques are available for solving it, such as a classic PI controller. We will use it in this text, however, to illustrate the design and operation of a fuzzy controller.

3. General outline of the fuzzy controller

We may conclude then that the procedure for implementing these fuzzy techniques to control systems consists of two very different stages:

1. First stage, to be completed before the control algorithm is executed, and consisting of:
a. Establishing the controller's input and output variables (linguistic variables).
b. Defining each variable's fuzzy sets.
c. Defining the sets' membership functions.
d. Establishing the rule base.
e. Defining the fuzzification, inference and defuzzification mechanisms.
2. Second stage, to be completed with each step of the control algorithm, and consisting of:
a. Obtaining the precise input values.
b. Fuzzification: Assigning the precise values to the fuzzy input sets and calculating the degree of membership for each of those sets.

c. Inference: Applying the rule base and calculating the output fuzzy sets inferred from the input sets.

d. Defuzzification: Calculating the precise output values from the inferred fuzzy sets. These precise values will be the controller's outputs (commands) and be applied to the system to be controlled.

This scheme is applied to classical feedback control techniques, as shown in Figure 3. The classical controller is replaced by a fuzzy controller, which performs the same function. The variables in lower case indicate precise values ('r' for the setpoint, 'e' for the error, 'u' for the command and 'y' for the output), while upper case letters indicate the corresponding fuzzy variables.

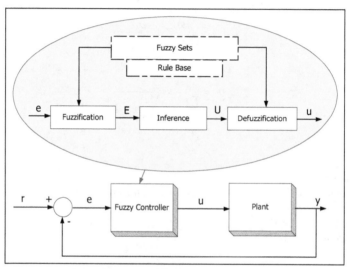

Fig. 3. Fuzzy controller in the feedback loop.

4. Fuzzy controller inputs and outputs

If we assume the presence of an expert in the feedback loop that controls the temperature system, as shown in Figure 4, then a fuzzy controller must be designed that automates the way in which the human expert carries out this control task. To do this, the expert must indicate (to the designer of the fuzzy controller) what information he receives as the input to his decision-making process. Assume that in the temperature control process, the expert observes the error and the variation in this error to carry out his control function; that is, he makes his decision based on the result obtained from Equation 4:

$$e(t) = r(t) - y(t) \tag{4}$$

Though there are many other variables that can be used as the input (e.g., the integral of the error), we will adopt this one since it is the one used by the expert.

We must next identify the variables to be controlled. For the temperature control case proposed, we can only control the amount of energy (q) supplied by the heating element.

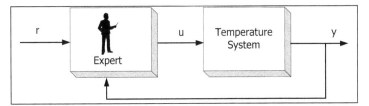

Fig. 4. Human control of a temperature system.

Once the fuzzy controller's inputs and outputs are selected, the next step is to determine the reference input desired, which in our case will be r=60 (step input of sixty).

The fuzzy control system, then, with its inputs and outputs, would be as shown in Figure 5.

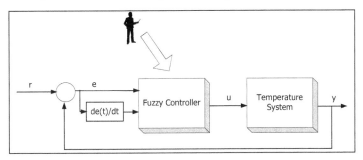

Fig. 5. Fuzzy controller for a temperature system.

5. Inclusion of control knowledge in the rule base

Assume that the human expert provides a description in his own words of the best way to control the plant. We will have to use this linguistic description to design the fuzzy controller.

5.1 Linguistic description

An expert uses linguistic variables to describe the time-varying inputs and outputs of the fuzzy controller. Thus, for our temperature system, we might have:

1. "error" to describe e(t)
2. "error variation" to describe de(t)/dt
3. "increase-energy-supplied" to describe $\Delta u(t)$

We used the quotes to emphasize how certain words or phrases. Though there are many possible ways to describe the variables linguistically, choosing one or another has no effect on how the fuzzy controller works, it only simplifies the task of constructing the controller using fuzzy logic.

Just as e(t) takes on a value, for example, 0.1 at t=2 (e(2)=0.1), so do linguistic variables take on "linguistic values", that is, the values of the linguistic variables change over time. For example, to control the temperature, we can have the "error", "error-variation" and "increase-energy-supplied" take on the following values:

1. LN   Large Negative
2. MN   Medium Negative
3. SN   Small Negative
4. ZE   Zero
5. SP   Small Positive
6. MP   Medium Positive
7. LP   Large Positive

a) Error = LN

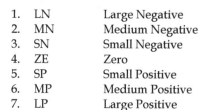

**b) Error=SN
Error-variation=SP**

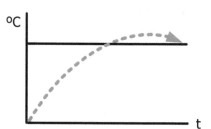

**c) Error = ZE
Error-variation = SN**

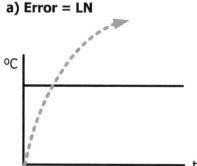

**d) Error = ZE
Error-variation = SP**

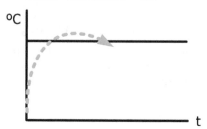

**e) Error = SP
Error-variation = SP**

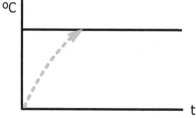

**f) Error = LP
Error-variation = LN**

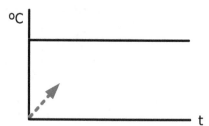

Fig. 6. Temperature system in different states.

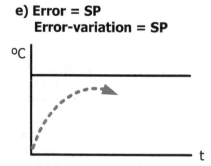

Let us now consider how we can describe the system's dynamics based on the linguistic variables and the values they assume. In the case of the temperature controller, each of the following phrases represents different system states:

1. The error is Large Negative, indicating that the temperature of the liquid is much higher than desired, Figure 6.a.
2. The error is Small Negative and the error-variation is Small Positive, indicating that the temperature of the liquid is somewhat higher than the setpoint and dropping to the desired value, Figure 6.b.
3. The error is Zero and the error-variation is Small Negative, indicating that the temperature of the liquid is more or less at the setpoint but rising, Figure 6.c.
4. The error is Zero and the error-variation is Small Positive, indicating that the temperature of the liquid is more or less at the setpoint but falling, Figure 6.d.
5. The error is Small Positive and the error-variation is Small Positive, indicating that the temperature of the liquid is below the setpoint and dropping further, Figure 6.e.
6. The error is Large Positive and the error-variation is Large Negative, indicating that the temperature of the liquid is well below the setpoint but increasing, Figure 6.f.

5.2 Rules

Next we will use the linguistic quantifiers defined earlier to craft a rule set that captures the expert's knowledge regarding how to control the system. Specifically, we have the following rules to control the temperature:

1. If the error is LN, MN or SN, then increase-energy-supplied is LN.

This rule quantifies the situation in which the liquid's temperature is above that desired, meaning heat must not be supplied.

2. If the error is LP and the error-variation is SP, then increase-energy-supplied is LP.

This rule quantifies the situation in which the liquid's temperature is far below the setpoint (undesired situation) and decreasing, requiring a substantial heat input.

3. If the error is ZE and the error-variation is SP, then increase-energy-supplied is SP.

This rule quantifies the situation in which the liquid's temperature is close to the desired temperature but decreasing slightly, meaning that heat must be supplied to correct the error.

Each of the three rules above is a "linguistic rule", since it uses linguistic variables and values. Since these linguistic values are not precise representations of the magnitudes they describe, then neither are the linguistic rules. They are merely abstract ideas on how to achieve proper control, and may represent different things to different people. And yet, experts very often use linguistic rules to control systems.

5.3 Rule base

Using rules of the type described above, we can define every possible temperature control situation. Since we used a finite number of linguistic variables and values, there is a finite number of possible rules. For the temperature control problem, given two inputs and seven linguistic variables, there are 72=49 possible rules (every possible combination of the values of the linguistic variables).

A convenient way of representing the set of rules when the number of inputs to the fuzzy controller is low (three or fewer) is by using a table. Each square represents the linguistic value of the consequent of a rule, with the left column and the top row containing the linguistic values of the antecedent's variables. A temperature control example is shown in Table 1. Note the symmetry exhibited by the table. This is not coincidental, and corresponds to the symmetrical behavior of the system to be controlled.

error/error-variation	LN	MN	SN	ZE	SP	MP	LP
LP	LN	LN	LN	LP	LP	LP	LP
MP	LN	LN	LN	MP	LP	LP	LP
SP	LN	LN	LN	SP	SP	LP	LP
ZE	LN	LN	LN	ZE	MP	MP	LP
SN	LN	LN	LN	SN	ZE	SP	MP
MN	LN	LN	LN	MN	SN	ZE	SP
LN	LN	LN	LN	LN	MN	SN	ZE

Table 1. Rule base for controlling temperature.

6. Fuzzy quantification of knowledge

Until now we have only quantified the expert's knowledge of how to control a system in an abstract manner. Next, we shall see how, using fuzzy logic, we can quantify the meaning of the linguistic descriptions so as to automate the control rules specified by the expert in a fuzzy controller.

6.1 Membership functions

Let us now quantify the meaning of the linguistic variables using the membership functions. Depending on the specific application and the designer (expert), we may select from various membership functions.

The fuzzy partitions for both the input variables (error and error-variation) and for the output variable (increase-energy-supplied) will consist of seven diffuse groups uniformly distributed in a normalized universe of discourse with range [-1,1]. Figure 7 shows the partition for the input variables, and Figure 8 that corresponding to the output variable.

The membership functions for the controller's input variables, at the edge of the universe of discourse, are saturated. This means that at a given point, the expert regards all values above a given value as capable of being grouped under the same linguistic description of "large-positive" or "large-negative". The membership function of the controller's output variable, however, cannot be saturated at the edge if the controller is to function properly. The basic reason is that the controller cannot tell the actuator that any value above a given value is valid; instead, a specific value must always be specified. Moreover, from a practical standpoint, we could not carry out a defuzzification process that considers the area of conclusion of the rule if, as an output, we have membership functions with an infinite area.

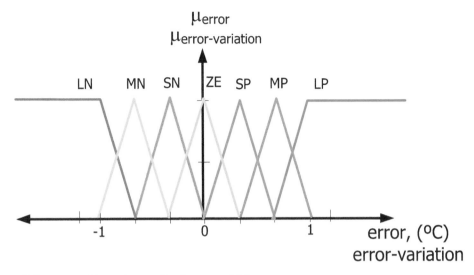

Fig. 7. Fuzzy partition of controller input variables.

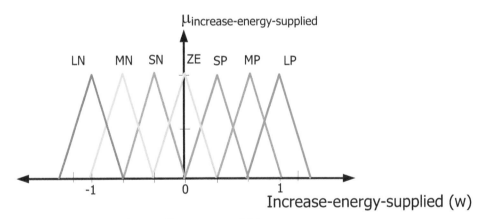

Fig. 8. Fuzzy partition of controller output variable.

7. Fuzzification, inference and defuzzification

In order to complete the design of the controller, we need to define the fuzzification, inference and defuzzification procedures.

In most practical applications of fuzzy control, the fuzzification process used is the "singleton", where the membership function is characterized by having degree 1 for a single value of its universe (input value) and 0 for the rest. In other words, the impulse function could be used to represent a membership function of this type, Figure 9. It is especially used in implementations because in the absence of noise, the input variables are guaranteed to equal their measured value. We also avoid the calculations that would be required if another membership function were used, such as Gaussian fuzzification, which requires constructing a Gaussian-shaped membership function to represent the exact value being provided by the sensor.

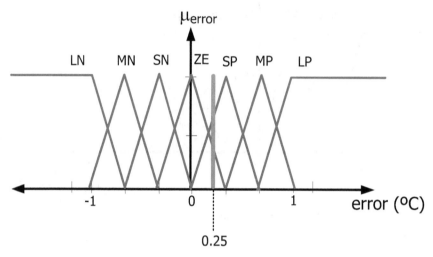

Fig. 9. Fuzzification process for the controller's input variable.

In order to define the inference mechanism, we have to determine how to carry out the basic operations. Since we are using Mandani's model, we have decided to implement the T-norm as the minimum and the S-norm as the maximum.

The last step is to define the defuzzification process. For this temperature control case, we will use the center of gravity.

8. Simulation of fuzzy temperature control

Normally, before proceeding with the implementation of the controller, a simulation is performed to evaluate its performance. The results of the simulation can aid in improving the design of the fuzzy controller and in verifying that it will work correctly when it is implemented. Such a simulation is shown below, implemented using Matlab (Sivanandam et al., 2007), specifically Simulink to simulate the control loop and fuzzy toolbox to implement the fuzzy controller.

The controller designed earlier is defined using the fuzzy toolbox in Matlab, yielding the fuzzy system shown in Figure 10. The fuzzy partition of the inputs and output is shown in Figure 11. As for the output surface, it is shown in Figure 12.

With this tool, we can see how the inference process is carried out, Figure 13.

The next step is to carry out a simulation with the temperature system to check the control system's performance. To do this, we will use the simulation tool Simulink, which allows us to implement the control loop in blocks and to use the fuzzy system made with the fuzzy toolbox as the controller. The diagram of the control system, then, is as shown in Figure 14.

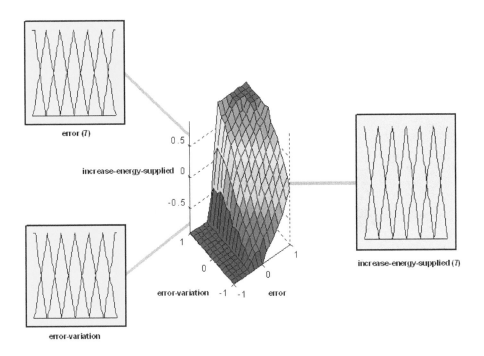

System cpi: 2 inputs, 1 outputs, 31 rules

Fig. 10. Fuzzy controller for the temperature system.

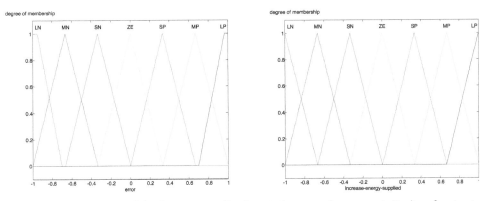

Fig. 11. Fuzzy partition of the fuzzy controller inputs (error and error-variation) and output (increase command).

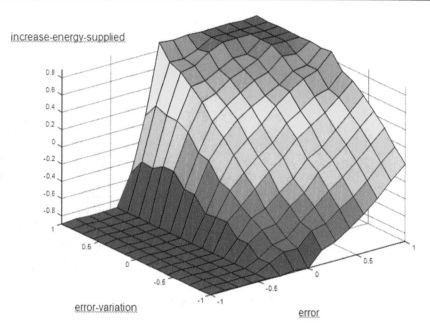

Fig. 12. Control surface.

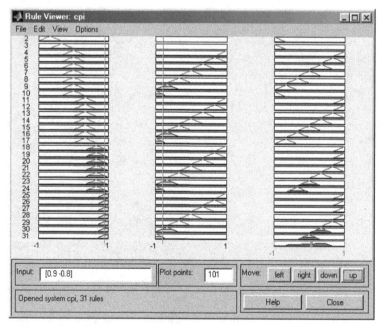

Fig. 13. Inference process for LP error (0.9) and LN error-variation (-0.8).

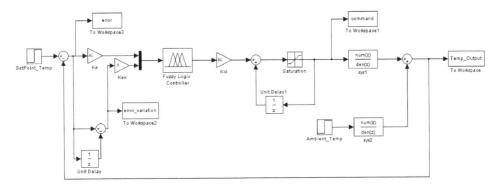

Fig. 14. Fuzzy temperature control.

A prerequisite step to studying the results of the fuzzy controller is to adjust its parameters. In other words, we used fuzzy partitions that were normalized between -1 and 1, and yet the error, the error variation and the commanded increase have to take on values within a different range. To do this, we use gains that scale these variables within the design range of the fuzzy controller, adjusting these gains to achieve the desired specifications. These gains are called gains of scale (g_s) and their effect is as follows:

1. If $g_s = 1$, there is no effect on the membership functions.
2. If $g_s > 1$, then the membership functions are uniformly contracted by a factor of $1/g_s$.
3. If $g_s < 1$, then the membership functions are uniformly expanded by a factor of $1/g_s$.

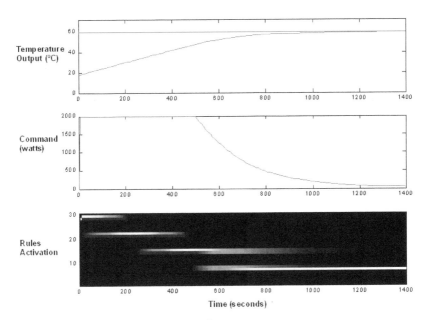

Fig. 15. Output of fuzzy temperature controller.

For the temperature controller, we have selected a gain of scale for the controller's error input of $K_e=0.0238$, of $K_{ev}=1$ for the error variation and of $K_{ci}=5000$ for the command increase. The values K_e and K_{ev} are needed to keep the error and the error variation bounded in the same margins. The K_{ci} value is used to match up the maximum command to the maximum value of resistance (2000 watts). The values used in the gains of scale have been selected through an adaptive method based on the results of successive simulations.

The results yielded by this system are as shown in Figure 15. By applying the maximum command (2000 watts), we can reach the setpoint value in 1000 seconds. The rules that are applied at first (trigger force equal to 0 is shown in black, with the brightness increasing to white as we progress to a trigger force equal to 1) correspond to rules 27-31, which involve LP. Then the 20-22 group takes over, these rules controlling MP errors and small error variations. Next to activate are those rules for dealing with SP errors. Lastly, rule 7, with trigger force 1, is activated for dealing with ZE error and ZE error variation.

If the setpoint is changed at t=2,200 seconds, the result is as shown in Figure 16. When the setpoint is changed, a new command is output since the MP and SP error rules are activated.

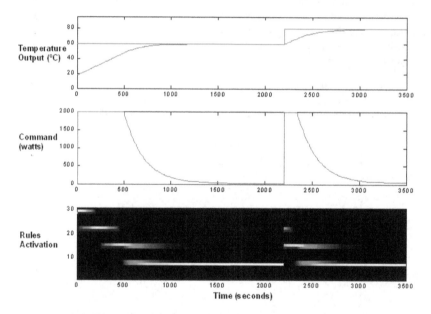

Fig. 16. Output of fuzzy temperature controller with change at t=2200 seconds.

9. Conclusions

Fuzzy logic is based on the method of reasoning that is typically used by experts to handle all kinds of systems, from the simplest to the very complex. This method (control) can be formulated with rules of the type if-then applied to inexact magnitudes such as "many", "fast", "cold", etc. Implementing this method of reasoning requires a representation of these vague magnitudes and an associated logic. These are the Theory of Diffuse Groups and Diffuse Logic, respectively.

In this chapter we have presented the steps required to implement fuzzy controllers. Such controllers, when integrated into systems that handle precise values, require a translation process before and after the reasoning method is applied. Hence the three-step structure of fuzzy controllers: fuzzification, inference and defuzzification.

The different stages were explained using an example involving temperature control. This is a trivial, academic problem that can be solved using many techniques, such as with a classical PI controller; in this chapter, however, we used this example to illustrate the design of a fuzzy controller, as well as its mode of operation.

10. References

Babuška R. (1998). *Fuzzy Modeling for Control*, Kluwer Academic Publishers, ISBN 978-0-7923-8154-9, Boston, USA

Cai X.-Z. (1997). Intelligent Control: Principles, Techniques and Applications, World Scientific Publishing Company, ISBN 978-9810225643, Singapore-New Jersey

Chen G. & Joo Y. H. (2009). Introduction to Fuzzy Control Systems, In: *Encyclopedia of Artificial Intelligence*, J. R. Rabul, J. Dorado, and A. Pazos (Eds.), 688-695, Hersh, ISBN 9781599048499, La Coruña, España

Horváth L. & Rudas I. J. (2004). *Modeling and Problem Solving Methods for Engineers*, Elsevier, Academic Press, ISBN 978-0126022506, New York

Jang J. S. R., Sun C. T. & Mizutani E. (1997). *Neuro-Fuzzy and Soft Computing*, Prentice Hall, ISBN 978-0132610667, New York

Jantzen J. (2007). *Foundations of Fuzzy Control*, Wiley, ISBN 978-0470029633, New York

Klir G. & Yuan B. (1995). *Fuzzy Sets and Fuzzy Logic*, Prentice Hall, ISBN 978-0131011717, Upper Saddle River, NJ

Li H. X. & Tong S.C. (2003). A hybrid adaptive fuzzy control for a class of nonlinear mimo systems. *IEEE Trans. Fuzzy Systems*, Vol.11, No.1, (February 2003), pp. 24–34, ISSN 1063-6706

Passino K. M. & Yurkovich S. (1998). *Fuzzy Control*, Addison Wesley Longman, Inc., ISBN 0 - 201 - 18074 - X, California

Pedrycz W. (1993). *Fuzzy Control and Fuzzy Systems*, Research Studies. Press/John Wiley, ISBN O-471-93475-5, Taunton, New York

Sala A., Guerra T. M. & Babuška R. (2005). Perspectives of Fuzzy Systems and Control. *Fuzzy Sets and Systems*, Vol.156, No.3, (December 2005), pp. 432-444, ISSN 0165-0114, North-Holland

Sala J., Picó J. & Bondia J. (2000) Tratamiento de la incertidumbre en modelado y control borrosos, *Revista Iberoamericana de Inteligencia Artificial.* Vol.4, No 10, (Summer 2000), pp. 119-126, ISSN 1137-3601, España

Sivanandam S.N., Sumathi S. & Deepa S.N. (2007). *Introduction to Fuzzy Logic using MATLAB*, Ed. Springer, ISBN 978-3540357803, Berlín, New York

Tanaka K. & Sugeno M. (1992). Stability Analysis and Design of Fuzzy Control Systems, *Fuzzy Sets and Systems*, Vol.45, No.2, (January 2002), pp. 135-156, ISSN 0165-0114, North-Holland

Tanaka K. & Wang H. O. (2001). *Fuzzy control systems design and analysis. A linear matrix inequality approach*, John Wiley & Sons, ISBN 978-0471323242, New York

Wang L. X. (1994). *Adaptative Fuzzy Systems and Control: Design and Stability Analysis,* Prentice Hall, Inc., ISBN 978-0130996312, Upper Saddle River, NJ

Yager R.R., Filev D.P. (1994). *Essentials of Fuzzy Modeling and Control,* Wiley, ISBN 978-0471017615, New York

Section 3

Application to Civil Engineering Problems

7

Neural Network and Adaptive Neuro-Fuzzy Inference System Applied to Civil Engineering Problems

Mohammed A. Mashrei

Thi-Qar University, College of Engineering, Civil Department
Iraq

1. Introduction

Soft computing is an approximate solution to a precisely formulated problem or more typically, an approximate solution to an imprecisely formulated problem (Zadeh, 1993). It is a new field appearing in the recent past to solve some problems such as decision-making, modeling and control problems. Soft computing is an emerging approach to computing which parallels the remarkable ability of the human mind to reason and learn in an environment of uncertainty and imprecision (Jang el at., 1997). It consists of many complementary tools such as artificial neural network (ANN), fuzzy logic (FL), and adaptive neuro-fuzzy inference system (ANFIS).

Artificial neural network (ANN) model is a system of interconnected computational neurons arranged in an organized fashion to carry out an extensive computing to perform a mathematical mapping (Rafiq et al., 2001). The first interest in neural network (or parallel distributed processing) emerged after the introduction of simplified neurons by McCulloch & Pitts, (1943). These neurons were presented as models of biological neurons and as conceptual components for circuits that could perform computational works. ANN can be most adequately characterized as a computational model with particular properties such as the ability to adapt or learn, to generalize, or to cluster or organize data in which the operation is based on parallel processing.

ANN has a large number of highly interconnected processing elements (nodes or units) that usually operate in parallel and are configured in regular architectures. The collective behavior of an ANN, like a human brain, demonstrates the ability to learn, recall, and generalize from training patterns or data. ANN is inspired by modeling networks of biological neurons in the brain. Hence, the processing elements in ANN are also called artificial neurons (Rafiq et al., 2001). Artificial neural network described in this chapter is mostly applied to solve many civil engineering applications such as structural analysis and design (Cladera & Mar, 2004a, 2004b; Hajela & Berke, 1991; Sanad & Saka, 2001), structural damage assessment (Feng & Bahng, 1999; Mukherjee et al., 1996), structural dynamics and control (Chen et al., 1995; Feng & Kim, 1998) and pavement condition-rating modeling (Eldin & Senouuci, 1995).

The adaptive neuro-fuzzy inference system (ANFIS), first proposed by Jang, 1993, is one of the examples of neuro-fuzzy systems in which a fuzzy system is implemented in the framework of adaptive networks. ANFIS constructs an input-output mapping based both on human knowledge (in the form of fuzzy if-then rules) and on generated input-output data pairs by using a hybrid algorithm that is the combination of the gradient descent and least squares estimates. Readers are referred to References (Jang, 1993; Mashrei, 2010) for more details on the ANFIS. After generated input-output by training, the ANFIS can be used to recognize data that is similar to any of the examples shown during the training phase .The adaptive neuro-fuzzy inference system has been used in the area of civil engineering to solve many problems (Abdulkadir et al., 2006; Akbulut et al., 2004; Fonseca el at., 2007; Tesfamariam & Najjaran, 2007).

Most of the problems solved in civil and structural engineering using ANFIS and ANN are prediction of behavior based on given experimental results that are used for training and testing data. The matter of modeling is to solve a problem by predicting which is obtained by mapping a set of variables in input space to a set of response variables in output space through a model as represented in Fig. 1. In the box representing a model in this figure, conventionally a mathematical model is used. However, the conventional modeling of the underlying systems often tends to become quite intractable and very difficult. Recently an alternative approach to modeling has emerged under the rubric of soft computing with neural network and fuzzy logic as its main constituents. The development of these models, however, requires a set of data. Fortunately, for many problems of civil engineering such data are available.

The purpose of this chapter is to investigate the accuracy of an adaptive neuro-fuzzy inference system and neural network to solve civil engineering problems: The ANN and ANFIS are used to predict the shear strength of concrete beams reinforced with fiber reinforced polymer (FRP) bars and shear strength of ferrocement members. The performance of the ANFIS and ANN models are compared with experimental values and with those of the other methods to assess the efficiency of these models. The study is based on the available databases.

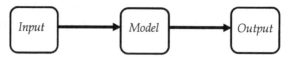

Fig. 1. An input-output mapping

2. Artificial neural network

One type of network sees the nodes as artificial neurons. These are called artificial neural network (ANN). An artificial neuron is a computational model inspired in by natural neurons. Natural neurons receive signals through *synapses* located on the dendrites or membrane of the neuron. When the signals received are strong enough (surpass a certain *threshold*), the neuron is *activated* and emits a signal through the *axon*. This signal might be sent to another synapse, and might activate other neurons (Gershenson, 2003). Fig. 2 shows a natural neuron.

The complexity of real neurons is highly abstracted when modeling artificial neurons. These basically consist of *inputs*(like synapses), which are multiplied by *weights* (strength of the respective signals), and then computed by a mathematical function which determines the *activation* of the neuron. Another function (which may be the identity) computes the *output* of the artificial neuron (sometimes independent on a certain *threshold*). ANN combines artificial neurons in order to process information (Gershenson, 2003).

Compared to conventional digital computing techniques, neural networks are advantageous because of their special features, such as the massively parallel processing, distributed storing of information, low sensitivity to error, their very robust operation after training, generalization and adaptability to new information (Waszczyszyn, 1998).

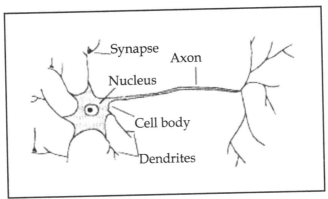

Fig. 2. Natural (biological) neurons

2.1 Learning process

An artificial neuron is composed of five main parts: inputs, weights, sum function, activation function and outputs. Inputs are information that enters the cell from other cells of from external world. Weights are values that express the effect of an input set or another process element in the previous layer on this process element. Sum function is a function that calculates the effect of inputs and weights totally on this process element. This function calculates the net input that comes to a cell (Topcu & Sarıdemir, 2007).

The information is propagated through the neural network layer by layer, always in the same direction. Besides the input and output layers there can be other intermediate layers of neurons, which are usually called hidden layers. Fig. 3 shows the structure of a typical neural network.

The inputs to the jth node are represented as an input factor, a, with component a_i (i=1 to n), and the output by bj. The values w_{1j}, w_{2j}, ..., and w_{nj} are weight factors associated with each input to the node. This is something like the varying synaptic strengths of biological neurons. Weights are adaptive coefficients within the network that determine the intensity of the input signal. Every input (a_1, a_2, ..., a_n) is multiplied by its corresponding weight factor (w_{1j}, w_{2j}, ..., w_{nj}), and the node uses this weighted input ($w_{1j} a_1$, $w_{2j} a_2$, ..., $w_{nj} a_n$) to perform further calculations. If the weight factor is positive, ($w_{ij}a_i$) tends to excite the node. If the weight factor is negative, ($w_{ij}a_i$) inhibits the node. In the initial setup of a neural network, weight factors may be chosen according to a specified statistical distribution. Then these weight factors are adjusted in the development of the network or "learning" process.

The other input to the node is the node's internal threshold, T_j. This is a randomly chosen value that governs the "activation" or total input of the node through the following equation (Baughman & Liu, 1995).

Total Activation: $$x_i = \sum_{i=1}^{n}(w_{ij}).a_i - T_j \tag{1}$$

The total activation depends on the magnitude of the internal threshold T_j. If T_j is large or positive, the node has a high internal threshold, thus inhibiting node-firing. If T_j is zero or negative, the node has a low internal threshold, which excites node-firing. If no internal threshold is specified, a zero value is assumed. This activity is then modified by transfer function and becomes the final output (b_j) of the neuron (Baughman & Liu, 1995).

$$b_j = f(x_i) = f(\sum_{i=1}^{n}(w_{ij}).a_i - T_j) \tag{2}$$

This signal is then propagated to the neurons (process elements) of the next layer. Fig. 4 depicts this process.

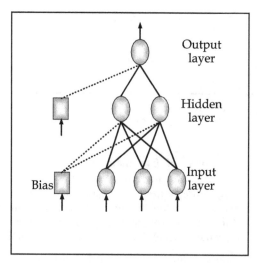

Fig. 3. Structure of a typical neural network

A back-propagation neural network has been successfully applied in various fields such as in civil engineering problems. A learning with back-propagation technique starts with applying an input vector to the network, which is propagated in a forward propagation mode which ends with an output vector. Next, the network evaluates the errors between the desired output vector and the actual output vector. It uses these errors to shift the connection weights and biases according to a learning rule that tends to minimize the error. This process is generally referred to as "error back- propagation" or back-propagation. The adjusted weights and biases are then used to start a new cycle. A back-propagation cycle, also known as an epoch, in a neural network is illustrated in Fig. 5. For a number of epochs the weights and biases are shifted until the deviations from the outputs are minimized.

Transfer functions are the processing units of a neuron. The node's output is determined by using a mathematical operation on the total activation of the node. These functions can be linear or non-linear. Three of the most common transfer functions are depicted in Fig. 6.

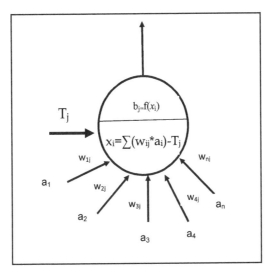

Fig. 4. A single neuron

The mathematical formulation of the functions is given as follows (Matlab Toolbox, 2009):

Pure-Linear: $$f(x) = x \tag{3}$$

Log sigmoid: $f(x) = 1/1 + e^{-x}$ $\qquad 0 \leq f(x) \leq 1$ (4)

Tangent sigmoid: $f(x) = \tanh(x) = e^{x} - e^{-x}/e^{x} + e^{-x}$ $\quad -1 \leq f(x) \leq 1$ (5)

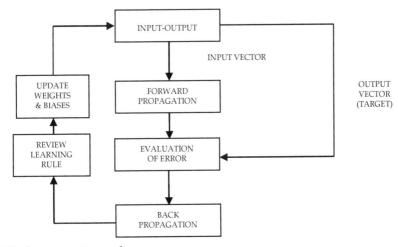

Fig. 5. Back-propagation cycle

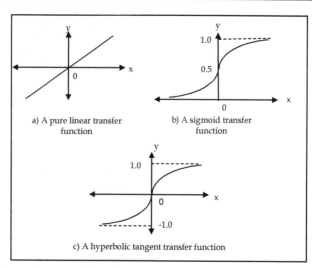

Fig. 6. Commonly used transfer function

2.2 Generalization

After the training is completed, the network error is usually minimized and the network output shows reasonable similarities with the target output, and before a neural network can be used with any degree of confidence, there is a need to establish the validity of the results it generates. A network could provide almost perfect answers to the set of problems with which it was trained, but fail to produce meaningful answers to other examples. Usually, validation involves evaluating network performance on a set of test problem that were not used for training. Generalization (testing) is so named because it measures how well the network can generalize what it has learned and form rules with which to make decisions about data it has not previously seen. The error between the actual and predicted outputs of testing and training converges upon the same point corresponding to the best set of weight factors for the network. If the network is learning an accurate generalized solution to the problem, the average error curve for the test patterns decreases at a rate approaching that of the training patterns. Generalization capability can be used to evaluate the behavior of the neural network.

2.3 Selecting the number of hidden layers

The number of hidden layers and the number of nodes in one hidden layer are not straightforward to ascertain. No rules are available to determine the exact number. The choice of the number of hidden layers and the nodes in the hidden layer(s) depends on the network application. Determining the number of hidden layers is a critical part of designing a network and it is not straightforward as it is for input and output layers (Rafiq el at., 2001).

To determine the optimal number of hidden layers, and the optimal number of nodes in each layer, the network is to be trained using various configurations, and then to select the configuration with the fewest number of layers and nodes that still yields the minimum mean-squares error (MSE) quickly and efficiently. (Eberhard & Dobbins, 1990) recommended the number of hidden-layer nodes be at least greater than the square root of the sum of the number of the components in the input and output vectors. (Carpenter & Barthelemy, 1994; Hajela & Berke, 1991) suggested that the number of nodes in the hidden layer is between the sum and the average of the number of nodes in the input and output layers.

The number of nodes in the hidden layer will be selected according to the following rules:

1. The maximum error of the output network parameters should be as small as possible for both training patterns and testing patterns.
2. The training epochs (number of iteration) should be as few as possible.

2.4 Pre-process and post-process of the training patterns

Neural networks require that their input and output data are normalized to have the same order of magnitude. Normalization is very critical; if the input and the output variables are not of the same order of magnitude, some variables may appear to have more significance than they actually do. The normalization used in the training algorithm compensates for the order-of-differences in magnitude of variables by adjusting the network weights. To avoid such problems, normalization all input and output variables is recommended. The training patterns should be normalized before they are applied to the neural network so as to limit the input and output values within a specified range. This is due to the large difference in the values of the data provided to the neural network. Besides, the activation function used in the back-propagation neural network is a sigmoid function or hyperbolic tangent function. The lower and upper limits of the function are 0 and 1, respectively for sigmoid function and are -1 and +1 for hyperbolic tangent function. The following formula is used to pre-process the input data sets whose values are between -1 and 1(Baughman & Liu, 1995).

$$x_{i,norm.} = 2.\frac{x_i - x_{i,min.}}{x_{i,max.} - x_{i,min.}} - 1 \qquad (6)$$

where:
$x_{i,norm}$: the normalized variable.
$x_{i,min}$: the minimum value of variable xi (input).
$x_{i,max}$: the maximum value of variable xi (input).

However, for the sigmoid function the following function might be used.

$$O_{i,norm} = \frac{t_i - t_{i,min}}{t_{i,max} - t_{i,min}} \qquad (7)$$

where:
$t_{i,min}$: the minimum value of variable t_i (output).
$t_{i,max}$: the maximum value of variable t_i (output).

3. Adaptive neuro-fuzzy inference system (ANFIS)

The fuzzy set theory developed by (Zadeh, 1965) provides as a mathematical framework to deal with vagueness associated with the description of a variable. The commonly used fuzzy inference system (FIS) is the actual process of mapping from a given input to output using fuzzy logic.

Fuzzy logic is particularly useful in the development of expert systems. Expert systems are built by capturing the knowledge of humans: however, such knowledge is known to be qualitative and inexact. Experts may be only partially knowledgeable about the problem domain, or data may not be fully available, but decisions are still expected. In these situations, educated guesses need to be made to provide solutions to problems. This is where fuzzy logic can be employed as a tool to deal with imprecision and qualitative aspects that are associated with problem solving (Jang, 1993).

A fuzzy set is a set without clear or sharp boundaries or without binary membership characteristics. Unlike a conventional set where object either belongs or do not belong to the set, partial membership in a fuzzy set is possible. In other words, there is a softness associated with the membership of elements in a fuzzy set (Jang, 1993).A fuzzy set may be represented by a membership function. This function gives the grade (degree) of membership within the set. The membership function maps the elements of the universe on to numerical values in the interval [0, 1]. The membership functions most commonly used in control theory are triangular, trapezoidal, Gaussian, generalized bell, sigmoidal and difference sigmoidal membership functions (Jang et al., 1997; Matlab toolbox, 2009; Zaho & Bose, 2002).

As mentioned previously, the fuzzy inference system is the process of formulating the mapping from a given input to an output using fuzzy logic. The dynamic behavior of an FIS is characterized by a set of linguistic description rules based on expert knowledge.

The fuzzy system and neural networks are complementary technologies.The most important reason for combining fuzzy systems with neural networks is to use the learning capability of neural network. While the learning capability is an advantage from the view point of a fuzzy system, from the viewpoint of a neural network there are additional advantages to a combined system. Because a neuro-fuzzy system is based on linguistic rules, we can easily integrate prior knowledge in to the system, and this can substantially shorten the learning process. One of the popular integrated systems is an ANFIS, which is an integration of a fuzzy inference system with a back-propagation algorithm (Jang et al., 1997; Lin & Lee 1996).

There are two types of fuzzy inference systems that can be implemented: Mamdani-type and Sugeno-type (Mamdani & Assilian, 1975; Sugeno, 1985). Because the Sugeno system is more compact and computationally more efficient than a Mamdani system, it lends itself to the use of adaptive techniques for constructing the fuzzy models. These adaptive techniques can be used to customize the membership functions so that the fuzzy system best models the data. The fuzzy inference system based on neuro-adaptive learning techniques is termed adaptive neuro-fuzzy inference system (Hamidian & Seyedpoor, 2009).

In order for an FIS to be mature and well established so that it can work appropriately in prediction mode, its initial structure and parameters (linear and non-linear) need to be tuned or adapted through a learning process using a sufficient input-output pattern of data. One of the most commonly used learning systems for adapting the linear and non-linear parameters of an FIS, particularly the first order Sugeno fuzzy model, is the ANFIS. ANFIS is a class of adaptive networks that are functionally equivalent to fuzzy inference systems (Jang, 1993).

3.1 Architecture of ANFIS

Fig. 7 shows the architecture of a typical ANFIS with two inputs X_1 and X_2, two rules and one output f, for the first order Sugeno fuzzy model, where each input is assumed to have two associated membership functions (MFs). For a first-order Sugeno fuzzy model a typical rule set with two fuzzy if–then rules can be expressed as (Jang, 1993):

Rule (1): If X_1 is A_1 and X_2 is B_1, then $f_1 = m_1 X_1 + n_1 X_2 + q_1$,
Rule (2): If X_1 is A_2 and X_2 is B_2, then $f_2 = m_2 X_1 + n_2 X_2 + q_2$.

where: m_1, n_1, q_1 and m_2, n_2, q_2 are the parameters of the output function.

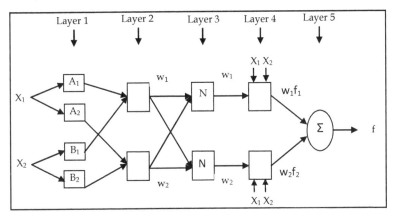

Fig. 7. Structure of the proposed ANFIS model

The architecture of the proposed (ANFIS), it contains five layers where the node functions in the same layer are of the same function family. Inputs, outputs and implemented mathematical models of the nodes of each layer are explained below.

Layer 1: The node function of every node i in this layer take the form:

$$O_i^1 = \mu A_i(X) \tag{8}$$

where X is the input to node i, μA_i is the membership function (which can be triangular, trapezoidal, gaussian functions or other shapes) of the linguistic label A_i associated with this node and O_i is the degree of match to which the input X satisfies the quantifier A_i. In the current study, the Gaussian shaped MFs defined below are utilized.

$$\mu A_i(X) = exp\left\{-\frac{1}{2}\frac{(X-c_i)^2}{\sigma_i^2}\right\} \tag{9}$$

where $\{c_i, \sigma_i\}$ are the parameters of the MFs governing the Gaussian functions. The parameters in this layer are usually referred to as premise parameters.

Layer 2: Every node in this layer multiplies the incoming signals from layer 1 and sends the product out as follows,

$$w_i = \mu A_i(X_1) \times \mu B_i(X_2), i = 1,2 \tag{10}$$

where the output of this layer (w_i) represents the firing strength of a rule.

Layer 3: Every node i in this layer is a node labeled N, determine the ratio of the i-th rule's firing strength to the sum of all rules' firing strengths as:

$$\bar{w_i} = \frac{w_i}{w_1 + w_2} \tag{11}$$

where the output of this layer represent the normalized firing strengths.

Layer 4: Every node i in this layer is an adaptive node with a node function of the form:

$$O_i^4 = \bar{w_i} f_i = \bar{w_i}(m_i X_1 + n_i X_2 + q_i), i = 1,2 \tag{12}$$

where $\bar{w_i}$ is the output to layer 3, and $\{m_i, n_i, q_i\}$ is the parameter set of this node. Parameters in this layer are referred to as consequent parameters.

Layer 5: There is only a single node in this layer that computes the overall output as the weighted average of all incoming signals from layer 4 as:

$$O_i^5 = \sum_i \bar{w_i} f_i = \frac{\sum_i w_i f_i}{\sum_i w_i}, i = 1,2 \tag{13}$$

3.2 Learning process

As mentioned earlier, both the premise (non-linear) and consequent (linear) parameters of the ANFIS should be tuned, utilizing the so-called learning process, to optimally represent the factual mathematical relationship between the input space and output space. Normally, as a first step, an approximate fuzzy model is initiated by the system and then improved through an iterative adaptive learning process. Basically, ANFIS takes the initial fuzzy model and tunes it by means of a hybrid technique combining gradient descent back-propagation and mean least-squares optimization algorithms. At each epoch, an error measure, usually defined as the sum of the squared difference between actual and desired output, is reduced. Training stops when either the predefined epoch number or error rate is obtained. There are two passes in the hybrid learning procedure for ANFIS. In the forward pass of the hybrid learning algorithm, functional signals go forward till layer 4 and the consequent parameters are identified by the least squares estimate. In the backward pass, the error rates propagate backward and the premise parameters are updated by the gradient descent. When the values of the premise parameters are learned, the overall output (f) can be expressed as a linear combination of the consequent parameters (Jang, 1993):

$$f = \frac{w_1}{w_1 + w_2} f_1 + \frac{w_2}{w_1 + w_2} f_2 = \bar{w_1} f_1 + \bar{w_2} f_2 \tag{14}$$

$$= (\bar{w_1} X_1) m_1 + (\bar{w_1} X_2) n_1 + (\bar{w_1}) q_1 + (\bar{w_2} X_2) m_2 + (\bar{w_2} X_2) n_2 + (\bar{w_2}) q_2$$

which is linear in the consequent parameters m_1, n_1, q_1, m_2, n_2 and q_2.

4. Cases studies

There are two case studies considered in this chapter:

1.   Predicting of shear strength of ferrocement members using ANN and ANFIS.

2. Predicting of shear strength of concrete beams reinforced with FRP bars using ANN and ANFIS.

4.1 Case study 1

In this study the back-propagation neural networks (BPNN) model and adaptive neuro-fuzzy inference system (ANFIS) are utilized to predict the shear strength of ferrocement members. A database of the shear strength of ferrocement members obtained from the literature alongside the experimental study conducted by the author is used for the development of these models. The models are developed within MATLAB using BPNN and Sugeno ANFIS.

4.1.1 Review of shear strength of ferrocement members

In recent years, ferrocement has been widely accepted and utilized. Research and development on ferrocement has progressed at a tremendous pace. Many innovative applications are being explored and constructed throughout the world. The application of ferrocement in low cost housing is well known. However, as ferrocement elements are thin, their use for roofing and exterior walls raises doubts regarding the thermal comfort inside the building (Naaman, 2000). Ferrocement is a composite material constructed by cement mortar reinforced with closely spaced layers of wire mesh (Naaman, 2000; Shah, 1974). The ultimate tensile resistance of ferrocement is provided solely by the reinforcement in the direction of loading. The compressive strength is equal to that of the unreinforced mortar. However, in case of flexure and shear, the analysis and design of ferrocement elements is complex and are based primarily on the reinforced concrete analysis using the principles of equilibrium and compatibility.

Few methods have been proposed for the estimation of the shear strength of ferrocement specimens. One of these methods is considered in this study which is given by Rao et al., (2006). They proposed an empirical expression to estimate the shear strength of ferrocement elements by considering the shear resistance of ferrocement elements as the sum of shear resistance due to mortar and reinforcement. The shear resistance of ferrocement element (V_u) was given as:

$$\frac{V_u}{b.d} = \frac{\sqrt{f_c'}}{a/d}\left\{0.0856 + 0.0028\frac{v_f f_y}{\sqrt{f_c'}}\right\}$$ (15)

4.1.2 ANN for predicted the shear strength of ferrocement members

An artificial neural network was developed to predict the shear strength of ferrocement. This section describes the data selection for training and testing patterns, the topology of the constructed network, the training process and the verification of the neural network results. A relative importance is carried out which is based on the artificial neural network predictions. Finally, the results of the shear strength of ferrocement members predicted by BPNN and ANFIS are compared with the results of the experimental program and empirical method. The empirical method was proposed by (Rao et al., 2006).

4.1.2.1 Selection of the training and testing patterns

The experimental data that are used to train the neural network are obtained from literature (Mansur & Ong, 1987; Mashrei, 2010; Rao et al., 2006) as shown in Table A in appendix. The data used to build the neural network model should be divided into two subsets: training set and testing set. The testing set contains approximately 13% from total database. The training phase is needed to produce a neural network that is both stable and convergent. Therefore, selecting what data to use for training a network is one of the most important steps in building a neural network model. The total numbers of 69 test specimens was utilized. The training set contained 60 specimens and the testing set was comprised of 9 specimens.

Neural networks interpolate data very well. Therefore, patterns chosen for training set must cover upper and lower boundaries and a sufficient number of samples representing particular features over the entire training domain (Rafiq et al., 2001).An important aspect of developing neural networks is determining how well the network performs once training is complete. The performance of a trained network is checked by involving two main criteria:

1. How well the neural network recalls the predicted response from data sets used to train the network (called the recall step). A well trained network should be able to produce an output that deviates very little from desired value.
2. How well the network predicts responses from data sets that were not used in the training (called the generalization step). Generalization is affected by three factors: the size and the efficiency of the training data set, the architecture of the network, and the physical complexity of the problem. A well generalized network should be able to sense the new input patterns.

To effectively visualize how well a network performs recall and generalization steps, the learning curve is generated which represents the mean square error (MSE) for both the recall of training data sets and generalization of testing set with the number of iteration or epoch. The error between the training data sets and the generalization of testing sets should converge upon the same point corresponding to the best set of weight factors for the network.

4.1.2.2 Input and output layers

In the developed neural network model there is an input layer, where input data are presented to the network, and an output layer of one neuron representing the shear strength of ferrocement member. In this study the parameters which may be introduced as the components of the input vector consist of six inputs: the total depth of specimens cross

Parameters	Range
Width of specimens (b) (mm)	100-200
Total depth of specimens (d) (mm)	25-50
Shear span to depth ratio (a/d)	1-7
Compressive strength of mortar (f_c')	26.5-44.1
yield strength of wire mesh (f_y) (MPa)	380-410
Volume fraction of wire mesh (v_f) %	0-5.7

Table 1. Range of parameters in the database

section (d), the width of specimens cross section (b),yield tensile strength of wire mesh reinforcement (f_y), cylinder compressive strength of mortar (fc'), total volume fraction of wire mesh (v_f) and shear span to depth ratio (a/d). The shear strength of ferrocement member represents the target variable. Table 1 summarizes the ranges of each different variable.

4.1.2.3 Normalizing input and output data sets

Normalization (scaling down) of input and output data sets within a uniform range before they are applied to the neural network is essential to prevent larger numbers from overriding smaller ones, and to prevent premature saturation of hidden nodes, which impedes the learning process. The limitation of input and output values within a specified range are due to the large difference in the values of the data provided to the neural network. Besides, the activation function used in the back-propagation neural network is a hyperbolic tangent function, the lower and upper limits of this function are -1 and +1 respectively. In this study Eq. 5 mentioned above is used to normalize the input and output parameters. That equation gives the required results with a certain mean square error by a small number of epochs.

4.1.2.4 Number of hidden layers and nodes in each hidden layer

The network is tested with an increasing number of nodes in hidden layer. It is found that one-hidden layer network with four nodes gives the optimal configurations with minimum mean square error (MSE). As an activation function, a hyperbolic tangent function is selected for the hidden layer and a purelin function is used for the output layer.

In this study the initial weights are randomly chosen. The network has been trained continually through updating weights until the final error achieved is $8.48*10^{-4}$.

Fig. 8 shows the performance for training and generalization (testing) sets using resilient back-propagation training algorithm, the network is trained for 420 epochs to check if the performance (MSE) for either training or testing sets might diverge. The network performance with resilient back-propagation training algorithm have been tested for training and generalizing patterns, as shown in Fig. 9 (a) and (b). A good agreement has been noted in the predicted values compared with the actual (targets) values.

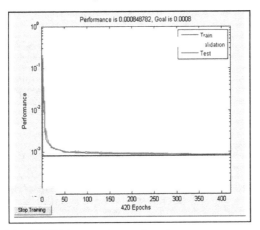

Fig. 8. Convergence of the BPNN for training and testing sets

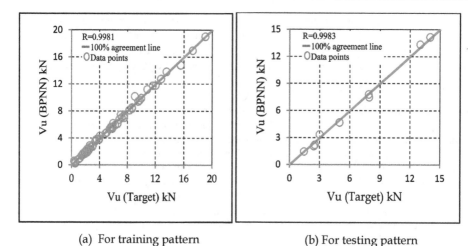

(a) For training pattern   (b) For testing pattern

Fig. 9. Comparison between BPNN results and target results

4.1.2.5 Relative importance

Once the artificial neural network has been trained, a relative importance is used to investigate the influence of the various parameters on the shear strength. The effect of each parameter on the shear strength of ferrocement is clear in Table 2. After training all the data sets with the final model, the relative importance of each input variable is evaluated. The methodology suggested by Garson, (1991) is used. The relative importance of the various input factors can be assessed by examining input-hidden-output layer connection weights. This is carried out by partitioning the hidden-output connection weights into components connected with each input neuron. Table 2 lists the relative importance of the input variables in the BPNN model. It can be observed that for shear strength of the ferrocement member, the shear span to depth ratio $(^a/_d)$ is the most important factor among the input variables and volume fraction of wire mesh is the second most important factor comparing with the others. Therefore, it can be concluded that $(^a/_d)$ ratio has the most influence on the shear strength of ferrocement.

Input variables	b (mm)	d (mm)	f_c' (MPa)	f_y (MPa)	$^a/_d$	v_f (%)
RI (%)	7.11	20.0	8.89	5.28	38.32	20.4

Table 2. Relative importance (RI) (%) of BPNN model

4.1.3 Adaptive neural fuzzy inference system (ANFIS) model

In the developed ANFIS, six variables consisting of width (b) and depth (d) of the specimens, yield tensile strength of wire mesh reinforcement (f_y), cylinder compressive strength of mortar (f_c'), total volume fraction of wire mesh (v_f) and shear span to depth ratio $(^a/_d)$ are selected as input variables to predict the shear strength of ferrocement members, which is the target variable. In this investigation the subtractive clustering technique introduced by (Chiu, 1994)with (genfis2) function was used. Given separate sets of input and output data, the genfis2 uses a subtractive clustering method to generate a Fuzzy Inference System (FIS). When there is only one output, genfis2 may be used to generate an initial FIS for ANFIS training by first implementing subtractive clustering on the data. The genfis2 function uses the subclust function to estimate the antecedent membership functions and a set of rules. This function returns an FIS structure that contains a set of fuzzy rules to cover the feature space (Fuzzy Logic Toolbox, 2009). For a given set of data, subtractive clustering method was used for estimating the number of clusters and the cluster centers in a set of data. It assumes each data point is a potential cluster center and calculates a measure of the potential for each data point based on the density of surrounding data points. The algorithm selects the data point with the highest potential as the first cluster center and then delimits the potential of data points near the first cluster center. The algorithm then selects the data point with the highest remaining potential as the next cluster center and delimits the potential of data points near this new cluster center. This process of acquiring a new cluster center and delimiting the potential of surrounding data points repeats until the potential of all data points falls below a threshold. The range of influence of a cluster center in each of the data dimensions is called cluster radius. A small cluster radius will lead to finding many small clusters in the data (resulting in many rules) and vice versa (Jang, 1997; Jonic', 1999). Membership functions (MFs) and numbers are appropriately decided when testing data set.

4.1.3.1 Database

The adaptive neuro-fuzzy inference system model is developed to predict the shear strength of ferrocement members. The same database of (69) specimens as in the previous BPNN model is used for the development of this model. The total data is divided at random into two groups (training data set, and testing data set), as shown in Table A in Appendix.

4.1.3.2 Modeling and results

The ANFIS model is developed to predict shear strength of ferrocement specimens with MFs of type (gussmf) for all input variables and linear for the output. The number of MFs assigned to each input variable is chosen by trial and error. After training and testing, the

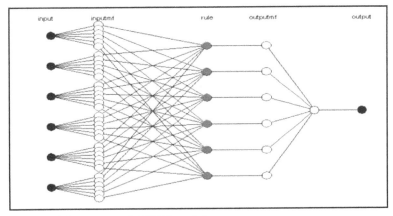

Fig. 10. Structure of the proposed ANFIS model

number of MFs is fixed as six MFs for each input variable. This is chosen when the ANFIS model reaches an acceptable satisfactory level. The structure of ANFIS model is developed as shown in Fig. 10. The basic flow diagram of computations in ANFIS is illustrated in Fig. 11. A comparison between the prediction from ANFIS and target value for each of training and testing data set is shown in Fig. 12(a) and (b) respectively. The predictions appear to be quite good with correlation coefficient R approaches one.

4.1.4 Comparison between experimental and theoretical results

The predictions of shear strength of ferrocement members as obtained from BPNN, ANFIS, and the empirical available method (Eq.15) (Rao et al., 2006) are compared with the experimental results and shown for both training and testing sets in Figs.13 and 14 and Table 3 . In Table 3 the ratios of experimental (V_e) to theoretical predictions of the shear strength (V_i) of the ferrocement specimens are calculated. The theoretical predications include those obtained by BPNN (V_1), ANFIS (V_2), and empirical method (Eq.15) (V_3). The average and the standard deviation of the ratios V_e/V_i are given in this table for both training and testing set. It can be seen that BPNN and ANFIS models give average values of V_e/V_1 and V_e/V_2 of 1.01 and standard deviations of 0.14 and 0.13, respectively for training set and the average values of V_e/V_1 and V_e/V_2 of 1.03 and standard deviations of 0.09 and 0.08, respectively for testing set , which are better than the values obtained for the empirical method. Figs. 13 and 14 confirm the same conclusion the predictions of BPNN and ANFIS

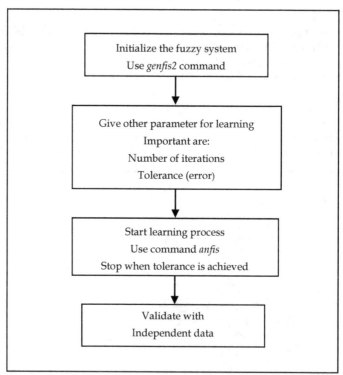

Fig. 11. The basic flow diagram of computations in ANFIS

models are better than those of the empirical method. Also in Table 3 the correlation coefficient R of predicted shear strength by BPNN, ANFIS, and the empirical method are summarized. As shown in Table 4, both ANFIS and BPNN produce a higher correlation coefficient R as compared with the empirical method. Therefore, the BPNN as well as ANFIS can serve as reliable and simple tools for the prediction of shear strength of ferrocement.

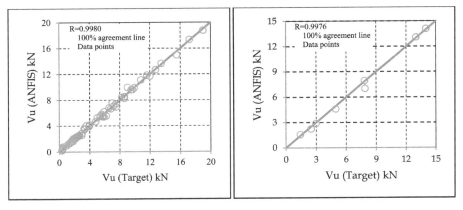

(a) For training pattern   (b) For training pattern

Fig. 12. Comparison between ANFIS results and target results

Specimens	No.	Average of of V_e / V_i			STDEV of V_e / V_i		
		$\dfrac{V_e}{V_1}$	$\dfrac{V_e}{V_2}$	$\dfrac{V_e}{V_3}$	$\dfrac{V_e}{V_1}$	$\dfrac{V_e}{V_2}$	$\dfrac{V_e}{V_3}$
Training set	60	1.01	1.01	1.21	0.14	0.13	0.27
Testing set	9	1.03	1.03	1.23	0.09	0.08	0.31

Table 3. Comparison between experimental and predicted results for training and testing sets

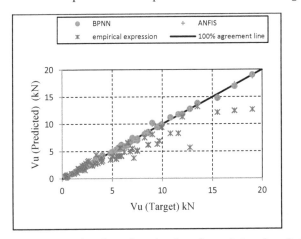

Fig. 13. Comparison experimental and predicted values for training data Set

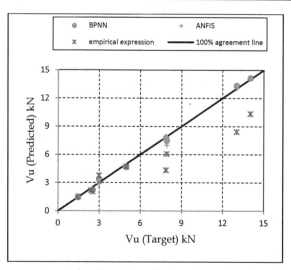

Fig. 14. Comparison experimental and predicted values for testing data Set

Type	Correlation R	
	Training	Testing
BPNN	0.9981	0.9983
ANFIS	0.9980	0.9976
Empirical Method	0.9500	0.9600

Table 4. Comparison summary of correlation R

4.2 Case study 2

In this part the PBNN and ANFIS models are developed to predict the shear strength of concrete beams reinforced with FRP bars. A database from tests on concrete beams reinforced with FRP bars obtained from the review of literature is used in this study. The structure of ANN and ANFIS models and the results of this study will be described below.

4.2.1 Review on shear strength of concrete beams reinforced with FRP bars

An FRP bar is made from filaments or fibers held in a polymeric resin matrix binder. The FRP Bar can be made from various types of fibers such as Glass (GFRP) or Carbon (CFRP). FRP bars have a surface treatment that facilitates a bond between the finished bar and the structural element into which they are placed (Bank, 2006).

During the last two decades, fiber reinforced polymer (FRP) materials have been used in a variety of configurations as an alternative reinforcement for new and strengthening civil engineering structures and bridges. The attractiveness of the material lies mainly in their high corrosion resistance, high strength and fatigue resistance. In some cases, the non-magnetic characteristics became more important for some special structures. An important application of FRP, which is becoming more popular (Tan, 2003, as cited in Al-Sayed et at.,

2005a) is the use of FRP for reinforcement in concrete structures. The use of FRP in concrete structures include: (a) the internal reinforcing (rod or bar) which is used instead of the steel wire (rod) equivalent; and (b) the external bonded reinforcement, which is typically used to repair/strengthen the structure by plating or wrapping FRP tape, sheet or fabric around the member (Wu & Bailey, 2005).

There are fundamental differences between the steel and FRP reinforcements: the latter has a lower modulus of elasticity, the modulus of elasticity for commercially available glass and aramid FRP bars is 20 to 25 % that of steel compared to 60 to 75 % for carbon FRP bars (Bank, 2006) linear stress–strain diagram up to rupture with no discernible yield point and different bond strength according to the type of FRP product. These characteristics affect the shear capacity of FRP reinforced concrete members. Due to the relatively low modulus of elasticity of FRP bars, concrete members reinforced longitudinally with FRP bars experience reduced shear strength compared to the shear strength of those reinforced with the same amounts of steel reinforcement.

Some of empirical equations have been developed to estimate shear strength of concrete beams reinforced with FRP. Most of the shear design provisions incorporated in these codes and guides are based on the design formulas of members reinforced with conventional steel considering some modifications to account for the substantial differences between FRP and steel reinforcement. These provisions use the well-known $V_c + V_s$ method of shear design, which is based on the truss analogy. This section reviews the concrete shear strength of members longitudinally reinforced with FRP bars, V_{cf}, as recommended by the American Concrete Institute (ACI 440.1R-03, 2003), Tureyen and Frosch Equation (2003), and the proposed equation by El-Sayed et al. (2005a).

4.2.1.1 American Concrete Institute (ACI 440.1R-03)

The equation for shear strength proposed by the American Concrete Institute (ACI 440.1R-03), can be expressed as follows:

$$V_{cf} = \frac{\rho_f E_f}{90 \beta_1 f_c'} \left(\frac{\sqrt{f_c'}}{6} b_w d \right) \le \frac{\sqrt{f_c'}}{6} b_w d \tag{16}$$

4.2.1.2 Tureyen and Frosch equation (2003)

This equation was developed by Tureyen and Frosch, 2003. It was developed from a model that calculates the concrete contribution to shear strength of reinforced concrete beams. The equation was simplified to provide a design formula applicable FRP reinforced beams as follows:

$$V_{cf} = \frac{2}{5} \left(\frac{\sqrt{f_c'}}{6} b_w c \right) \tag{17}$$

where: $c = kd$ = cracked transformed section neutral axis depth (mm).

$$k = \sqrt{2 \rho_f n_f + (\rho_f n_f)^2} - \rho_f n_f \tag{18}$$

4.2.1.3 El-Sayed et al. equation (2005a)

They applied the same procedure in ACI 440.1R-03 to derive Eq. 1 above, with some modification for proposing the Eq. below:

$$V_{cf} = 0.037 \left(\frac{\rho_f E_f \sqrt{f_c'}}{\beta_1}\right)^{1/3} b_w d \leq \frac{\sqrt{f_c'}}{6} b_w d \qquad (19)$$

According to ACI 440.1R-03, the factor β_1 in the denominator of Eq. 3 is a function of the concrete compressive strength. It can be simply expressed by the following equation:

$$0.85 \geq \beta_1 = 0.85 - 0.007(f_c' - 28) \geq 0.65 \qquad (20)$$

4.2.2 Shear strength database

From the review of literature (Deitz, et al., 1999; El-Sayed et al. , 2005b, 2006a, 2006b, 2006c; Gross et al., 2003, 2004; Omeman et al., 2008; Razaqpur et al., 2004; Tariq & Newhook, 2003; Tureyen & Frosch, 2002, 2003; Wegian & Abdalla , 2005; Yost et al., 2001), a number (74) of shear strength tests are used for developing the ANN and ANFIS as shown in Table B in appendix. All specimens were simply supported and were tested in three-point loading. The main reinforcement of all specimens is FRP. All specimens had no transverse reinforcement and failed in shear. These data are divided into two sets: a training set containing 64 members, and testing set comprised of 10 members. Six input variables are selected to build the ANN and ANFIS models. These variables are width (b_w), and depth (d) of the beams, modulus of elasticity of FRP (E_f), compressive strength of concrete (f_c'), reinforcement ratio of FRP (ρ_f) and the shear span to depth ratio (a/d). The output value is the shear strength of concrete beams reinforced with FRP bars. Table 5 summarizes the ranges of each different variable.

Parameters	Range
Width of beams (b_w) mm	89-1000
Effective depth of beams (d) mm	143-360
Shear span to depth ratio (a/d)	1.3-6.5
Compressive strength of concrete (f_c') MPa	24-81
Modulus of elasticity of FRP (E_f) (GPa)	37-145
Reinforcement ratio of FRP (ρ_f)	0.25-2.63

Table 5. Summarizes the ranges of the different variables.

4.2.3 ANN model and results

ANN is used to investigate the shear strength of concrete beams reinforced with FRP bars. The configuration and training of neural networks is a trail-and-error process due to such undetermined parameters as the number of nodes in the hidden layer, and the number of training patterns. In the developed ANN, there is an input layer, where six parameters are presented to network and an output layer, with one neuron representing shear strength of concrete beams reinforced with FRP bars. One hidden layer as intermediate layer is also included. The network with one hidden layer and four nodes in the hidden layer gave the optimal configuration with minimum mean square error (MSE).

The back-propagation neural network model used for this study is trained by feeding a set of mapping data with input and target variables as explained previously. After the errors are minimized, the model with all the parameters including the connection weights is tested with a separate set of "testing" data that is not used in the training phase.

The network has trained continually through updating of the weights until error goal of 15.1*10-4 is achieved. Fig. 15 shows the performance for training and generalization (testing). A resilient back propagation training algorithm is used to train the network, for 800 epochs to check if the performance (MSE) for either training or testing sets might diverge.

The network performance with resilient back propagation training algorithm have been tested for training and testing patterns, as shown in Fig. 16 (a) and (b). A good agreement has been noted in the predicting values compared with the actual (targets) values.

Based on the same idea used to study the effect of the parameters on shear strength of ferrocement members, the effect of each parameter used in the input layer on shear strength of concrete beams reinforced with FRP bars is investigated. Table 6 lists the relative importance of the input variables in BPNN model. It can be observed that for shear strength of concrete beams reinforced with FRP, the shear span to depth ratio($^a/_d$) is also the most important factor among the input variables. This result is very match with the experimental results of many papers published in this field.

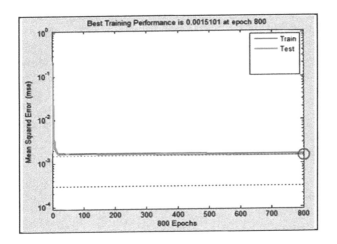

Fig. 15. Convergence of the BPNN for training and testing sets

Input variables	b_w (mm)	d (mm)	f_c' (MPa)	E_f (MPa)	$^a/_d$	ρ_f (%)
RI (%)	24.76	18.26	11.11	5.23	37.50	3.19

Table 6. Relative importance (RI) (%) of BPNN model

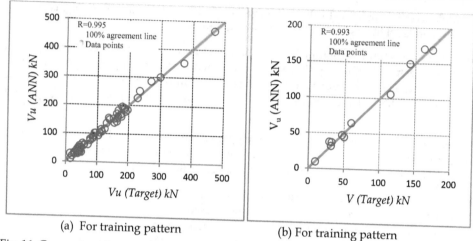

(a) For training pattern (b) For training pattern

Fig. 16. Comparison between BPNN results and target results

4.2.4 ANFIS model and results

The same technique used to build the ANFIS to predict shear strength of ferrocement members is used to build of ANFIS to predict the shear strength of concrete beams reinforced with FRP bars. Fig. 17 presents the structure of an adaptive neuro-fuzzy inference system developed to predict shear strength of concrete beams reinforced with FRP bars. The membership functions (MFs) of type (Gauss) for all input variables and linear for output present the best prediction in this study. The number of MFs assigned to each input variable is chosen by trial and error. After training and testing the number of MFs was fixed at two MFs for each input variable, when the ANFIS model reaches an acceptable satisfactory level. A comparison between the predictions from ANFIS and target value for both the training and testing data set is presented in Fig. 18(a) and(b) respectively. A good agreement has been noted in the predicting values compared with the experimental (target) values with reasonably high correlation R.

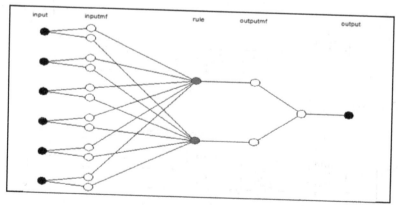

Fig. 17. Structure of the proposed ANFIS model

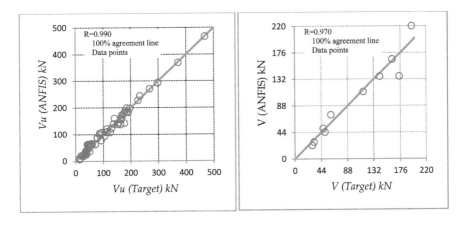

(a) For training pattern   (b) For training pattern

Fig. 18. Comparison between BPNN results and target results

4.2.5 Comparison between experimental and theoretical results

The predictions of shear strength of beams reinforced with FRP as that obtained from BPNN, ANFIS, ACI 440.1R-03, Tureyen and Frosch's equation, and the proposed equation by El-Sayed et al. (2005a), are compared with the experimental results and shown for both training and testing sets in Figs. 19 and 20 and Table 7.

In Table 6 the ratios of experimental (V_e) to theoretical (V_i) predictions of the shear strength of beams reinforced with FRP are calculated, the theoretical predictions include those obtained by BPNN (V_1), ANFIS (V_2), proposed equation by El-Sayed et al. (V_3), ACI 440.1R-03 (V_4), and Tureyen and Frosch's equation (V_5). The average and the standard deviation of the ratios V_e/V_i are also given in this table. It can be seen that the BPNN and ANFIS models give average values for the testing set of V_e/V_1 and V_e/V_2 of 0.97 and 1.03 and standard deviations of 0.1 and 0.167 respectively which are much better than the values obtained from other methods as shown in table 7. Figs. 19 and 20 confirm the same conclusion that the predictions of the ANN and ANFIS models are better than those of the other methods.

Also in Table 8 the correlation coefficient R of predicted shear strength that was evaluated by BPNN, ANFIS and the other methods are summarized. As shown in Table 8, the BPNN and ANFIS produces a higher correlation coefficient R as compared with the other methods. These results indicate that the BPNN and ANFIS is a reliable and simple model for predicting the shear strength of beams reinforced with FRP bars.

Specimens	No	Average of of V_e / V_i					STDEV of V_e / V_i				
		$\dfrac{V_e}{V_1}$	$\dfrac{V_e}{V_2}$	$\dfrac{V_e}{V_3}$	$\dfrac{V_e}{V_4}$	$\dfrac{V_e}{V_5}$	$\dfrac{V_e}{V_1}$	$\dfrac{V_e}{V_2}$	$\dfrac{V_e}{V_3}$	$\dfrac{V_e}{V_4}$	$\dfrac{V_e}{V_5}$
Training set	64	1.01	1.04	2.30	5.32	3.17	0.16	0.23	2.31	3.94	2.98
Testing set	10	0.96	1.03	2.01	3.93	2.73	0.103	0.17	1.72	1.62	2.27

Table 7. Comparison between experimental and Predicted results for training and testing sets

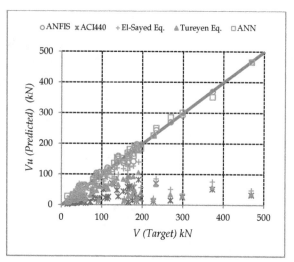

Fig. 19. Comparison experimental and predicted values for testing data set

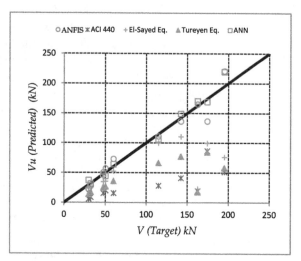

Fig. 20. Comparison experimental and predicted values for testing data set

Type	Correlation R	
	Training	Testing
ANN	0.995	0.993
ANFIS	0.99	0.97
El-Sayed's Eq.	0..32	0.63
ACI 440	0.51	0.78
Tureyen and Frosch's Eq.	0.37	0.69

Table 8. Comparison summary of correlation R

5. Conclusion

Two civil engineering applications are preformed using back-propagation neural network (BPNN)and adaptive neuro fuzzy inference system (ANFIS). The models were developed by predicting the shear strength of ferrocement members and the shear strength of concrete beams reinforced with fiber reinforced polymer (FRP) bars using BPNN and ANFIS based on the results of experimental lab work conducted by different authors. From the results of this study, the following conclusions can be stated:

1. BPNN and ANFIS have the ability to predict the shear strength of ferrocement members and the shear strength of concrete beams reinforced with FRP with a high degree of accuracy when they are compared with experimental and available methods results.
2. The relative importance of each input parameter is estimated using ANN. The relative importance study indicated that the predicted shear strength for both ferrocement and concrete beams with FRP by ANN models are in agreement with the underlying behavior of shear strength prediction based on the prior knowledge.
3. The ANN and ANFIS techniques offer an alternative approach to conventional techniques and, from them, some advantages can be obtained. Conventional models are based on the assumption of predefined empirical equations dependent on unknown parameters. However, in problems for which the modeling rules are either not known or extremely difficult to discover, such as in our problem, the conventional methods do not work well as shown in results. By using artificial neural network and the adaptive neuro fuzzy inference system, these difficulties are overcome since they are based on the learning and generalization from experimental data. ANN and ANFIS models can serve as reliable and simple predictive tools for the prediction of shear strength for both ferrocement and concrete beams with FRP of ferrocement members. Therefore, these models can be applied to solve most of civil engineering problems as a future research.

6. Nomenclature

V_u: Shear strength.
V_{cf}: The shear resistance of members reinforced with FRP bars as flexural reinforcement.
b: Width of the specimen.
d: Depth of the specimen.
v_f: Volume fraction of the mesh reinforcement ($100 * A_{ls}/$ bd).
A_{ls}: Cross sectional area of the longitudinal reinforcing mesh
b_w: Width of the concrete specimen reinforced wih FRP
ρ_f: Reinforcement ratio of flexural FRP.
E_f: Modulus of elasticity of fiber reinforced polymers.
n_f: Ratio of the modulus of elasticity of FRP bars to the modulus of elasticity of concrete.
f_c': Compressive strength of concrete or mortar.
f_y: Yield strength of reinforcement (wire mesh or FRP).
a/d: Shear span to depth ratio.
β_1: Is a function of the concrete compressive strength.

6.1 Appendix

Test No.	b (mm)	d (mm)	f_c' (MPa)	f_y (MPa)	a/d	v_f %	V_u (kN)	Reference
1	100	40	35.20	410.00	1.00	1.80	8.60	
2	100	40	35.20	410.00	1.50	1.80	5.40	
3	100	40	35.20	410.00	2.00	1.80	3.90	
4	100	40	35.20	410.00	2.50	1.80	3.00	
5	100	40	35.20	410.00	3.00	1.80	2.50	
6	100	40	35.20	410.00	1.00	2.72	10.80	
7	100	40	35.20	410.00	1.50	2.72	7.00	
8	100	40	35.20	410.00	2.00	2.72	5.70	
9	100	40	35.20	410.00	2.50	2.72	4.00	
10	100	40	35.20	410.00	3.00	2.72	3.30	*Mansur Ong,* 1987
11	100	40	36.00	410.00	1.00	3.62	14.00	
12	100	40	36.00	410.00	1.50	3.62	9.70	
13	100	40	36.00	410.00	2.00	3.62	7.50	
14	100	40	36.00	410.00	2.50	3.62	5.90	
15	100	40	36.00	410.00	3.00	3.62	4.80	
16	100	40	36.00	410.00	1.00	4.52	17.20	
17	100	40	36.00	410.00	1.50	4.52	11.60	
18	100	40	36.00	410.00	2.00	4.52	8.60	
19	100	40	36.00	410.00	2.50	4.52	6.80	
20	100	40	36.00	410.00	3.00	4.52	5.60	
21	100	40	44.10	410.00	1.00	4.52	19.00	
22	100	40	44.10	410.00	1.50	4.52	13.00	
23	100	40	44.10	410.00	2.00	4.52	9.50	
24	100	40	44.10	410.00	2.50	4.52	7.50	
25	100	40	44.10	410.00	3.00	4.52	5.90	*Mansur & Ong,* 1987
26	100	40	26.50	410.00	1.00	4.52	15.50	
27	100	40	26.50	410.00	1.50	4.52	9.00	
28	100	40	26.50	410.00	2.00	4.52	7.90	
29	100	40	26.50	410.00	2.50	4.52	6.20	
30	100	40	26.50	410.00	3.00	4.52	5.00	
31	150	25	32.20	0	1.00	0	1.84	
32	150	25	32.20	380.00	1.00	2.85	8.24	*Rao et al.,* 2006
33	150	25	32.20	380.00	1.00	3.80	9.93	
34	150	25	32.20	380.00	1.00	4.75	12.00	

Test No.	b (mm)	d (mm)	f_c' (MPa)	f_y (MPa)	a/d	v_f %	V_u (kN)	Reference
35	150	25	32.20	380.00	1.00	5.70	13.50	
36	150	25	32.20	380.00	2.00	0	0.93	
37	150	25	32.20	380.00	2.00	2.85	3.92	
38	150	25	32.20	380.00	2.00	3.80	4.95	
39	150	25	32.20	380.00	2.00	4.75	5.79	
40	150	25	32.20	380.00	2.00	5.70	6.57	
41	150	25	32.20	0	3.00	0	0.49	
42	150	25	32.20	380.00	3.00	2.85	2.20	
43	150	25	32.20	380.00	3.00	3.80	2.55	
44	150	25	32.20	380.00	3.00	4.75	2.97	
45	150	25	32.20	380.00	3.00	5.70	3.36	
46	150	25	32.20	0	4.00	0	0.44	
47	150	25	32.20	380.00	4.00	2.85	1.60	
48	150	25	32.20	380.00	4.00	3.80	1.99	
49	150	25	32.20	380.00	4.00	4.75	2.35	
50	150	25	32.20	380.00	4.00	5.70	2.65	
51	150	25	32.20	0	5.00	0	0.40	
52	150	25	32.20	380.00	5.00	2.85	1.42	
53	150	25	32.20	380.00	5.00	3.80	1.86	
54	150	25	32.20	380.00	5.00	4.75	2.16	
55	150	25	32.20	380.00	5.00	5.70	2.40	
56	150	25	32.20	0	6.00	0	0.34	
57	150	25	32.20	380.00	6.00	2.85	1.37	
58	150	25	32.20	380.00	6.00	3.80	1.84	
59	150	25	32.20	380.00	6.00	4.75	2.15	
60	150	25	32.20	380.00	6.00	5.70	2.40	
61	200	50	33.80	390.00	7.00	0.25	1.16	
62	200	50	33.80	390.00	7.00	0.50	1.47	
63	200	50	36.90	390.00	7.00	0.99	2.25	
64	200	50	40.40	390.00	3.00	0.25	2.94	
65	200	50	40.40	390.00	3.00	0.50	3.53	Mashrei, 2010
66	200	50	40.40	390.00	3.00	0.99	7.16	
67	200	50	41.20	390.00	2.00	0.25	5.40	
68	200	50	41.20	390.00	2.00	0.50	7.85	
69	200	50	41.20	390.00	2.00	0.99	12.75	

Table A. Experimental data used to construct the BPNN and ANFIS for shear strength of ferrocement members

Test No.	b (mm)	d (mm)	f_c' (MPa)	ρ_f %	E_f (Gpa)	a/d	V_u (kN)	Reference
1	1000	165.3	40	0.39	114	6.05	140	El-Sayed et al., 2005b
2	1000	159	40	1.7	40	6.29	142	
3	1000	165.3	40	0.78	114	6.05	167	
4	1000	160.5	40	1.18	114	6.23	190	
5	1000	162.1	40	0.86	40	6.16	113	
6	1000	162.1	40	1.71	40	6.16	163	
7	1000	159	40	2.44	40	6.29	163	
8	1000	154.1	40	2.63	40	6.49	168	
9	250	326	44.6	1.22	42	3.07	60	El-Sayed et al., 2006a, 2006b
10	250	326	50	0.87	128	3.07	77.5	
11	250	326	50	0.87	39	3.07	70.5	
12	250	326	44.6	1.24	134	3.07	104	
13	250	326	43.6	1.72	134	3.07	124.5	
14	250	326	43.6	1.71	42	3.07	77.5	
15	250	326	63	1.71	135	3.07	130	
16	250	326	63	2.2	135	3.07	174	
17	250	326	63	1.71	42	3.07	87	
18	250	326	63	2.2	42	3.07	115.5	
19	200	225	40.5	0.25	145	2.67	36.1	Razaqpur et al., 2004
20	200	225	49	0.5	145	2.67	47	
21	200	225	40.5	0.63	145	2.67	47.2	
22	200	225	40.5	0.88	145	2.67	42.7	
23	200	225	40.5	0.5	145	3.56	49.7	
24	200	225	40.5	0.5	145	4.22	38.5	
25	127	143	60.3	0.33	139	6.36	14	Gross et al., 2004
26	159	141	61.8	0.58	139	6.45	20	
27	121	141	81.4	0.76	139	6.45	15.4	
28	160	346	37.3	0.72	42	2.75	59.1	Tariq & Newhook, 2003
29	160	346	43.2	1.1	42	3.32	44.1	
30	160	325	34.1	1.54	42	3.54	46.8	
31	130	310	37.3	0.72	120	3.06	47.5	
32	130	310	43.2	1.1	120	3.71	50.15	
33	130	310	34.1	1.54	120	3.71	57.1	
34	203	225	79.6	1.25	40.3	4.06	38	Gross et al., 2003
35	152	225	79.6	1.66	40.3	4.06	32.53	
36	165	224	79.6	2.1	40.3	4.08	35.77	
37	203	224	79.6	2.56	40.3	4.08	46.4	

Test No.	b (mm)	d (mm)	f_c' (MPa)	ρ_f %	E_f (Gpa)	a/d	V_u (kN)	Reference
38	457	360	39.7	0.96	40.5	3.39	108.1	Tureyen & Frosch, 2002
39	457	360	40.3	0.96	47.1	3.39	114.8	
40	457	360	39.9	0.96	37.6	3.39	94.7	
41	457	360	42.3	1.92	40.5	3.39	137	
42	457	360	42.5	1.92	37.6	3.39	152.6	
43	457	360	42.6	1.92	47.1	3.39	177	
44	229	225	36.3	1.11	40.3	4.06	38.13	Yost et al., 2001
45	229	225	36.3	1.66	40.3	4.06	44.43	
46	279	225	36.3	1.81	40.3	4.06	45.27	
47	254	224	36.3	2.05	40.3	4.08	45.1	
48	229	224	36.3	2.27	40.3	4.08	42.2	
49	178	279	24.1	2.3	40	2.69	53.4	
50	178	287	24.1	0.77	40	2.61	36.1	
51	178	287	24.1	1.34	40	2.61	40.1	
52	305	157.5	28.6	0.73	40	4.5	26.8	Deitz et al., 1999
53	305	157.5	30.1	0.73	40	5.8	28.3	
54	305	157.5	28.2	0.73	40	5.8	28.5	
55	305	157.5	27	0.73	40	5.8	29.2	
56	305	157.5	30.8	0.73	40	5.8	27.6	
57	150	150	34.7	1.13	134	1.55	185.2	Omeman et al.,2008
58	150	150	38.9	1.13	134	1.83	154.9	
59	150	150	37.4	1.7	134	1.83	162.3	
60	150	150	40.6	1.13	134	2.33	91.5	
61	150	150	39.6	2.26	134	1.83	185.5	
62	150	250	41.7	1.35	134	1.41	298.1	
63	150	350	37.6	1.21	134	1.36	468.2	
64	150	150	63.1	1.13	134	1.83	226.9	
65	250	326	40	0.78	134	1.69	179.5	Al-Sayed, 2006
66	250	326	40	0.78	40	1.69	164.5	
67	250	326	40	1.24	40	1.69	175	
68	250	326	40	1.24	134	1.69	195	
69	250	326	40	1.71	134	1.69	233.5	
70	250	326	40	1.71	40	1.69	196	
71	250	326	40	1.24	134	1.3	372	
72	250	326	40	1.24	40	1.3	269	
73	1000	112	60	0.95	41.3	8.93	42.6	Wegian& Abdalla, 2005
74	1000	162	60	0.77	41.3	6.17	86.1	

Table B. Experimental data used to construct the BPNN and ANFIS for shear strength of concrete beams reinforced with FRP.

7. References

Adeli, H. & Park, H. (1995). A Neural Dynamic Model for Structural Optimization-Theory. *Journal of Computer and Structure*, Vol.57, No.3, pp. 383–390, ISSN 0045-7949

Abudlkudir, A.; Ahmet, T.& Murat, Y. (2006). Prediction of Concrete Elastic Modulus Using Adaptive Neuro-Fuzzy Inference System. *Journal of Civil Engineering and Environmental Systems*, Vol.23, No.4, pp.295–309, ISSN 1028-6608

Akbuluta, S.; Samet, H. & Pamuk S. (2004). Data Generation for Shear Modulus and Damping Ratio in Reinforced Sands Using Adaptive Neuro-Fuzzy Inference System. *Journal of Soil Dynamics and Earthquake Engineering*, Vol. 24, No.11, pp. 805–814, ISSN 0267-7261

Alkhrdaji, T.; Wideman, M.; Belarbi, A. & Nanni, A. (2001). Shear Strength of GFRP RC Beams and Slabs, *Proceedings of the International Conference, Civil Construction International Conference (CCC) 2001, Composites in Construction*, pp. 409-414, Porto/Portugal

Bank .L. (2006). *Composites for Construction: Structural Design with FRP Materials*, John Wiley, ISBN 0471681261, New Jersey

Baughman, D. & Liu, Y. (2005). *Neural Network in Bioprocessing and Chemical Engineering*. Academic Press,. ISBN 0120830302. San Diego, CA

Carpenter, W.& Barthelemy, J. (1994). Common Misconceptions about Neural Networks as Approximators. *Journal of Computing in Civil Engineering*, Vol.8, No.3, pp. 345-358

Chen, S. & Shah, K. (1992). Neural Networks in Dynamic Analysis of Bridges. Proceedings, 8th Confernce. *Computing in Civil Engineering and Geographic Information System Symposium* ASCE, PP.1058–1065, New York, USA.

Chiu S. (1994). Fuzzy Model Identification Based on Cluster Estimation. *Journal of Intelligent and Fuzzy System*, Vol.2, No.3, pp.267-278.

Cladera, A. & Mar A. (2004). Shear Design Procedure for Reinforced Normal and High-Strength Concrete beams Using Artificial Neural Networks. Part I: Beams Without Stirrups. *Journal Engineering Structure*, Vol.26, No.7 pp. 917-926, ISSN 0141-0296

Cladera, A. & Mar A. (2004). Shear Design Procedure for Reinforced Normal and High-Strength Concrete beams Using Artificial Neural Networks. Part II: Beams With Stirrups. *Journal Engineering Structure*, Vol. 26, No.7pp. 927-936, ISSN 0141-0296

Deitz, D.; Harik, I. & Gesund, H. (1999). One-Way Slabs Reinforced with Glass Fiber Reinforced Polymer Reinforcing Bars, *Proceedings of the 4th International Symposium, Fiber Reinforced Polymer Reinforcement for Reinforced Concrete Structures*, pp. 279-286, Maryland, USA

Eberhart, R. & Dobbins, R. (1990). *Neural Network PC Tools A Practical Guide*. Academic Press, ISBN0-12-228640-5, San Diego, CA

Eldin, N. & Senouci, A.(1995), A Pavement Condition-Rating Model Using Back Propagation Neural Networks. *Microcomputers in Civil Engineering*, Vol.10, No.6, pp. 433–441

El-Sayed, A.; El-Salakawy, E. & Benmokrane, B. (2004). Evaluation of Concrete Shear Strength for Beams Reinforced with FRP Bars, *5th Structural Specialty Conference of the Canadian Society for Civil Engineering*, CSCE, Saskatoon, Saskatchewan, Canada

El-Sayed, A.; El-Salakawy, E. & Benmokrane, B. (2005a). Shear Strength of Concrete Beams Reinforced with FRP Bars: Design Method, ACI- SP-230 − 54, pp.955-974

El-Sayed, A.; El-Salakawy, E. & Benmokrane, B. (2005b). Shear Strength of One-way Concrete Slabs Reinforced with FRP Composite Bars. *Journal of Composites for Construction*, ASCE, Vol.9, No.2, pp.147-157, ISSN 1090-0268

El-Sayed, A.; El-Salakawy, E. & Benmokrane, B. (2006a). Shear Strength of FRP Reinforced Concrete Beams without Transverse Reinforcement. *ACI Structural Journal*, Vol.103, No.2, pp.235-243, ISSN 0889-3241

El-Sayed, A.; El-Salakawy, E. & Benmokrane, B. (2006b). Shear Capacity of High-Strength Concrete Beams Reinforced with FRP Bars. *ACI Structural Journal*,Vol.103, No.3, pp.383-389, ISSN 0889-3241

El-Sayed, A. (2006c),Concrete Contribution to the Shear Resistance of FPR- Reinforced Concrete beams, PhD Thesis, Sherbrook University, Canada.

Feng, M. & Kim, J. (1998). Identification of a Dynamic System Using Ambient Vibration Measurements. *Journal of Applied Mech*anic, Vo.65, No.2, pp. 1010– 1023, ISSN 0021-8936

Feng, M. & Bahng, E. (1999). Damage Assessment of Jacketed RC Columns Using Vibration Tests. *Journal of Structure Engineering*, Vol.125, No.3, pp. 265–271, ISSN 0733-9445

Fonseca, E.; Vellasco, S. & Andrade S. (2008). A Neuro-Fuzzy Evaluation of Steel Beams Patch Load Behaviour. *Journal of Advances in Engineering Software*, Vol.39, No.7, pp.535-555, ISSN 0965-9978

Fuzzy Logic Toolbox User's Guide for Use with MATLAB 2009.

Gershenson C. Artificial Neural Networks for Beginners. Cognitive and Computing Sciences, University of Sussex, Available from, http:// cgershen@vub.ac.be

Garson, G. (1991). Interpreting Neural-Network Connection Weights. *AI Expert*, Vol.6, No.7, pp. 47-51, ISSN 0888-3785

Gagarin, N.; Flood, I., & Albrecht, P. (1994). Computing Truck Attributes with Artificial Neural Networks. *Journal of Computing in Civil Engineering*, Vol.8, No.2, ISSN 0887-3801

Guide for the Design and Construction of Concrete Reinforced with FRP Bars (ACI 440.1R-03), Reported by ACI Committee 440, 2003

Gross, S.; Dinehart, D.; Yost, J. & Theisz, P. (2004). Experimental Tests of High-Strength Concrete Beams Reinforced with CFRP Bars, *Proceedings of the 4th International Conference on Advanced Composite Materials in Bridges and Structures (ACMBS-4)*, Calgary, Alberta, Canada, July 20-23, 8p.

Gross, S. P.; Yost, J.; Dinehart, D. W.; Svensen, E. & Liu, N. (2003). Shear Strength of Normal and High Strength Concrete Beams Reinforced with GFRP Reinforcing Bars, Proceedings of the International Conference on High Performance Materials in Bridges, ASCE, 426-437.

Hajela, P. & Berke, L. (1991). Neurobiological Computational Models in Structural Analysis and Design. *Computers and Structures*, Vol.41, No.4, pp. 657-667, ISSN 0045-7949

Hamidian D. & Seyedpoor M. (2010). Shape Optimal Design of Arch Dams Using an Adaptive Neuro-Fuzzy Inference System and Improved Particle Swarm Optimization. *Jornal of Applied Mathematical Modelling.* Vol.34, No.6. pp.1574-1585.

Jang, S.; Sun T. & Mizutani E. (1997). *Neuro-Fuzzy and Soft Computing A Computational Approach to Learning and Machine intelligence*, Prentice Hall, Inc. ISBN 0132610663

Jang S. (1993). Adaptive network-based Fuzzy Inference System. *IEEE Journal*, Vol.23, No.3, PP.665-685, ISSN 0018-9472

Jeon J. (2007). Fuzzy and Neural Network Models for Analyses of Piles. PhD thesis, Civil Engineering, NCSU, USA.

Jonic', S.; Jankovic', T.; Gajic', V. & Popovic', D. (1999). Three Machine Learning Techniques for Automatic Determination of Rules to Control Locomotion. *Journal of IEEE*, Vol.46, No.3, pp.300-310, ISSN 0018-9294.

Lin. C. & Lee. C. (1996). *Neural Fuzzy Systems-A Neuro Fuzzy Synergism to Intelligent Systems*. Prentice Hall P T R. Upper Saddle River, N.J., ISBN 0-13-235169-2

Lin, J.; Hwang, M.; Becker, J. (2003). A Fuzzy Neural Network for Assessing the Risk of Fraudulent Financial Reporting. *Managerial Auditing Journal*, Vol.18, No.8, pp. 657-665, ISSN 0268-6902

Mamdani, E. & Assilian, S. (1975). An experiment in linguistic synthesis with a fuzzy logic controller. *International Journal of Man Machine Studies*, Vol.7, No.1, pp. 1-13, ISSN 00207373

Mansur, M. & Ong, K. (1987). Shear Strength of Ferrocement Beams. *ACI Structural Journal*, Vol.84, No.1, pp. 10-17.

Mansour, M.; Dicleli, M.; Lee, J. & Zhang, J. (2004). Predicting the Shear Strength of Reinforced Concrete Beams Using Artificial Neural Networks. *Journal of Engineering Structures*, Vol.26, No.6, pp.781–799, ISSN 0141-0296

Malhotra, R. & Malhotra, D. (1999). Fuzzy Systems and Neuro-Computing in Credit Approval. *Journal of Lending & Credit Risk Management*, Vol.81, No.11, pp. 24-37.

Mashrei, M. (2010). Flexure and Shear Behavior of Ferrocement Members: Experimental and Theoretical Study, PhD thesis, Civil Engineering, Basrah University, Iraq.

McCulloch and Pitts, W. (1943). A Logical Calculus of the Ideas Immanent in Nervous Activity. *Bulletin of Mathematical Biophysics*, Vol.(5), pp. 115-133, ISSN 0092-8240

Mukherjee, A.; Deshpande, J. & Anmada, J. (1996). Prediction of Buckling Load of Columns Using Artificial Neural Networks. *Journal of . Structural Engineering*, Vol.122, No.11, pp. 1385–1387, ISSN 0733-9445

Naaman, A. (2000. *Ferrocement and Laminated Cementitious Composites*. Ann Arbort, Michigan, Techno Press 3000, USA 2000. ISBN 0967493900

Neural Network Toolbox User's Guide for Use with MATLAB, 2009

Omeman, Z.; Nehdi, M. & El-Chabib, H. (2008). Experimental Study on Shear Behavior of Carbon-Fiber-Reinforced Polymer Reinforced Concrete Short Beams without Web Reinforcement. *Canadian Journal of Civil Engineering*, Vol.35, No.1, pp.1-10.

Rafiq, M.; Bugmann, G. & Easterbrook, D. (2001). Neural Network Design for Engineering Applications, *Journal of Computers and Structures*, Vol.79, No. 17, pp.1541-1552.

Rao, C.; Rao, G. & Rao, R. (2006). An Appraisal of the Shear Resistance of Ferrocement Elements. *ASIAN Journal of Civil Engineering (Building and Housing)*, Vol.7, No.6, pp. 591-602.

Razaqpur, A.; Isgor, B.; Greenaway, S. & Selley, A. (2004). Concrete Contribution to the Shear Resistance of Fiber Reinforced Polymer Reinforced Concrete Members. *Journal of Composites for Construction*, ASCE, Vol.8, No.5, pp. 452-460,ISSN 1090-0268

Sanad, A. & Saka, M. (2001). Prediction of Ultimate Shear Strength of Reinforced Concrete Deep Beams using neural Networks. *Journal of Structural Engineering*, Vol.127, No.7, pp. 818-828, ISSN 0733-9445

Shah, S. (1974). New Reinforcing Materials in Concrete. *Journal of ACI*, Vol.71, No.5, pp. 257-262.

Sugeno, M.(1985). *Industrial applications of fuzzy control*, Elsevier Science Pub, ISBN0444878297, NY, USA

Topcu, I. & Sarıdemir M. (2007). Prediction of Compressive Strength of Concrete Containing Fly Ash Using Artificial Neural Networks and Fuzzy Logic. *Computational Materials Science*, Vol.41, No.3, pp.305-311, ISSN0927-0256

Tariq, M. & Newhook, J. (2003). Shear Testing of FRP reinforced Concrete without Transverse Reinforcement, *Proceedings of Canadian Society for Civil Engineering (CSCE)Anuual Conference*, Moncton, NB, Canada, 10p.

Tesfamariam, S. & Najjaran, H. (2007). Adaptive Network-Fuzzy Inferencing to Estimate Concrete Strength Using Mix Design. *Journal of Materials in Civil Engineering*, Vol.19, No.7, pp. 550-560, ISSN 0899-1561

Tully, S. (1997). Neural Network Approach for Predicting the Structural Behaviour of Concrete Slabs. M.Sc Thesis, College of Engineering and Applied Science, University of Newfoundland.

Turban, E. & Aronson, J. (2000). *Decision Support Systems and Intelligent Systems*, 6th edition, Prentice-Hall, Englewood Cliffs, NJ, ISBN: 0130894656.

Tureyen, A. & Frosch, R. (2002). Shear Tests of FRP-Reinforced Concrete Beams without Stirrups. *ACI Structural Journal*, Vol.99, No.4, pp.427-434, ISSN 0889-3241

Tureyen, A. & Frosch, R. (2003). Concrete Shear Strength: Another Perspective. *ACI Structural Journal*. Vol.100, No.5, pp. 609-615.

Waszczyszyn, Z.; Pabisek, E. & Mucha, G., (1998). Hybrid Neural Network/Computational Program to the Analysis of Elastic- Plastic Structures, *Neural networks in Mechanics of Structures and Materials*, Udine, Italy, pp. 19-23.

Wegian, F.& Abdalla, H. (2005). Shear Capacity of Concrete Beams Reinforced with Fiber Reinforced Polymers. *Journal of Composite Structures*, Vol.71, No.1, pp. 130–138, ISSN 0263-8223

Wu, Z. & Bailey, C. (2005). Fracture Resistance of a Cracked Concrete Beam Post Strengthened with FRP Sheets. *International Journal of Fracture*, Vol.135, No.(1-4), pp.35–49, ISSN 0376-9429

Yost, J.; Gross, S. & Dinehart, D. (2001). Shear Strength of Normal Strength Concrete Beams Reinforced with Deformed GFRP Bars. *Journal of Composites for Construction*, ASCE, Vol.5, No.4, pp. 268-275, ISSN 1090-0268

Zadeh L. (1965). Fuzzy sets. *Journal of Information and Control*, Vol.8, No.3, pp. 338-353.

Zadeh, L. Making Computers Think Like People. *IEEE Spectrum*. 1984; Vol.21, No.8 pp.26-32, ISSN 0018-9235

Zadih, L. (1993). Fuzzy Logic, Neural Networks and Soft Computing. *Microprocessing and Microprogramming*, Vol.38, No.1,pp.13, ISSN 0165-6074

Zadeh, L. (1994), Fuzzy Logic, Neural Networks and Soft Computing. Communication of the ACM, Vol.3, No.3, pp.77-84.

Zaho, J. & Bose, B. (2002). Evaluation of membership Functions for Fuzzy Logic Controlled Induction Motor Drive. *IEEE Journal*, Vo.1, No.pp.229-234, ISBN 0-7803-7474-6. S

8

Fuzzy Inference System as a Tool for Management of Concrete Bridges

Amir Tarighat

Civil Engineering Department, Shahid Rajaee Teacher Training University
Iran

1. Introduction

Bridges are important infrastructures all over the world. We have invested and spent a lot of money in constructing them. Also we assign big budgets for their maintenance, repair and strengthening annually. Since the number of bridges is increasing the amount of money needed to preserve the existing bridges at minimum standard level is considerable. In order to make decision for optimal budgeting we should know how bridges respond to various kinds of deteriorating factors and what their current and future conditions will be.

Why bridges need maintenance, repair and strengthening depend on many factors. Deterioration of bridges is due to aging, material deterioration under environmental conditions, increasing traffic volume and higher weights of vehicles. There are many factors which are responsible to make decision what the current condition and/or rating of a bridge is. Practically to make logical and defendable decisions the main action is to inspect bridges. Inspection provides a lot of collected data that should be stored and retrieved at any required time to obtain useful and practical information regarding the bridge condition and its immediate need. At this stage and by appropriate information in hand it can be possible to predict the remaining service lives of bridges.

Bridges are susceptible to many defects during their service lives. The main common defects that occur on cast-in-place concrete slab (deck) bridges include: cracking, scaling, delamination, spalling, efflorescence, honeycombs, pop-outs, wear, collision damage, abrasion, overload damage, reinforcing steel corrosion (Chen & Duan, 2000; Hartle et al., 2002). These defects are symptoms showing some kinds of deteriorations. Inspectors should report these symptoms and consequently type of deterioration(s) should be diagnosed.

Inspecting a concrete bridge deck includes visual and advanced inspection methods. The inspection of concrete bridge deck for symptoms like cracks, spallings, and other defects is primarily a visual activity. However, hammers and chain drags can be used to detect areas of delamination. In addition, several advanced techniques are available for concrete bridge deck inspection. Nondestructive methods include: acoustic wave sonic/ultrasonic velocity measurements, electrical methods, electromagnetic methods, rebound and penetration methods, carbonation and so many others if needed (Hartle et al., 2002).

Visual inspection is the primary method used to evaluate the condition of the majority of the existing bridges. Visual inspection is a subjective assessment and it may have a significant impact on the diagnosis and decisions to be made. For example a defect reported from one inspector may be different from the others. In order to overcome this unwilling fact nondestructive testing methods have been suggested for objective inspection in recent decades. Although these methods are more accurate than visual inspection, there are some kinds of problems. Interpretation of their results needs experience together with the knowledge about deteriorations of bridge material and damage types of its elements. Therefore results of visual inspection and some nondestructive testing methods are inherently uncertain and vague. It is to notify that the linguistically describing results are more uncertain and vague. Degree of uncertainty and level of vagueness depend on many parameters such as inspector's experience, definition of symptom or deterioration type, level of defect categorizations and many others.

Among many methods it seems that models based on artificial intelligence which apply soft computing methods are more attractive for dealing with uncertain and vague data in managing bridges. Fuzzy Inference System (FIS) is capable of being used in areas for decision making when data is uncertain. One of the most attractive advantages of FIS is its tolerability to noisy (uncertain and vague) data.

Based on the type of problems with uncertain and vague data, different FIS modeling types can be regarded as appropriate and easy methods for managing bridges (Tarighat & Miyamoto, 2009).

After introduction section this chapter continues with section 2 and its subsections showing the need for managing bridges and introduces Bridge Management System and Bridge Health Monitoring system. Ambiguity in diagnosis and decision making based on the collected data in above mentioned systems are discussed in section 3. Section 4 explains why fuzzy inference systems are suitable in managing systems. Its subsections are about fuzzy inference systems including Mamdani's method and Adaptive Neuro Fuzzy Inference System (ANFIS) method. Then some case studies and some typical applications of fuzzy inference system for managing bridges are included in section 5. Section 6 concludes this chapter.

2. Managing bridges

All the inspection data should be stored in inventory and inspection databases and they should be used to get information for what to do in the next step of managing bridges. Therefore a kind of managing system is required to use the data and making appropriate and logical decisions for further actions.

2.1 Bridge Management System

Bridge Management System (BMS) has great roles in managing bridges. The main feed into any BMS is inspection data. It is designed to provide information not easily available from available data. BMS can provide the following:

- Improvements in the type and quality of data that is collected, stored, managed, and used in a bridge system analysis
- A logical method for setting priorities for current needs
- Realistic and reliable forecasts of future needs
- Ways to implement changes in management philosophies and goals

It is obvious that how and to what extents the above mentioned items can be fulfilled by the available data.

In general, the condition of a BMS element is identified by condition states and corresponding condition state language. Each element has a range of minimum to maximum condition states. Information from each BMS element along with expert input to predict how the condition of that element will change over time is used in BMS computer programs. BMS programs can estimate future network funding levels based on the predicted future bridge conditions and the corresponding costs to repair or replace them (Washington State Bridge Inspection Manual, 2010).

The following outline provides a short BMS summary for a typical inspection:

- Identify the BMS elements that apply to the structure.
- Determine the total quantity for each element.
- Inspect bridge and record the deficient quantity for each element in the corresponding condition state.

2.2 Bridge Health Monitoring System

Generally in advanced BMS there is a module named Bridge Health Monitoring System (BHMS). BHMS can be considered as one of the most important parts of a practical BMS.

In bridge structures there are many different unforeseen conditions that we do not have enough information about them. Although in design codes we are forced to consider some parameters or factors affecting structural behavior there are even more items that we cannot consider them practically. Therefore it is probable to have some risk for not fulfilling the complete standards of safety. Presently health and performance are described based on subjective indices which are not precise. In addition there are some possibilities for unobserved and undiscovered symptoms, deteriorations, and damages in bridge structures due to limited or no accessibility to some elements. The immediate consequence is that the real health index is not that thought and considered. This unwilling fact impacts the effectiveness and reliability of any managerial decision irrespective of sophistication in the management process. Moreover, even experienced engineers may find visual signs of defects, deterioration and damage and cannot be able to diagnose the causative mechanisms, or their impact on the reliability of the bridge and its global health. The global health of a bridge as a whole system, inclusive of the performance criteria corresponding to each limit states is actually what is needed for effective managerial decisions. There are needs of periodic inspections to detect deterioration resulting from normal operation and environmental attack or inspections following extreme events, such as earthquakes or hurricanes. To quantify these system performance measures requires some means to monitor and evaluate the integrity of bridge structures while in service (Wang & Zong, 2002). BHMS can help managers to know about the healthiness of a bridge at any given time.

BHMS may also have other applications. For example any damage in some elements of a bridge has direct effect on its load bearing capacity especially vibration characteristics. In other words this effect can change the overall behavior of the bridge under loads which cause the bridge to vibrate. Based on this fact any method for damage detection which is capable of showing the location and severity of damage can be considered useful for bridge maintenance and repair departments (Haritos, 2000).

Bridge real time monitoring during service provides information on structural behavior under predicted loads, and also registers the effects of unpredicted overloading. Data obtained by monitoring is useful for damage detection, safety evaluation, and determination of the residual load bearing capacity of bridges. Early damage detection is particularly important because it leads to appropriate and timely interventions. If the damage is not detected, it continues to propagate and the bridge no longer guarantees required performance levels. Late detection of damage results in either very elevated refurbishment costs or, in some cases, the bridge has to be closed and dismantled. In seismic areas the importance of monitoring is more critical. Subsequent auscultation of a bridge structure that has not been monitored during its construction can serve as a basis for prediction of its present and future structural behavior. Based on these facts there are many applications for developing BHMS. As mentioned one of the most important applications of BHMS is damage detection. Among the attractive methods for damage detection problems are models based on artificial intelligence especially soft computing methods (Ou et al., 2006; Wu & Abe, 2003).

As it is used several times in above paragraphs, health can be defined as the reliability of a bridge structure to perform adequately for the required functionalities (Aktan et al., 2002). Some of these functionalities are:

- Utility
- Serviceability and durability
- Safety and stability of failure at ultimate limit states
- Safety at conditional limit states

It is not possible to quantify health and reliability of a bridge system for many of the limit states without extensive data that we often do not have. Based on a general definition monitoring is the frequent or continuous observation or measurement of structural conditions or actions (Wenzel & Tanaka, 2006). There is another definition which gives more detail: structural health monitoring is the use of in-situ, non-destructive sensing and analysis of structural characteristics, including the structural response, for detecting changes that may indicate damage or degradation [Housner & Bergman, 1997). Fig. 1 shows basic components of a typical BMS and BHMS.

In summary BMS and BHMS are used to:

- Structural management
- Increase of safety
- Knowledge improvement
- Rating the current condition of bridge or its components
- Predicting the remaining service life
- Structural/system identification
- Damage detection/diagnosis and damage localization
- Forced vibration-based damage detection
- Wind induced vibration-based damage detection
- Ambient vibration-based damage detection

- Remote sensing and wireless sensor networks
- Life cycle performance design

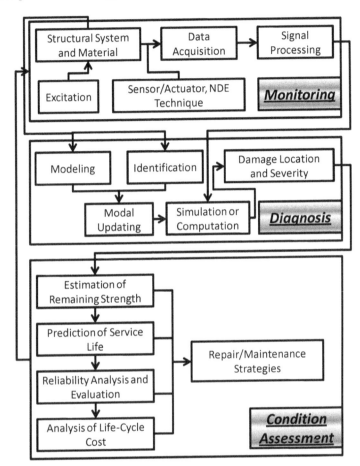

Fig. 1. Basic components of a typical BMS and BHMS

3. Ambiguity in diagnosis and decision making

Recently it is become obvious that although BMS and BHMS can be precisely used for managerial issues but there is an important fact about the collected data. Data is not perfect. It is found that the results and data-driven interpretations are prone to some degree of vagueness. Therefore, the obtained data that should be altered to information has inherently some degrees of uncertainty and vagueness (Tarighat & Miyamoto, 2009).

In managing a bridge we are concerned about condition state or standard level of a requirement. For example we want to know what the current condition state of a bridge is and to how it has been deviated from the previous and known condition state (Washington State Bridge Inspection Manual, 2010).

In most cases diagnosis is necessary to make decision for next action to return to a standard bridge condition state. Whenever we are going to diagnose, it is common to have circumstances in which we must make decision via ambiguous data and information. Practical diagnosis in managing bridges is the making of judgments about a bridge's condition state or damage detection using expert knowledge, but the observation of symptoms includes results of visual inspection and non destructive testing methods, bridge's history, and the circumstances of the diagnosis. For example, if we think about diagnosis during a regular inspection versus before a repairing operation, indications of possible deterioration or damage and need for retesting are important in the former, but in the latter, importance is placed on certainty rather than possibility. Normally a repairing operation is not performed without confirmation of the existence of deterioration or damage in the affected element of a bridge.

The words we use concerning symptoms often contain expressions of frequency and probability, such as *sever cracks* or *high corrosion*. In contrast to this kind of linguistic ambiguity, ambiguous circumstances exist in the distinguishing of the symptom, such as different inspectors' reporting differing symptoms.

When thinking about the ambiguity that originates in the characteristics discussed above, we must also consider the ambiguity that arises from the participation of experts in the bridge evaluation. In general, there is a large dependence on visual inspection results, which are subjective judgments. Since visual inspection is cheaper, faster and sometimes simpler than other inspecting methods it is more probable to have more ambiguity levels in data and interpretations (Terano et al., 1992).

Here are some more detailed explanations of the ambiguity in managing bridges. Condition rating is a judgment of a bridge component condition in comparison to its original as-built condition at a given time (Wang & Hu, 2006). Condition rating and damage detection are crucial methods and tools to conduct efficient maintenance and managing bridges. Condition rating indices are also useful for predicting future states which are completely time dependent. Based on the periodic inspections data at different time intervals deterioration rate of the material, elements and sometimes whole structure can be modeled. These models can be good tools for decision makers in future (Zadeh, 1976).

Related to condition rating definition there is another problem: what is the exact meaning of condition or health for material or bridge element in the structure? From practical point of view deterioration or damage symptoms should be easily distinguished. But in practice symptoms as signs of deteriorations cannot be easily distinguished and be reported or categorized in well-defined manner. Here, it becomes clear what the *subjective data* means. In other words the encoding of symptoms into condition rating is imprecise and involves *subjective judgments*.

Of greatest importance is the amount of variability found in the assignment of condition ratings at a given time. As an example results of the deck delamination survey conducted during some investigations indicate that this type of inspection does not consistently provide accurate results. In a case study the condition rating results analysis and the data revealed that the condition ratings were normally distributed. Table 1 shows the summary of statistical information from routine inspection for deck condition rating (Phares et al., 2000, 2001; Graybeal et al., 2001; Moore et al., 2001).

Bridge	Element	Average	Standard Deviation	Minimum	Maximum	Mode	N	Reference Rating
A	Deck	5.8	0.81	3	7	6	49	5
B	Deck	4.9	0.94	2	7	5	48	4
C	Deck	5.2	0.92	3	7	6	49	4
D	Deck	4.8	0.94	2	6	5	48	5
E	Deck	4.5	0.74	3	6	5	48	4
F	Deck	7.1	0.53	6	8	7	49	7
G	Deck	5.8	0.92	4	7	5	24	7

Table 1. Statistical information from routine inspection for deck condition rating (Phares et al., 2001).

The range of the results between min and max show the stochastic nature of the inspector's judgment. These stochastic representations show the fuzzy nature of the inspectors' judgments.

While current rating systems of concrete structures may give a fundamental understanding of structural deterioration conditions, their application is more or less limited in reflecting actual conditions. In some cases it is often difficult to cover complex structural behavior and environment in the real world. Uncertainties and fuzziness, along with complexity, add more difficulty to the estimation of condition rating by conventional methods. Therefore a better method may be a combination of logics and statistics. To take advantage of this approach in dealing with qualitative issues such as human factors, the influence of inspectors' judgment on structural condition rating and the effects of weather conditions on inspectors' judgment should be considered (Harris, 2006; Ma, 2006; Stephens, 2000; Wang et al., 2007; Yen & Langari, 1999).

Since the bridge inspection results are subjected to some degrees of imprecision and vagueness it is a good idea to use fuzzy set theory to overcome the shortcomings and problems of ordinary methods for prediction of condition of bridges. Fuzzy information or fuzzy data can be encountered in managing bridges. The main reasons for fuzzy data are imprecision in measured data and subjective judgments.

Knowledge engineering methods for dealing with uncertainty in many aspects of condition prediction are used to produce expert systems. Expert systems are expected to be effective for ill-defined problems (problems in which it is either difficult or impossible to define a method of approach).

In most cases, either the clear knowledge of ill-defined problems cannot be obtained, or completion of the knowledge set must be approached gradually. In other words, there are many cases in which knowledge is *ambiguous*. Meaning of the word *ambiguous* is also ambiguous and vague. Just as knowledge must be formulated and written down for a user to understand it, ambiguity must take some form before it can be dealt with technically. Therefore, ambiguity that is dealt with in knowledge engineering is classified and written down as follows:

- Nondeterminism
- Multiple meanings
- Uncertainty

- Incompleteness
- Fuzziness or imprecision

Uncertainty and fuzziness have a particularly close relationship with each other and systems that handle knowledge with fuzziness have been created even in the field of knowledge engineering (Terano et al., 1992).

One of the best ways of dealing with this kind of problems is the application of fuzzy inference system. Fuzzy inference system is capable of dealing with imprecise, imperfect, uncertain and vague data and information. Thus, it can be good candidate toward development of practical BMS and BHMS.

A measure of imprecision is advantageous for symptoms representation. Uncertainty characterizes a relation between symptoms and deteriorations/damages, while imprecision is associated with the symptoms representation.

4. Fuzzy inference systems and managing bridges

Fuzzy logic is an interesting and easy-to-use method for practical inference problems in engineering. It relates significance and precision to each other very well. Fuzzy logic-based inference systems enable the use of engineering judgment, experience and scarce field data to translate the level of deterioration or damage to condition rating (Rajani et al., 2006).

One of the best methods to deal with decision making problems such as condition rating of bridges is application of Fuzzy Inference System (FIS). In order to diagnose deterioration type or damage detection in concrete bridges and to increase accuracy and errors reduction caused by subjective human judgment fuzzy inferring is the appropriate choice (Wang & Hu 2006). Fuzzy sets can be used for modeling uncertainty of detection and imprecision of symptoms.

Detection support systems operate on rules with fuzzy premises, which represent imprecise symptoms. During inference fuzzy relations or implications are used, so conclusions are also represented in the form of fuzzy sets (Straszecka, 2006).

4.1 Fuzzy inference system

System modeling based on conventional mathematical tools (e.g., differential equations) is not well suited for dealing with ill-defined and uncertain systems. By contrast, a fuzzy inference system employing fuzzy *if-then* rules can model the qualitative aspects of human knowledge and reasoning processes without employing precise quantitative analyses. A Fuzzy Inference System (FIS) is a way of mapping an input space to an output space using fuzzy logic. A FIS tries to formalize the reasoning process of human language by means of fuzzy logic (that is, by building fuzzy IF-THEN rules). This *fuzzy modeling* or *fuzzy identification*, first explored systematically by Takagi and Sugeno, has found numerous practical applications in control different engineering application and fields.

Fuzzy if-then rules or *fuzzy conditional statements* are expressions of the form *IF A THEN B*, where A and B are labels of *fuzzy sets* characterized by appropriate membership functions. Due to their concise form, fuzzy if-then rules are often employed to capture the imprecise modes of reasoning that play an essential role in the human ability to make decisions in an environment of uncertainty and imprecision.

Another form of fuzzy if-then rule has fuzzy sets involved only in the premise part. By using Takagi and Sugeno's fuzzy if-then rule, we can use a relationship among variables or simply a formula. However, the consequent part is described by a nonfuzzy equation of the input variable.

Both types of fuzzy if-then rules have been used extensively in both modeling and control. Through the use of linguistic labels and membership functions, a fuzzy if-then rule can easily capture the spirit of a "rule of thumb" used by humans. From another angle, due to the qualifiers on the premise parts, each fuzzy if-then rule can be viewed as a local description of the system under consideration. Fuzzy if-then rules form a core part of the fuzzy inference system. Fig. 2 shows the general form of a Fuzzy Inference System (FIS) (Jang, 1993).

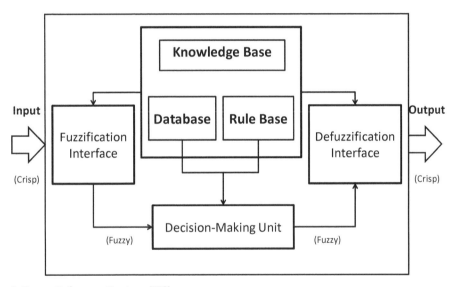

Fig. 2. Fuzzy Inference System (FIS)

4.1.1 Mamdani's method

Mamdani's method is the most commonly used in applications, due to its simple structure fuzzy calculations. This method as a simple FIS method is used to solve almost general decision making problems for practical issues.

Let X be the universe of discourse and its elements be denoted as x. In the fuzzy theory, fuzzy set A of universe X is defined by function $\mu_A(x)$ called the membership function of set.

$$m_A(x): X \in [0,1], \text{ where } \mu_A(x) = 1 \text{ if } x \text{ is totally in } A;$$
$$\mu_A(x) = 0 \text{ if } x \text{ is not in } A;$$
$$0 < \mu_A(x) < 1 \text{ if } x \text{ is partly in } A.$$

This set allows a continuum of possible choices. For any element x of universe X, membership function $\mu_A(x)$ equals the degree to which x is an element of set A. This degree, a value between 0 and 1, represents the degree of membership, also called membership value, of element x in set A. Any universe of discourse consists of some sets describing some attributes to the output. The main idea of fuzzy set theory is dealing with linguistic variables (Tarighat & Miyamoto, 2009).

A linguistic variable is a fuzzy variable. For example, the statement "a is b" implies that the linguistic variable a takes the linguistic value b. In fuzzy systems, linguistic variables are used in fuzzy rules. The range of possible values of a linguistic variable represents the universe of discourse of that variable. A fuzzy rule can be defined as a conditional statement in the form:

IF (x is a) THEN (y is b)

where x and y are linguistic variables; and a and b are linguistic values determined by fuzzy sets on the universe of discourses X and Y, respectively. The main and most important characteristic of fuzzy systems is that fuzzy rules relate fuzzy sets to each other. Fuzzy sets provide the basis for output estimation model. The model is based on relationships among some fuzzy input parameters (Baldwin, 1981).

All these definitions and arrangements are used to infer output based on the inputs. The most commonly used fuzzy inference technique is the so-called Mamdani method. Mamdani method is widely accepted for capturing expert knowledge. It allows describing the expertise in more intuitive, more human-like manner. However, Mamdani-type fuzzy inference entails a substantial computational burden.

The Mamdani-style fuzzy inference process is performed in four steps:

Step 1. Fuzzification of the input variables

The first step is to take the crisp inputs, $x1$ and $y1$, and determine the degree to which these inputs belong to each of the appropriate fuzzy sets.

Step 2. Rule evaluation

The second step is to take the fuzzified inputs and apply them to the antecedents of the fuzzy rules. If a given fuzzy rule has multiple antecedents, the fuzzy operator *(AND or OR)* is used to obtain a single number that represents the result of the antecedent evaluation. This number (the truth value) is then applied to the consequent membership function. Now the result of the antecedent evaluation can be applied to the membership function of the consequent. The most common method of correlating the rule consequent with the truth value of the rule antecedent is to cut the consequent membership function at the level of the antecedent truth.

Step 3. Aggregation of the rule outputs

Aggregation is the process of unification of the outputs of all rules. We take the membership functions of all rule consequents previously found and combine them into a single fuzzy set.

The input of the aggregation process is the list of found consequent membership functions, and the output is one fuzzy set for each output variable.

Step 4. Defuzzification

The last step in the fuzzy inference process is defuzzification. Fuzziness helps us to evaluate the rules, but the final output of a fuzzy system has to be a crisp number.

The input for the defuzzification process is the aggregate output fuzzy set and the output is a single number (Esragh & Mamdani, 1981).

Fig. 3 depicts the flowchart for fuzzy logic analysis based on Mamdani's fuzzy inference method (Symans & Kelly, 1999).

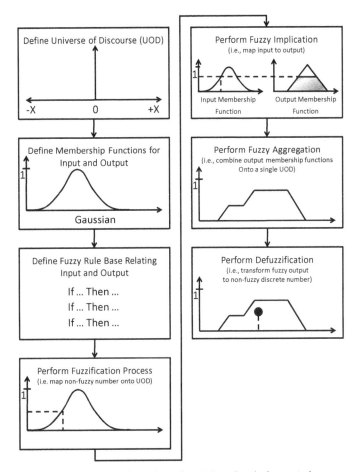

Fig. 3. Flowchart for fuzzy logic analysis based on Mamdani's fuzzy inference method (Symans & Kelly, 1999)

4.1.2 Adaptive Neuro Fuzzy Inference System (ANFIS) method

Adaptive Neuro Fuzzy Inference System (ANFIS) is a multilayer feed-forward network which uses neural network learning algorithms and fuzzy reasoning to map inputs into an output. It is a fuzzy inference system implemented in the framework of adaptive neural networks.

In order to explain ANFIS a fuzzy inference system with two inputs x and y and one output z is considered (Jang et al., 1997). In a first-order Sugeno fuzzy model with two fuzzy if-then rules we have:

Rule 1: If x is A_1 and y is B_1, then $f_1=p_1x+q_1y+r_1$

Rule 2: If x is A_2 and y is B_2, then $f_2=p_2x+q_2y+r_2$

Fig. 4 shows the reasoning procedure for the considered Sugeno model. Fig. 5 depicts the ANFIS architecture. As it is shown nodes of the same layer have similar functions. The output of the *ith* node in layer l is as $O_{l,i}$.

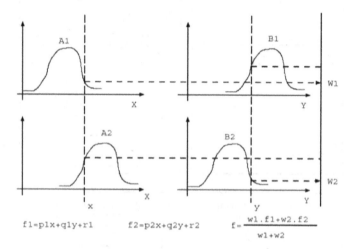

Fig. 4. A two-input first-order Sugeno fuzzy model with two rules

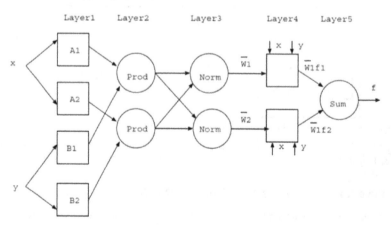

Fig. 5. Equivalent ANFIS architecture

Following few paragraphs contain brief description of the different layers:

Layer 1: Every node i in this layer is an adaptive node with a node function:

$$O_{1,i}=\mu_{Ai}(x), \qquad for\ i=1,\ 2,\ or$$
$$O_{1,i}=\mu_{Bi\text{-}2}(y), \qquad for\ i=3,\ 4$$

(1)

where x (or y) is the input to node i and A_i (or $B_{i\text{-}2}$) is an attribute associated with this node. In other words, $O_{1,i}$ is the membership grade of a fuzzy set A (= A_1, A_2, B_1 or B_2) and it specifies the degree to which the given input x (or y) satisfies the quantifier A. Here the membership function for A can be any appropriate parameterized membership function such as the generalized bell function:

$$\mu_A(x) = \frac{1}{1+\left|\dfrac{x-c_i}{a_i}\right|^{2b_i}}$$

(2)

where $\{a_i, b_i, c_i\}$ is the premise parameters set. Changing the values of these parameters leads to change of the bell-shaped function. Therefore various forms of membership functions for fuzzy set A are possible.

Layer 2: Every node in this layer is a fixed node labeled Prod, whose output is the product of all the incoming signals:

$$O_{2,i} = w_i = \mu_{Ai}(x)\,\mu_{Bi}(y),\ i = 1,\ 2$$

(3)

Each node output represents the firing strength of a rule. In general, any other T-norm operators that perform fuzzy AND can be used as the node function in this layer.

Layer 3: Every node in this layer is a fixed node labeled Norm. The ith node calculates the ratio of the ith rule's firing strength to the sum of all rules' firing strengths:

$$O_{3,i} = \overline{w}_i = \frac{w_i}{w_1+w_2} \qquad i=1,2$$

(4)

Outputs of this layer are called normalized firing strengths.

Layer 4: Every node i in this layer is an adaptive node with a node function

$$O_{4,i} = \overline{w}_i f_i = \overline{w}_i(p_i x + q_i y + r_i)$$

(5)

where $\overline{w}_i$ is a normalized firing strength from layer 3 and $\{p_i, q_i, r_i\}$ is the parameter set of this node. Parameters in this layer are referred to as consequent parameters.

Layer 5: The only node of this layer is a fixed node labeled Sum, which computes the overall output as the summation of all incoming signals:

$$overall\ output = O_{5,1} = \sum_i \overline{w}_i f_i = \frac{\sum_i w_i f_i}{\sum_i w_i}$$

(6)

It can be observed that the ANFIS architecture has two adaptive layers: Layers 1 and 4. Layer 1 has modifiable parameters $\{a_i, b_i, c_i\}$ and $\{a_j, b_j, c_j\}$ related to the input MFs. Layer 4 has modifiable parameters $\{p_{ij}, q_{ij}, r_{ij}\}$ pertaining to the first-order polynomial. The task of the learning algorithm for this ANFIS architecture is to tune all the modifiable parameters to make the ANFIS output match the training data. Learning or adjusting these modifiable parameters is a two-step process, which is known as the hybrid learning algorithm. In the forward pass of the hybrid learning algorithm, the premise parameters are hold fixed, node outputs go forward until layer 4 and the consequent parameters are identified by the least squares method. In the backward pass, the consequent parameters are held fixed, the error signals propagate backward and the premise parameters are updated by the gradient descent method. The detailed algorithm and mathematical background of the hybrid learning algorithm can be found in (Jang et al., 1997; Wang & Elhag, 2008).

The basic learning rule of ANFIS is the back propagation gradient descent, which calculates error signals (defined as the derivative of the squared error with respect to each node's output) recursively from the output layer backward to the input nodes. This learning rule is exactly the same as the back-propagation learning rule used in the common feed-forward neural networks. From the ANFIS architecture in Fig. 5, it is observed that given the values of premise parameters, the overall output f can be expressed as a linear combination of the consequent parameters. On the basis of this observation, a hybrid-learning rule is employed here, which combines the gradient descent and the least-squares method to find a feasible set of antecedent and consequent parameters. The details of the hybrid rule are given in (Jang et al., 1997), where it is also claimed to be significantly faster than the classical back-propagation method.

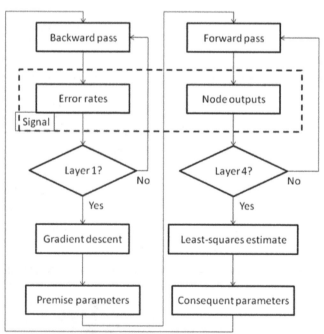

Fig. 6. Hybrid learning procedure of ANFIS

There are two passes in the hybrid-learning procedure for ANFIS. In the forward pass of the hybrid-learning algorithm, functional signals go forward till layer 4 and the consequent parameters are identified by the least-squares estimate. In the backward pass, the error rates propagate backward and the premise parameters are updated by the gradient descent. When the values of the premise parameters are fixed, the overall output can be expressed as a linear combination of the consequent parameters

$$f = \frac{w_1}{w_1 + w_2} f_1 + \frac{w_2}{w_1 + w_2} f_2$$
$$= \overline{w}_1 (p_1 x + q_1 y + r_1) + \overline{w}_2 (p_2 x + q_2 y + r_2) \qquad (7)$$
$$= (\overline{w}_1 x) p_1 + (\overline{w}_1 y) q_1 + (\overline{w}_1) r_1 + (\overline{w}_2 x) p_2 + (\overline{w}_2 y) q_2 + (\overline{w}_2) r_2$$

which is linear in the consequent parameters *p1, q1, r1, p2, q2, and r2* (Jang et al., 1997; Kandel & Langholz, 1993; Li et al., 2001; Sivanandam et al., 2007). A flowchart of hybrid learning procedure for ANFIS is shown schematically in Fig. 6 (Aydin et al., 2006).

5. Case studies and some typical applications of fuzzy inference system for managing bridges

As it is mentioned in earlier parts of this chapter and is shown in Fig. 1 the main concerns of bridge management systems are diagnosis of the encountered problems (deteriorations and/or damage detection) and finding the current condition of the bridge structure. It was also discussed that diagnosis and current condition determination accompany with ambiguity. In this section some case studies and applications are presented to show how fuzzy inference system can be used in bridge management issues.

5.1 A fuzzy system for concrete bridge damage diagnosis (DIASYN system)

Bridge management systems (BMSs) are being developed in recent years to assist various authorities on the decision making in various stages of bridge maintenance, which requires, first of all, appropriate preliminary deterioration diagnosis and modeling.

Diagnosis Synthesis (DIASYN) is a fuzzy rule-based inference system for bridge damage diagnosis and prediction which aims to provide bridge designers with valuable information about the impacts of design factors on bridge deterioration.

DIASYN is supposed to be a concept demonstration system for providing the bridge maintenance engineers and the bridge design engineers with assistance to obtain preliminary but important knowledge on individual bridge defects.

The DIASYN system incorporates a fuzzy reasoning process containing a rule base with its acquisition and update facility and a fuzzy inference engine with an explanation facility, and a user interface with option selecting capacity. Fuzzy logic is utilized to handle uncertainties and imprecision involved. The rules are if-then statements that describe associations between fuzzy parameters. Given the required input data, the inference engine evaluates the rules and generates an appropriate conclusion. Users can choose to make diagnoses of new cases or to update the rule base with new training data through the user interface.

The fuzzy rules provide associations between observed bridge conditions and damage causes. They are created by a rule generation algorithm that can convert crisp training data into fuzzy statements. The training data are collected from bridge inspection records and formalized into standard vectors. In the operational mode, the system reads a state vector of observed bridge condition and the inference engine performs damage cause implication through evaluation of the rules. The output of this implication procedure is a linguistic variable that describes the possible damage cause with a confident degree. This linguistic variable can be defuzzified by the explanation facility if a crisp output is desired. In the updating mode, new training vectors are input to generate new rules together with the existing training data. New rules, if any, will be installed in the rule base before the system gives a prompting of *updating finished* as output.

Inputs of DIASYN are:

- Design factors, i.e. structural type, span length, deck width, number of spans, wearing surface type, skew angle, etc.,
- Environmental factors, i.e. humidity and precipitation, climate region, traffic volume, temperature variations, etc.,
- Other factors, such as structure age, function class and location of damages.

The inference engine in DIASYN basically executes Mamdani's original reasoning procedure. The overall firing strength of the individual rule whose antecedents are connected with an *AND* operator, the intersection, is typically determined by taking the minimum value of the individual firing strengths of the antecedents.

After system training it is ready to be used to diagnose new bridge deterioration case. Two test examples are use for system verification, one for crack diagnosis and one for spalling diagnosis. The input data of the bridge including survey and inspection information which shows that a crack occurs in superstructure with a specific condition mark, and a spalling in support-structure with another given condition mark. The inference results, along with expert opinions indicate that the particular crack was caused by 'loads and its likes' with a confidence degree of 'very true', and that the spalling was caused by 'others' with a confidence degree of very true. Both of the results are in accordance with the expert opinion, which suggests 'overloaded' and 'aging' are the causes of the crack and spalling, respectively (Zhao & Chen, 2001, 2002).

5.2 An adaptive neuro-fuzzy inference system for bridge risk assessment

Bridge risks are often evaluated periodically so that the bridges with high risks can be maintained timely. Modeling bridge risks is a challenging job facing Highways Agencies because good mathematical models can save them a significant amount of cost and time.

In this case study an adaptive neuro-fuzzy system (ANFIS) using 506 bridge maintenance projects for bridge risk assessment is introduced. The system can help British Highways Agency to determine the maintenance priority ranking of bridge structures more systematically, more efficiently and more economically in comparison with the existing bridge risk assessment methodologies which require a large number of subjective judgments from bridge experts to build the complicated nonlinear relationships between bridge risk score and risk ratings.

The 506 bridge maintenance projects dataset is randomly split into two sample sets: training dataset with 390 projects and testing dataset with 116 projects. Both the training and testing datasets cover all levels and types of bridge risks.

Inputs to the ANFIS are safety risk rating (SRR), functionality risk rating (FRR), sustainability risk rating (SURR), and environment risk rating (ERR). All inputs range from 0 to 3 with 0 representing *no risk*, 1 *low risk*, 2 *medium risk* and 3 *high risk*. Output to the ANFIS is the risk scores (RSs) of the 506 bridge projects, which ranges from 5 to 99.

With the 390 training dataset, two generalized bell-shaped membership functions are chosen for each of the four inputs to build the ANFIS, which leads to 16 if-then rules containing 104 parameters to be learned. Fig. 7 shows the model structure of the ANFIS that is to be built for bridge risk assessment in this study.

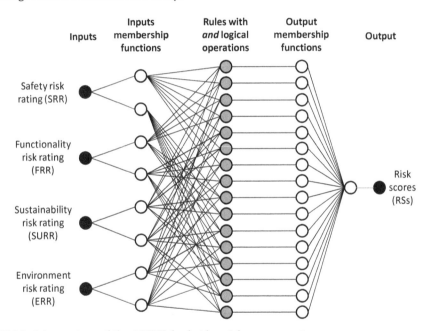

Fig. 7. Model structure of the ANFIS for bridge risk assessment

The developed ANFIS system for bridge risk assessment learns the if–then rules between bridge risk scores and risk ratings from the past bridge maintenance projects and memorizes them for generalization and prediction. It has been observed that ANFIS outperforms artificial neural networks to perform better than multiple regression models (Wang & Elhag, 2007). Differing from artificial neural network, ANFIS is transparent rather than a black box. Its if–then rules are easy to understand and interpret. In this case study the performances of the ANFIS and ANN in modeling bridge risks are compared, where the two models are trained using the same training dataset and validated by the same testing dataset. Comparison shows that the ANFIS has smaller root mean squared error and mean absolute percentage error as well as bigger correlation coefficient for both the training and testing datasets than the ANN model. In other words, the ANFIS achieves better performances than the ANN model. Therefore, ANFIS is a good choice for modeling bridge risks. Moreover, ANN is a black box in nature and its relationships between inputs and outputs are not easy to be interpreted, while ANFIS is transparent and its if–then rules are very easy to understand and interpret. But the drawback of ANFIS is its limitation to the number of outputs. It can only model a single output. In summary, ANFIS is a good choice and powerful tool for modeling bridge risks (Wang & Elhag, 2008).

5.3 Fuzzy concrete bridge deck condition rating method for practical bridge management system

Bridge management system (BMS) is a tool for structured decision making and planning/scheduling for bridge infrastructure inspection, maintenance and repair or retrofit. Any BMS is basically constructed based on data stored in inventory and inspection databases. One of the important and crucial efforts in managing bridges is to have some criteria to show the current condition of the elements of bridges based on the results from inspection data. As the results are not precise and are related to the depth and extent of the inspectors' expertise, there are some uncertainties in any evaluation. On the other side condition of bridges are rated linguistically in many cases with some kinds of vagueness in description of the bridge element conditions. Based on these facts in this case study a new fuzzy method is introduced to deal with these shortcomings from the uncertain and vague data. The fuzzy bridge deck condition rating method is practically based on both subjective and objective results of existing inspection methods and tools. The parameters of the model are selected as fuzzy inputs with membership functions found from some statistical data and then the fuzziness of the condition rating is calculated by the fuzzy arithmetic rules inherent in the fuzzy expert system. Since one of the most proven and experienced advantages of fuzzy inference systems is the tolerability for noisy (uncertain and vague) data it is believed that this proposed system can be an alternative method for current rating indices amongst many others which are almost used deterministically.

In this case study Fuzzy Inference System is used to translate the concrete bridge deck inspection results to condition rating (Tarighat & Miyamoto, 2009).

In literature the proposed rating methods are resulted from either visual inspection or nondestructive tests. Here, in order to enhance the capabilities of both methods (visual inspection and nondestructive tests) a hybrid inspection results is used to calculate the condition rating of the concrete bridge deck. Fig. 8 shows the type of inspection results.

The linguistic attributes of observed symptoms are defined as following fuzzy sets.

$A1 = \{No; Yes\}$
$A2 = \{NoCracks; HairlineCracks; WideCracks\}$
$A3 = \{No; Maybe; Yes\}$
$A4 = \{Firm; Moderately; Hollow; Very Hollow\}$
$A5 = \{Low; Moderate; High\}$

Considering Gaussian membership functions for inputs and applying Mamdani's method as fuzzy inference system Fig. 9 shows the proposed system for predicting of bridge deck condition rating. For design of fuzzy inference system 162 rules are defined based on the experts' experience and available facts from previous inspection results. Finally Fig. 10 can be used to convert the crisp condition rating result to linguistic term.

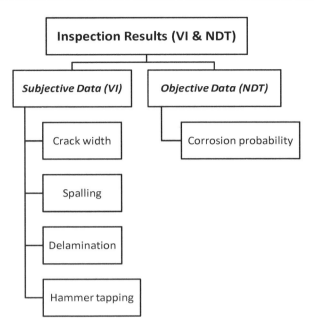

Fig. 8. Type of inspection results

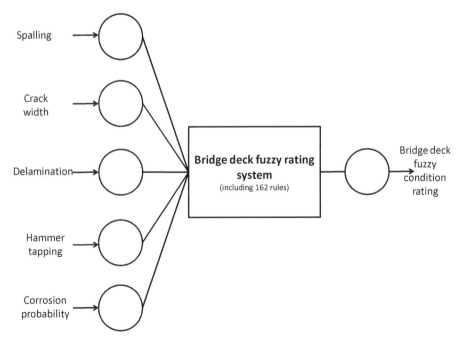

Fig. 9. Proposed fuzzy system for bridge deck condition rating.

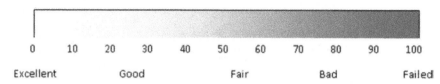

| 0 | 10 | 20 | 30 | 40 | 50 | 60 | 70 | 80 | 90 | 100 |

Excellent   Good   Fair   Bad   Failed

Fig. 10. Concrete bridge deck condition rating in linguistic terms.

To verify the proposed method an inspected concrete bridge deck is used. The layout of inspection is shown in Fig. 11. The proposed method is applied to the red slab and green haunch girder of the deck shown in Fig. 11.

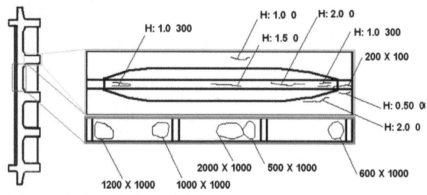

Fig. 11. Concrete bridge deck inspection layout.

Fuzzy condition rating method facilitates data collection in inspection process. No area calculation is required and it needs only the good judgment of the inspector to find out the condition rating. The inspection data is shown in Table 2. Since the symptoms and deterioration/damages of girders and slabs of a deck are totally similar the proposed model can be used for them during bridge inspection process.

Deck element	Spalling condition	Crack width condition	Delamination condition	Hammer tapping condition	Corrosion probability condition	Fuzzy condition rating
Slab (Red Area)	20	50	90	50	10	75.2
Girder (Green Area)	80	70	40	70	90	78.9

Table 2. Inspection data for typical slab and haunch girder of the reinforced concrete bridge deck.

To compare these results with a well-defined and in-use condition rating method the following seven-state rating scale, which reflects the different damage states associated with chloride-induced corrosion is used (Federal Highway Administration (FHWA), 1995; Morcous, Lounis, & Mirza, 2003). Table 3 provides a summary description of the adopted condition rating system as the benchmark.

Description	Condition rating (CR)
Excellent condition: no contamination; no corrosion; no repaired area	1
Very good condition: minor cracks, no spalls or delaminations; chloride contaminated or repaired areas 62% (of total deck area)	2
Satisfactory condition: spalls or delaminations 62%; cracked, corroded, contaminated, or repaired area 610%	3
Fair condition: spalls or delaminations 65%; cracked, corroded, contaminated, or repaired area 620%	4
Poor condition: spalls or delaminations 610%; cracked, corroded, contaminated, or repaired area 625%	5
Critical condition: spalls or delaminations 615%; cracked, corroded, contaminated, or repaired area P25%	6
Failed condition (total loss of serviceability or functionality): extensive spalling, delamination, repaired areas P30%; maintenance required	7

Table 3. Condition rating system for concrete bridge decks (Federal Highway Administration (FHWA), 1995; Morcous et al., 2003).

Based on Table 3 the condition rating for typical slab and haunch girder under consideration are 6 and 5. Scaling is required to be able to compare the results, therefore the above mentioned numbers should be multiplied by 14.28 to get a 100-based score system. Table 4 provides the comparison. It is shown that results from proposed method can estimate the condition rating very well.

Deck Component	Proposed fuzzy condition rating system		Scaled (to 100) Condition Rating based on the selected references		Absolute value Difference of the proposed method to the selected references
	Numerical value	Linguistically index	Numerical value	Linguistically index	
Slab CR	75.2	Bad	85.7	Critical condition	10.5
Girder CR	78.9	Bad	71.4	Poor condition	7.5

Table 4. Comparison of the condition ratings from two methods.

5.4 A two stage method for structural damage identification using an adaptive neuro-fuzzy inference system and practice swarm optimization

All the above three case studies are of diagnosis and assessment types. As declared earlier another important task of any BMS or BHMS is the possibility to locate damaged area or components. The present case study is about damage detection (Fallahian & Seyedpoor, 2010).

In this case study, an efficient methodology is proposed to accurately detect the sites and extents of multiple structural damages. The proposed methodology has two main phases combining the adaptive neuro-fuzzy inference system (ANFIS) and a particle swarm optimization (PSO) as an optimization solver. In the first phase, the ANFIS is employed to quickly determine the structural elements having the higher probability of damage from the original elements. In the second phase, the reduced damage problem is solved via the particle swarm optimization (PSO) algorithm to truthfully determine the extents of actual damaged elements.

Structural damage detection techniques can be generally classified into two main categories. They include the dynamic and static identification methods requiring the dynamic and static test data, respectively. Furthermore, the dynamic identification methods have shown their advantages in comparison with the static ones. Among the dynamic data, the natural frequencies of a structure can be found as a valuable data. Determining the level of correlation between the measured and predicted natural frequencies can provide a simple tool for identifying the locations and extents of structural damages. Two parameter vectors are used for evaluating correlation coefficients. A vector consists of the ratios of the first n_f vector natural frequency changes ΔF due to structural damage, i.e.

$$\Delta F = \frac{F_h - F_d}{F_h} \tag{8}$$

where F_h and F_d denote the natural frequency vectors of the healthy and damaged structure, respectively. Similarly, the corresponding parameter vector predicted from an analytical model can be defined as:

$$\delta F(X) = \frac{F_h - F(X)}{F_h} \tag{9}$$

where $F(X)$ is a natural frequency vector that can be predicted from an analytic model and $X^T = \{x_1, ..., x_i, ..., x_n\}$ represents a damage variable vector containing the damage extents $(x_i, i=1, ..., n)$ of all n structural elements.

Given a pair of parameter vectors, one can estimate the level of correlation in several ways. An efficient way is to evaluate a correlation-based index called the multiple damage location assurance criterion (MDLAC) expressed in the following form:

$$MDLAC(X) = \frac{\left|\Delta F^T . \delta F(X)\right|^2}{(F^T . \Delta F)[\delta F^T(X).\delta F(X)]} \tag{10}$$

The MDLAC compares two frequency change vectors, one obtained from the tested structure and the other from an analytical model of the structure. The MDLAC varies from a minimum value 0 to a maximum value 1. It will be maximal when the vector of analytical frequencies is identical to the frequency vector of damaged structure, i.e., $F(X) = F_d$.

The key point of this case study is that ANFIS concept can be effectively utilized to determine the most potentially damaged element (MPDE) of an unhealthy structure. For this, some sample structures having the damaged elements are randomly generated based on the damage vector X as the input and the corresponding $MDLAC(X)$ as the output. In other words some scenarios are defined for damaged structures. Then, an exhaustive search is performed using the ANFIS within the available input-output data to arrange the structural elements according to their damage potentiality. Essentially, the exhaustive search technique builds an ANFIS network for each damage variable from original ones and trains the network for a little epoch and reports the performance achieved. The step by step summary of the exhaustive search algorithm for determining the MPDE of an unhealthy structure is as follows:

a.   Establish the pre-assigned parameters of the intact structure.
b.   Randomly generate a number of sample structures having some damaged elements within the allowed space of damage variables X.
c.   Determine the natural frequencies of the sample structures using a conventional finite element analysis.
d.   Estimate the level of correlation between unhealthy structure and each sample structure by evaluating the MDLAC(X) index via equation (10).
e.   Randomly split the sample structures into two sets with some samples for training and remaining samples for testing the ANFIS, respectively.
f.   Build an ANFIS model for each damage variable as the input and the MDLAC(X) as the output. This leads to n ANFIS models equal to the total number of structural elements.
g.   Calculate the root mean square error (RMSE) for training and testing sets as:

$$RMSE = \sqrt{\frac{1}{n_t}\sum_{i=1}^{n_t}(ac_i - pr_i)^2} \qquad (11)$$

where ac and pr represent the actual and predicted values of the MDLAC(X), also n_t is the number of training or testing samples.

a.   Sort the structural elements according to increasing their training RMSE values and select the first m arranged elements, having the least RMSE errors, as the reduced damage vector, denoted here by $X_r^T = \{x_{r1}, x_{r2}, ..., x_{rm}\}$.
b.   End of the algorithm.

Now it is time to identify damage using optimization algorithms. As mentioned above, the MDLAC index will reach to a maximum value 1 when the structural damage occurs. This concept can be utilized to estimate the damage vector using an optimization algorithm. For this aim, the unconstrained optimization problem with discrete damage variables reduced may be stated as:

Find $X_r^T = \{x_{r1}, x_{r2}, ..., x_{rm}\}$
Minimize : $w(X_r) = -MDLAC(X_r)$ $\qquad (12)$
                          $x_{ri} \in R^d, \quad i = 1, ..., m$

where R^d is a given set of discrete values and the damage extents x_{ri} (i= 1, ...,m) can take values only from this set. Also, w is an objective function that should be minimized.

The selection of an efficient algorithm for solving the damage optimization problem is a critical issue. Needing fewer structural analyses for achieving the global optimum without trapping into local optima must be the main characteristic of the algorithm. In this study, a particle swarm optimization (PSO) algorithm working with discrete design variables is proposed to properly solve the damage problem.

In order to show the capabilities of the proposed methodology for identifying the multiple structural damages, two illustrative test examples are considered. The first example is a cantilever beam discussed in detail and the second one is a bending plate discussed in brief. The numerical results for these examples demonstrate that the combination of the ANFIS and PSO can produce an efficient tool for correctly detecting the locations and sizes of damages induced (Fallahian & Seyedpoor, 2010).

6. Conclusion

Fuzzy logic inference methods can be used for managing bridges. Models based on FIS consider simultaneously several facts or knowledge combinations as rules and indicate the final answer or guess which is very close to practical existing situation as the hypothesis of the greatest belief. The reasoning process is very clear and easy to understand by users who are not experts in the performance of decision support systems. For bridge inspection no deteriorated area calculation is needed and the only requirement is the good inspector's judgment. It should be noted that fuzzy systems can tolerate some noise to predict the outputs. This means that during bridge deck inspection if in some cases judgment is not correct, but close to real condition, the proposed method can estimate the condition very well without a major difference from practical point of view. It is clear that in deterministic methods incorrect judgment or decision changes the category of the predefined condition and overall condition rating drastically. Another point that should be notified is that FIS can be applied in areas with high nonlinearity. When nonlinearity is high the prediction accuracy is expected to be improved by using ANFIS comparing to Mamdani's method. Accuracy of the method can be improved when an adaptive optimization method is used for constructing similar model based on the training data from inspections. FIS modeling is suitable for prioritization of repairing bridges and budgeting tasks in which relatively simple and practical reasoning is required for decision makers. Even in cases that human expertise is not available, we can still set up intuitively reasonable initial membership functions and start the learning process to generate a set of fuzzy if-then rules to approximate a desired data set. The efficiency of rule-based reasoning can be improved by comparing different inference methods. Generally the inferred results are in agreement with the expert's opinion, and can provide substantial assistance to authorities in their planning.

7. References

Aktan, A. E., Pervizpour, M., Catbas, N., Grimmelsman, K., Barrish, R., Curtis, J. & Qin, X. (2002). *Information technology research for health monitoring of bridge systems*, Drexel University Intelligent Infrastructure and Transportation Safety Institute, Philadelphia, USA

Aydin, A. C., Tortum, A. & Yavuz, M. (2006). Prediction of concrete elastic modulus using adaptive neuro-fuzzy inference system. *Civil Engineering and Environmental Systems*, Vol. 23, No. 4, December 2006, pp. 295–309Baldwin, J. F. (1981). Fuzzy logic and fuzzy reasoning. *In E. H. Mamdani & B. R. Gaines (Eds.), Fuzzy reasoning and its applications*, Academic Press, London

Chen, W. F. & Duan, L. (2000). *Bridge engineering handbook*. CRC Press

Esragh, F. & Mamdani, E. H. (1981). A general approach to linguistic approximation. *In E. H. Mamdani & B. R. Gaines (Eds.), Fuzzy reasoning and its applications*, Academic Press, London

Fallahian, A. & Seyedpoor, S. M. (2010). A two stage method for structural damage identification using an adaptive neuro-fuzzy inference system and particle swarm optimization. *Asian Journal of Civil Engineering (Building and Housing)*, Vol. 11, No. 6, pp. 795-808

Federal Highway Administration (FHWA). (1995). *Recording and coding guide for the structure inventory and appraisal of the nations' bridges. Report FHWA-PD-96-001*, Washington, D.C.

Graybeal, B., Rolander, D., Phares, B., Moore, M., Washer, G. (2001). Reliability and Accuracy of In-Depth Inspection. *Transportation Research Record*, No. 1749, pp. 93-99

Haritos, N. (2000). Dynamic testing techniques for structural identification of bridge superstructures, *Proceedings of the International Conference on Advances in Structural Dynamics*, The Hong Kong Polytechnic University, Hong Kong, December 2000

Harris, J. (2006). *Fuzzy logic applications in engineering science*. Springer

Hartle, R. A., Ryan, T. W., Eric Mann, J., Danovich, L. J., Sosko, W. B., & Bouscher, J. W. (2002). *Bridge inspector's reference manual*. Federal Highway Administration

Housner, G. W. & Bergman, L. A., et al. (1997). Structural control: Past, present, and future. *Journal of Engineering mechanics, ASCE*, Vol. 123, No. 9, September 1997, pp. 897-971

Jang J. S. R. (1993). ANFIS:Adaptive-Network-Based Fuzzy Inference System. *IEEE Trans. on Systems, Man and Cybernetics*, Vol. 23, No. 3, May 1993, pp. 665-685

Jang, J. S. R., Sun, C. T. & Mizutani, E. (1997). *Neuro-Fuzzy and Soft Computing A Computational Approach to Learning and Machine Intelligence*, Prentice Hall, USA

Kandel, A. & Langholz, G. (1993). *Fuzzy Control Systems*, CRC Press

Li, H., Chen, C. L. P. & Huang, H. P. (2001). *Fuzzy Neural Intelligent Systems: Mathematical Foundation and the Applications in Engineering*, CRC Press

Ma, Z. (2006). *Fuzzy database modeling of imprecise and uncertain engineering information*. Berlin, Heidelberg: Springer-Verlag

Moore, M., Phares, B., Graybeal, B., Rolander, D. & Washer, G. (2001). Reliability of visual inspection for highway bridges. *Federal Highway Administration*, Vols. I & II

Morcous, G., Lounis, Z. & Mirza, M. S. (2003). Identification of environmental categories for Markovian deterioration models of bridge decks. *Journal of Bridge Engineering, ASCE*, Vol. 8. No. 6, pp. 353-361

Ou, J. P., Li, H. & Duan, Z. D. (2006). Structural Health Monitoring and Intelligent Infrastructure, *Proceedings of the second international conference*, Shenzhen, China, 2006

Phares, B. M., Rolander, D. D., Graybeal, B. A. & Washer, G. A. (2000). Studying the reliability of bridge inspection. *US Department of Transportation, Federal Highway Administration, Public Roads*, Vol. 64, No. 3, November/December 2000

Phares, B. M., Rolander, D. D., Graybeal, B. A. & Washer, G. A. (2001). Reliability of visual bridge inspection. *US Department of Transportation, Federal Highway Administration, Public Roads*, Vol. 64, No. 5, March/April 2001

Rajani, B., Kleiner, Y. & Sadiq, R. (2006). Translation of pipe inspection results into condition ratings using the fuzzy synthetic evaluation technique. *International Journal of Water Supply Research and Technology: Aqua*, Vol. 55, No. 1, pp. 11–24

Sivanandam, S. N., Sumathi, S. & Deepa, S. N. (2007). *Introduction to Fuzzy Logic using MATLAB*, Springer-Verlag, Berlin Heidelberg Straszecka, E. (2006). Combining uncertainty and imprecision in models of medical diagnosis. *International Journal of Information Sciences*, Vol. 176, pp. 3026–3059

Stephens, H. M., Jr. (2000). NDE reliability – human factors – basic considerations. *15th WCNDT*, Roma, Italy

Symans, M. D. & Kelly, S. W. (1999). Fuzzy logic control of bridge structures using intelligent semi-active seismic isolation systems. *Earthquake Engineering and Structural Dynamics*, Vol. 28, pp. 37-60

Tarighat, A. & Miyamoto, A. (2009). Fuzzy concrete bridge deck condition rating method for practical bridge management system. *Expert Systems with Applications*, Vol. 36, 2009, pp. 12077–12085

Terano, T., Asai, K. & Sugeno, M. (1992). *Fuzzy systems theory and its applications*. Academic Press

Wang, T. T. L. & Zong, Z. (2002). *Final Report: Improvement of evaluation method for existing highway bridges*, Department of Civil & Environmental Engineering, Florida International University, USA

Wang, J. & Hu, H. (2006). Vibration-based fault diagnosis of pump using fuzzy technique. *International Journal of Measurement*, 39, pp. 176–185

Wang, X., Nguyen, M., Foliente, G. & Ye, L. (2007). An approach to modeling concrete bridge condition deterioration using a statistical causal relationship based on inspection data. *Structure and Infrastructure Engineering*, Vol. 3, No. 1, pp. 3–15

Wang, Y. M., & Elhag, T. M. S. (2007). A comparison of neural network, evidential reasoning and multiple regression analysis in modeling bridge risks. *Expert Systems with Applications*, Vol. 32, pp. 336–348

Wang, Y. M. & Elhag, T. M. S. (2008). An adaptive neuro-fuzzy inference system for bridge risk assessment. *Expert Systems with Applications*, Vol. 34, pp. 3099–3106

Washington State Department of Transportation. (February 2010). Washington State Bridge Inspection Manual, In: *Manuals*, M 36-64.02, Available from: http://www.wsdot.wa.gov/Publications/Manuals/M36-64.htm

Wenzel. H. & Tanaka, H. (2006). *SAMCO monitoring glossary: Structural dynamics for VBHM of bridges*, Austria

Wu, Z.S. & Abe, M. (2003). Structural Health Monitoring and Intelligent Infrastructure, *Proceedings of the First international conference*, Tokyo, Japan, 2003

Yen, J. & Langari, R. (1999). *Fuzzy logic: Intelligence, control, and information*. Prentice-Hall

Zadeh, L. A. (1976). A fuzzy-algorithmic approach to the definition of complex or imprecise concepts. *International Journal of Man–Machine Studies*, 8, pp. 249–291

Zhao, Z. & Chen, C. (2001). Concrete bridge deterioration diagnosis using fuzzy inference system. *Advances in Engineering Software*, Vol. 32, pp. 317-325

Zhao, Z. & Chen, C. (2002). A fuzzy system for concrete bridge damage diagnosis. *Computers and Structures*, Vol. 80, pp. 629–641

Permissions

The contributors of this book come from diverse backgrounds, making this book a truly international effort. This book will bring forth new frontiers with its revolutionizing research information and detailed analysis of the nascent developments around the world.

We would like to thank Professor (Dr.) Mohammad Fazle Azeem, for lending his expertise to make the book truly unique. He has played a crucial role in the development of this book. Without his invaluable contribution this book wouldn't have been possible. He has made vital efforts to compile up to date information on the varied aspects of this subject to make this book a valuable addition to the collection of many professionals and students.

This book was conceptualized with the vision of imparting up-to-date information and advanced data in this field. To ensure the same, a matchless editorial board was set up. Every individual on the board went through rigorous rounds of assessment to prove their worth. After which they invested a large part of their time researching and compiling the most relevant data for our readers. Conferences and sessions were held from time to time between the editorial board and the contributing authors to present the data in the most comprehensible form. The editorial team has worked tirelessly to provide valuable and valid information to help people across the globe.

Every chapter published in this book has been scrutinized by our experts. Their significance has been extensively debated. The topics covered herein carry significant findings which will fuel the growth of the discipline. They may even be implemented as practical applications or may be referred to as a beginning point for another development. Chapters in this book were first published by InTech; hereby published with permission under the Creative Commons Attribution License or equivalent.

The editorial board has been involved in producing this book since its inception. They have spent rigorous hours researching and exploring the diverse topics which have resulted in the successful publishing of this book. They have passed on their knowledge of decades through this book. To expedite this challenging task, the publisher supported the team at every step. A small team of assistant editors was also appointed to further simplify the editing procedure and attain best results for the readers.

Our editorial team has been hand-picked from every corner of the world. Their multi-ethnicity adds dynamic inputs to the discussions which result in innovative outcomes. These outcomes are then further discussed with the researchers and contributors who give their valuable feedback and opinion regarding the same. The feedback is then collaborated with the researches and they are edited in a comprehensive manner to aid the understanding of the subject.

Apart from the editorial board, the designing team has also invested a significant amount of their time in understanding the subject and creating the most relevant covers. They scrutinized every image to scout for the most suitable representation of the subject and create an appropriate cover for the book.

The publishing team has been involved in this book since its early stages. They were actively engaged in every process, be it collecting the data, connecting with the contributors or procuring relevant information. The team has been an ardent support to the editorial, designing and production team. Their endless efforts to recruit the best for this project, has resulted in the accomplishment of this book. They are a veteran in the field of academics and their pool of knowledge is as vast as their experience in printing. Their expertise and guidance has proved useful at every step. Their uncompromising quality standards have made this book an exceptional effort. Their encouragement from time to time has been an inspiration for everyone.

The publisher and the editorial board hope that this book will prove to be a valuable piece of knowledge for researchers, students, practitioners and scholars across the globe.

List of Contributors

Zohreh Souzanchi Kashani
Young Researchers Club, Mashhad Branch, Islamic Azad University, Mashhad, Iran

Rasli and Fauzi
Universiti Teknologi Malaysia, Malaysia

Hussain
Universiti Kebangsaan Malaysia, Malaysia

Thair Mahmoud, Daryoush Habibi, Octavian Bass and Stefan Lachowics
School of Engineering, Edith Cowan University, Australia

Cheng-Jian Lin and Chun-Cheng Peng
National Chin-Yi University of Technology, Taiwan, R. O. C.

Ahmed Ali Abadalla Esmin
Lavras Federal University, Brazil

Marcos Alberto de Carvalho
José do Rosário Vellano University, Brazil

Carlos Henrique Valério de Moraes and Germano Lambert-Torres
Itajuba Federal University, Brazil

R.M. Aguilar, V. Muñoz and Y. Callero
University of La Laguna, Spain

Mohammed A. Mashrei
Thi-Qar University, College of Engineering, Civil Department, Iraq

Amir Tarighat
Civil Engineering Department, Shahid Rajaee Teacher Training University, Iran

Printed in the USA
CPSIA information can be obtained
at www.ICGtesting.com
JSHW011359221024
72173JS00003B/347

9 781632 380920